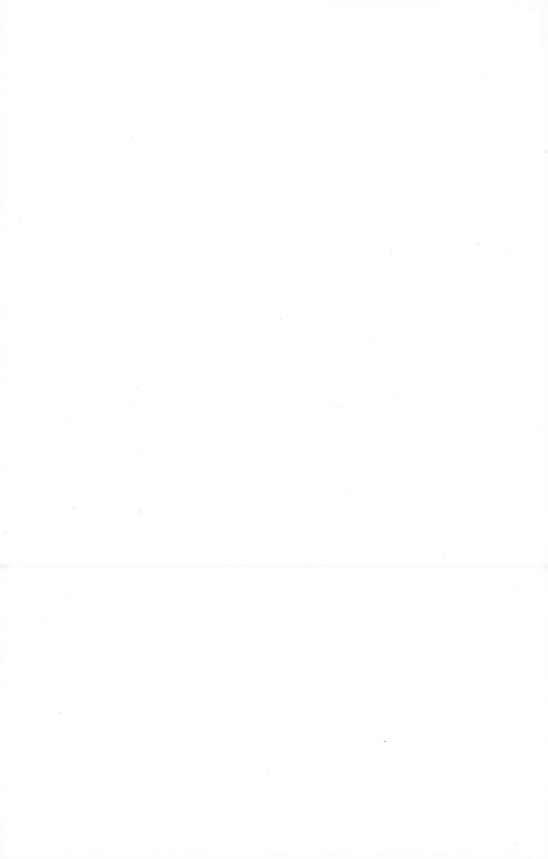

Productivity in Local Government

Productivity in Local Government

Frederick O'R. Hayes

Lexington Books
D.C. Heath and Company
Lexington, Massachusetts
Toronto

Library of Congress Cataloging in Publication Data

Hayes, Frederick O'R
  Productivity in local government.

  Includes index.
  1. Municipal officials and employees—United States.
United States—Labor productivity. I. Title.
2. Civil service—United States—Labor productivity.
I. Title.
JS363.H39   352'.005'1470973   76-20400
ISBN 0-669-00883-4

Published simultaneously in Canada

Printed in the United States of America

International Standard Book Number: 0–669–00883–4

Library of Congress Catalog Card Number: 76–20400

To my father to whom
I owe my earliest and
most enduring education in
the world of politics and
government.

Contents

List of Exhibits

Acknowledgments

This book had its origins in discussions with Vice-President Mitchell Sviridoff and Robert Goldman of the Ford Foundation. The initial concern was the need for an evaluation of six Ford-funded projects concerned with various aspects of productivity in state and local government. As the discussion evolved, we reached the conclusion that a broader survey of efforts to improve state and local government productivity made far more sense. We also agreed that the evaluation of the Foundation's projects would be best done as part of such a survey. The eventual result was that I applied for—and the Foundation approved—a grant to finance a study of local government productivity programs.

When I wished to expand the project to provide for more field work, my plans proved to be in close accord with the interests of the National Commission on Productivity and Work Quality in the preparation and publication of analyses of model local government productivity programs. On the recommendation of Nancy Hayward, director of the Commission's public sector staff, additional financing was provided by the Commission to expand the study.

Beyond the customary (and felt) gratitude for those who provided the funding, the arrangement proved an unusually satisfying one for me. My financiers, especially Goldman and Hayward, shared my enthusiasm for the project and reinforced it throughout the study. They gave me ideas, read and commented on my drafts, and were nearly always ready to talk about productivity.

During the initial stage of the study in the summer of 1975, the Battelle Seattle Research Center generously provided me with office space, the excellent secretarial services of Renate Lammerman, and a summer intern, Dan Rubin, as a research assistant. Rubin was an industrious and meticulous researcher but, more important, he had good judgment and he could write. He is credited as coauthor of the chapters on Palo Alto and Tacoma, but this understates his contribution. Tacoma is both the most difficult to analyze and the most exhaustively researched of all the case studies; it is 90 percent Rubin and 10 percent Hayes.

In every local government, I was dependent on city officials and staff to guide my way, to review my drafts, and to correct my mistakes. They gave me yeoman service. I am especially grateful to Harvey Singleton and Regina Glenn in Tacoma; George Barbour and Ed Everett in Palo Alto; Charles Hill, Harry Kelman, and Patrick Manion in Phoenix; James Favour, Dean Vanderbilt, and John Moren in Dallas; Edward Whitney, Marion Kammerer, and Walter Simko in Milwaukee; John Cox in Detroit and Robert DauffenBach, then at Wayne State University; Justin Renz and Vincent Macri in Nassau County; James Cavanagh and Robert Bott in New York City; and Professor Walter Balk of the Productivity Project at the State University of New York at Albany. And in each of these governments, there were many more who contributed time and effort to my education.

From the autumn of 1975 until the edited manuscript finally went to the publisher nearly a year later, the typing was done by Valerie Shepherd. Ours has become a mail order relationship, dependent on her cryptographic skills in the deciphering of my handwriting and her patience in working the message over again and again.

I leave until last my gratitude to Gregory Farrell, Director of the Fund for the City of New York who has provided me with office space and office services for much of my work on city government.

Introduction

Most of the improvements that have been or could be made in the performance of local government are, in a technical sense, neither complex nor esoteric. In an environment other than government, only a few of the projects and programs of productivity improvement in local government would be worth much discussion.

In local government, however, any management improvement effort that is both significant and conspicuous is a phenomenon with a scarcity value. Such an effort, if not unnatural, is uncommon enough to occasion questions as to the causes of its generation. I have attempted to discover, in each of eight local governments, why productivity or performance improvement programs came into existence, why they survived or failed, and what they accomplished.

Productivity programs can be regarded as a special case of the broader issue of innovation in government. This issue is my principal concern. I undertook the study in the hope it would cast some light on the characteristics of situations conducive to managerial change and innovation in local government.

I framed my inquiry in each of the eight local governments to accord with a simple five-stage model of innovation described in Chapter 1. The results have been written as descriptive case histories, organized in whatever manner seemed most appropriate for the particular case. I have attempted to analyze each case to identify causal factors and limitations. The analysis is straightforward and judgmental. It became evident very early in the work that a more structured analytic approach would not be worth pursuing.

I have looked at productivity programs primarily from the perspective of their protagonists and those associated with them. I did not, for example, interview union leaders or council members.

I have taken considerable pains to assure the accuracy of my accounts including a review of drafts by officials in each of the local governments. Where there were differences in perspective, these are reflected in the case histories. I believe the resulting accounts are, by and large, fair and objective as well as accurate. But, I concede limitations to the extent to which an outsider with a limited time schedule can do this. If there are problems, they are most likely in those governments where the conduct of the productivity programs has been controversial.

Chapter 1, "An Introduction to Government Productivity," is a preliminary discussion of productivity and the processes of change in local government by which productivity improvement is obtained. Chapters 2 through 9 are case studies of productivity improvement programs in eight local governments—Dallas, Detroit, Milwaukee, Nassau County, New York City, Palo Alto, Phoenix, and Tacoma.

Chapter 10, "The Unions," is broader in its coverage drawing on the literature

of productivity bargaining as well as the experience of the eight surveyed governments. Chapter 11, "What Makes Productivity Programs Work?" attempts to
draw conclusions from the eight cases. Chapter 12, "Research and Technical Assistance," covers the productivity research programs aided by Ford Foundation
programs and the federally financed research and technical assistance bearing on
local government productivity. The final chapter, "For the Future," is a brief
statement of recommendations for national policy.

1

An Introduction to Government Productivity

Background

Productivity crept into the national vocabulary sometime since World War II as one of the symbols for our concern for our seeming inability to reach and sustain per capita rates of growth in the Gross National Product that matched either our own expectations or the impressive performance of the Japanese and West German economies. The expression of that concern in the politics of 1960 was, in essence, a demand for more stimulative macroeconomic policies by the federal government as a means of inducing the expansion of gross national product by engaging resources—labor, capital, and materials—then unemployed.

During the 1960s productivity emerged as the key word for a related but different problem. This problem was the growing inability of American manufacturers to compete with their Japanese and West German counterparts in the manufacture of radios, television sets, phonographs, tape recorders, typewriters, and many other items. That failure did not mean, of course, that average American productivity on any or all of the items involved was necessarily below that of their foreign competitors but rather that higher American factor costs were no longer matched by a parallel margin in productivity. The growing American international payments deficit, although dominated by nontrade items, added to the productivity concern, as did the devaluations of the American dollar. A final input was the obvious fact that increased productivity would offset in part the sustained inflation we have endured since 1965.

In 1970, the Congress established a National Commission on Productivity, clearly a child of its times, to study problems and make recommendations on the means by which national productivity might be increased. The Commission was concerned primarily with productivity in the private sector but it elected to also devote significant attention to governmental productivity. It worked with other federal agencies on a federal government productivity program and initiated a number of studies on productivity improvement in state and local services. Despite some real contributions, the commission barely survived its passage through the Congress in 1973 indicating that productivity had been, despite the attention, a side show at best. The agency emerged with a new name, the Commission on

1

Productivity and Work Quality (and, still later, in 1976, as the National Center
for Productivity and Quality of Working Life) reflecting the still newer concern for worker alienation illustrated by the problems of the General Motors
Lordstown plant and by the Department of Health, Education and Welfare
report, *Work in America.*

The first local government productivity program to be so titled was announced by Mayor John V. Lindsay of New York City early in 1972. The
program established a series of quarterly performance targets for most agencies
under the Mayor's direction. Needless to say, the New York City program did
little for our balance of payments problem or our competition with Japan. It
did, however, promise an effort to obtain performance from municipal workers
that would be more consistent with the high wage and fringe benefit levels the
employee unions had won in a succession of collective bargaining agreements
in the late 1960s. The program was widely applauded and widely publicized
through the press and through meetings with other cities on municipal productivity. The idea acquired a certain cachet and was emulated in a number of other
local governments.

By 1975, a host of productivity programs had blossomed in state and local
governments. Some scarcely deserved the name. Productivity was a new governmental gambit, an easily applied label of apparent political value and not always
supported by the effort or the serious attention necessary to achieve results. But
there were efforts conscientiously pursued in New York, Detroit, Nassau County,
Dallas, Phoenix, Palo Alto, and other local governments. Many of the states
also undertook productivity programs including New York, Washington, Florida,
Wisconsin, Vermont, and others.

A longer perspective of state and local government would see the productivity programs as only the last of a series of programs to improve the performance of state and local governments dating back to at least the beginning of
this century. Many have concentrated on the budget process. We have had
periods almost as marked as the cycle of style in fashions with performance
budgeting, program budgeting, and most recently the planning, programming,
budgeting system (PPBS), with numerous variations on each major motif.   There
have also been a succession of organizational and structural changes to modern-
ize government. The introduction of executive budgets and budget bureaus, the
city manager movement, the strong mayor charter and numerous other measures
have all been justified by the need to develop better performing and more efficient government. The federal government's Hoover Commissions spawned a
host of little Hoover Commissions in state and sometimes local government. The
list is endless, a history of American dissatisfaction with the performance of
local government and, to a lesser extent, of state government as well.

How are productivity programs different from their numerous antecedents?
They differ, first, from the many budgetary programs in their relatively narrow
focus on operations or activities rather than programs. Productivity efforts tend

to be the domain of the industrial engineer rather than the budget analyst and to center on discrete work processes rather than the budgetary grouping of activities serving a broad program or purpose. Furthermore, unlike many of the prior efforts to improve state and local management, productivity programs place little importance on government organization or reorganization. There is, however, a strong kinship between productivity programs and numerous earlier work measurement and work performance projects. Moreover, while productivity programs take far different points of departure than do the innovative budgetary systems, much of the analysis of issues and activities developed under the PPBS rubric closely resembles the analytic aspects of the productivity programs.

The meaning of "productivity" would appear to be obvious, but productivity programs have, in fact, had several different objectives, including some that might be excluded from a narrow concept of productivity. In the narrowest sense, a productivity improvement can be regarded as an increase in the amount of output in relation to the amount of input. But the quality of program output is also important. In fact, concern in productivity programs with the quality of output seems almost as great as interest in the quantity produced in relation to inputs. A program objective, for example, may be to increase the timeliness of service or to reduce undesirable side effects. Some of the projects included in the New York city program are concerned with accomplishing some stated objective in accordance with a schedule and without explicit regard for the inputs required to do this. There are others aimed at increasing the high-value output of certain composite services, presumably by reducing lower-value outputs.

Rather than undertake any lengthy exploration of what a productivity program should cover, it is better to simply recognize that most productivity programs will in fact be productivity and performance improvement programs. Many of the projects will be solely concerned with performance improvements yielding no clearly measurable productivity gain (in the narrow sense) nor any savings for the budget.

State and Local Productivity in the National Economy

We know very little on a national basis about productivity in either state or local governments. The gross national product accounts simply carry state and local output valued at input costs. When expenditures increase, the product or output rises *pari passu*. Hence, productivity is assumed to be essentially unchanging. (This may, in fact, be a reasonable approximation to the true situation.) Despite the lack of systematic evidence, most Americans regard the productivity of government workers as low and the anecdotal evidence and the opinion of the experts both tend to support this view.

Productivity programs would seem to have an immense potential for state and local government. These governments spent in 1970 an aggregate of $133.2 billion and employed over 8.5 million people. The services provided by local government—the primary target for productivity efforts—employed 6.6 million in that year. By 1974 state and local expenditures totaled $204.5 billion and employment was nearly a million higher. But these magnitudes overestimate the base to which productivity efforts are likely to be applied.

Payrolls accounted for only 54 percent of all state and local government expenditures. For state governments alone the proportion was 40 percent and for local governments, 62 percent. To the extent that productivity programs are aimed at work performed by state and local governments by their own employees, the target is consequently only a little more than half of aggregate expenditures. Alternatively, the situation suggests the importance of including in productivity improvement efforts expenditures for other than personal services. It is true that many of these expenditures are for fixed costs, such as debt service, but the increasing use by government of both private business and nonprofit institutions to provide services is also an important factor. Productivity in the private hospitals and nursing homes used by Medicaid patients, the contract day care centers, head start programs, drug addiction treatment centers, and the many others may be as important to state and local budgets as productivity in any program manned by civil servants.

The high proportion of state and local expenditures representing other than payroll costs is not the only limiting fact on state and local productivity programs. A second and important factor is the distribution of expenditures among programs. Discussions of productivity in local government seem to revolve around programs such as refuse collection, street repair and paving, fire fighting, and law enforcement. All these functions taken together constitute only a modest fraction of local expenditures and an even smaller part of total state and local expenditures.

Almost exactly half of all state and local expenditures are attributable to education, where reductions in manpower per student in the schools are almost universally regarded not as an indication of increased productivity but rather as a symptom of reduced quality. The issue is, of course, more complicated than the comment would imply if only because our school systems, in addition to their educational programs, must spend money on maintenance and operation of buildings, preparation and serving of school lunches, provision of transportation to and from school, various supplementary recreation and adult education programs, as well as a multitude of supporting services. Moreover, even in the basic education program, there may be opportunities for greater productivity without changing the average class size, the most commonly used surrogate for education quality. Despite the range of possibilities, productivity improvement efforts in education face, because of the "quality" issue, some unusually difficult problems.

It is more to the point that education is a second local government, typically wholly independent from general local government and with its own independent taxation authority. Even where education is dependent on general local government for financing, the jealously guarded tradition of education's independence from "politics" makes it difficult for the related local government to intervene in any of the specific aspects of administration and management of the schools. The prospect is that this half of state and local government will remain outside the purview of state and local productivity programs unless the boards of education are persuaded to participate or undertake similar efforts.

Education's 4,258,000 employees in 1970 far exceeded employment in any other function. The next largest were hospitals with 830,000 employees and highways with 568,000. State employment accounted for slightly more than half of the total in each of these functions. The traditional local responsibilities were all smaller. State and local employment in police protection was 450,000 employees, fire protection employed 190,000, health 120,000, sewage disposal 61,000, sanitation 125,000, and local parks and recreation 117,000. Employment in all these functions was heavily concentrated in local government. Other major functions were: local utilities with 267,000, public welfare with 250,000 (three-fifths local), general control with 254,000 (six-sevenths local), and financial administration with 211,000 (57 percent local).

It is noteworthy that police, fire, and sanitation—the focus of discussion of local productivity programs—had a national total of only 725,000 employees, less than 9 percent of all state and local government employment. Productivity gains permitting an average reduction of 10 percent employment in these functions would reduce total state and local employment by less than 1 percent.

These data suggest that one measure of the importance of local productivity programs is breadth. A significant impact in national terms depends on successful efforts in a large proportion of state and local governments and in a large number of different functions. A comprehensive program in a typical city would still leave outside the effort more than half of the local expenditures and employment if the boards of education did not make a comparable effort. A concentration on direct manpower use in all local units of government including school boards would exclude the third of all expenditures that are spent on other than personal services.

How Is Productivity Increased?

How is productivity increased? Historically, the great increases in the output per capita in the western world have been associated with investments in capital equipment incorporating new technologies.[1] Today's worker in any manufacturing industry produces much more than his counterpart of a century ago (or even a quarter of a century ago), primarily because he is assisted by a far larger stock of far more efficient capital appliances. The increase in productivity has over a long period of time been sufficient to permit both the recovery of invested capital and a continuing increase in the real wages of workers.

The experience in manufacturing is more commonly cited but the results of labor-saving investment in agriculture have been equally dramatic. The services—private and governmental—on which we spend a large and necessary part of national income are thought more resistant to capital substitution. This is only half true; one might, for example, cite the case of the computer and its marked impact on production in clerical paper processing and record keeping. In local government, the large paper-processing units have already been impacted by the computer, and there are still substantial further gains to be realized.

This process of capital accumulation has been perhaps the single most important factor in the development of the western world during the past two centuries. It is a process so complex and varied that generalizations incur the risk of oversimplification. With this qualification, a few common or nearly common aspects of the dynamics of the process have some relevance to our concern for productivity in government.

First, the productivity resulting from increased capital investment and technological advances has made possible substantial increases in the wages of labor. At the same time, increases in the cost of labor have created further incentives for labor-saving capital investments. Higher wages and salaries may make economic previously uneconomic investments in equipment and will create inducements for the invention or development of facilities that promise even greater reductions in labor needs. For example, major investments in the automation of American coal mines came after John L. Lewis' United Mine Workers made the labor of miners an expensive commodity. In the same economic terms, the absolute and relative increase in the compensation of American municipal workers over the last decade has increased the potential return from labor-saving investments. This should create not only greater pressure on mayors and city managers to effect such investments but also added inducement to industry to develop labor-saving equipment with municipal applications.

Second, the growth of technology and capital in industry has tended to result not in the more efficient development of the same product but in the development of new products. The evidence suggests that the application of new technologies to local government has had some similar effects, with hospitals constituting the best example. This is worth noting if only because we tend in considering governmental productivity to think in the simpler terms of the production of the same product.

Third, the changing technology has also tended to change industrial organization. For example, the optimum size of a firm manufacturing automobiles has become very large, and small firms have all but disappeared. Municipal government is organized on the basis of political rather than economic forces and lacks the same capacity to adjust to an optimum size configuration, if such exists. One may only guess as to the importance of this factor, but would seem clearly to have significant implications for the many small local governments.

Fourth, the process of technological change has been fueled by enormous industrial investments in research and development designed to produce new technologies and new products and in the market research designed to identify the character and magnitude of consumer demands. There is little comparable activity in state and local government, and it may have adverse effects on the speed of technological change in government.

A second means of increasing productivity is through the redesign of work processes. The "efficiency expert" came on the American scene in the first quarter of this century. Frederick Taylor, the father of the effort, used time and motion studies to establish the most productive techniques for work performance and to set work standards. Taylorism has long since lapsed into disfavor as efficiency experts found more opportunities in broader issues of organizing complex work processes. Operations research and systems analysis techniques have, since World War II, added to the basic kit of tools. The reorganization and redesign of work processes has become widely accepted in both industry and government as a means for improving work efficiency and effectiveness. In the process, the management consultant has become an established element in the economy, and many staffs have been established in government agencies as well as in large businesses to provide the same skills in-house.

Management consultants, efficiency experts, and the like do not enjoy much popularity among government officials, but there is little doubt that work redesign can frequently increase productivity. The opportunity arises in part from the complexity of many work processes with numerous parallel and/or sequential actions necessary to the delivery of a product or service. The efficiency of such processes often cannot be "seen" clearly save through the analytic techniques of the so-called management sciences. Moreover, work arrangements tend to become obsolete with new developments. The classic case cited by the operations researchers is their discovery in World War II that British gun crews still included one man whose original function was to hold the horses during firing.

In some measure, improvements in productivity proceed from the introduction and gradual spread of new ideas. The good management analyst has a professional interest in new ideas and makes it his business to learn of them; he tends as a result to become a vehicle for more rapid transmission of new approaches. The outside management consultant reinforces this role from experience in analyzing comparable problems in other settings. By the same token, the management analysts are sometimes more likely than operating officials to be aware of new developments in more efficient hardware.

Work redesign need not, of course, be done by management analysts or industrial engineers. Many improvements in processes and tools have been made by those working in the process and by their foremen and supervisors. Some improvements arise simply from the natural interest and imagination of those engaged in the work. But a more comprehensive interest probably must be stimulated by enlisting worker participation in work design under a format that promises to elicit an adequate response.

A third approach to productivity increases is more primitive. This is the Stakhanovite approach, so named after the World War II Ukranian coal miner who was motivated to extraordinary production—simply by working harder. It is still possible in many cultures to exhort workers to higher productivity through appeals to patriotism, pride in community or company. Herman Kahn cites, in this connection, a Japanese company song articulating a dedication to that company rather reminiscent of older American college fight songs. Kahn's point is that the same attitude is virtually inconceivable in America.

Yet, one cannot dismiss the opportunity to increase productivity by just getting more work from the work force. Indeed, it happens. Sometimes it happens for no better reason than the fact that management demands it. Particularly in government, there are frequently situations where the amount of work actually performed is simply left to workers and their foremen. Standards tend to evolve through some kind of group consensus, sometimes never articulated. Management may be able to introduce more productive performance standards, especially if they are either inherently credible or supported by acceptable outside indications that they are reasonable. Or they may be acceptable with some quid pro quo of additional compensation or benefits for workers. Even in America, an appeal to worker pride in performance may have favorable results.

The Mayo-Roethlischberger experiments at the Hawthorne plant of the Western Electric Company are nearly half-a-century behind us. Yet, they provide lasting evidence of the responsiveness of workers to outside interest in, concern for, and attention to their problems. The Hawthorne experiments provide the most telling indication of the importance of the human factor and the limitations to scientific design of technique and process. At the other end of the spectrum, the difficulties of General Motors at its superefficient Lordstown assembly line give equally strong indication that workers today will not readily accept the tedium and dullness of very fine divisions of labor combined with the pressure of high productivity targets. All of this suggests only the guarded observation that workers may sometimes be more productive or will respond to higher productivity goals under circumstances where they are happier with their jobs. And these circumstances may often involve job designs that do not meet the standards of efficiency experts.

Fourth, the improvement in national productivity has benefited from an increase in the average quality of labor and by shifts of labor from low productivity sectors to higher productivity sectors. This has occurred largely in ways that have little direct application to the consideration of productivity improvements within a governmental jurisdiction or agency. Yet, personnel shifts and improving labor quality do have some relevance. For example, police departments carry out their law enforcement functions through a variety of different methods, some of which are more effective than others. When, for example, the New York City Police Department experiments demonstrated a markedly higher number of felony arrests from plainclothes patrol than from uniformed patrol, it suggested that further shifts to plainclothes patrol might increase the productivity and effectiveness of the department's operations. One might put in the same category the effort made in some police departments to substitute lower-salaried civilians for police officers in desk assignments to increase the number of patrolmen on higher-value functions. Training programs may improve the quality of labor and hence add to productivity.

Productivity and Its Measurement

There are serious and difficult problems in measuring productivity. Most of these problems concern output. These are not simply difficulties in measuring output but often problems in determining what output is.

Even in the more straightforward climate of manufacturing industry, output definition and measurement is not always easy. This year's Chevrolet is not the same as last year's model, and, even in current model production, station wagons are not the same as two-door sedans, and any one body style may come with several dozen significant variations in equipment configurations. A comparable product variation is common in any governmental service program where service is tailored to client needs, say social casework. Many of these problems are satisfactorily, albeit roughly, solved by assuming that average workload per unit of service delivered is roughly the same.

Output also varies in quality, an important issue in view of the possibility that an increased quantity of output may be obtained by reducing its quality rather than by higher productivity. One of the most significant problems arises from the large number of governmental service areas where quality has traditionally been measured by input levels. As we have already noted, the quality of public elementary and secondary education is judged to vary inversely with the ratio of pupils to teachers or the average class size. Colleges and universities are similarly assessed. Hospitals, likewise, tend to be evaluated in terms of staff per patient bed. The quality of police patrol tends to be judged largely by the density of personnel or patrol units relative to area, population, or street mileage.

The reliance on input ratios as a surrogate of quality is, in effect, an indication that output measures are inadequate. One child-year of fifth grade education is not the same as another child-year of similar education at a different school with a different teaching program. Logically, however, we should measure the quality of education (and other programs) by its results, i.e., what the children know and are able to do. This is a formidable undertaking because learning gains must be calibrated against the varying capacities of the children involved. There is wide interest in this problem and a burgeoning literature on so-called educational production functions, which attempt to relate educational inputs to educational performance levels. Typically, the emphasis is on the proportion of children reading below grade level. It is fair to say that no solutions, certainly no simple and workable solutions, emerge from the various investigations. To the substantial but limited extent to which we can regard standardized educational performance tests as a measure of output, we can treat as unambiguous productivity increases only two cases: an increase in education performance obtained without increased inputs per child-year, or a reduction in inputs per child-year without measured losses in educational performance. The area in between is ambiguous, where one can only assess the subjective value of the results against costs or gains.

Police protection and law enforcement pose even more difficult problems. A substantial part of police patrol time is spent in crime-inhibiting surveillance. The value of patrol in reducing crime is subject to considerable doubt. National Crime Commission data showed that a typical officer on patrol would actually witness a serious crime in process of commission only once every fourteen years. The more recent Kansas City experiment in variations in intensity of police patrol failed to show any significant effects on crime from either large increases in police patrol or its total elimination from the experimental neighborhoods.

There are some indications that crime can be reduced by police deployment strategies more tailored to the particular crime problem. But even here, the crime rate will depend far more upon the incidence of criminal behavior of the population. In the climate of the rising criminality of the last decade and a half, the most effective police performance was unlikely to do more than produce an unmeasurable reduction, not in the crime rate, but in the rate of increase in the crime rate.

Police arrest rates are another measure of police productivity. A police panel organized by the National Commission on Productivity has suggested, as one measure, the number of felony arrests surviving the first judicial screening. Crime clearance rates pose many problems of reliability but perhaps also have some usefulness in appraising police productivity. But police action against serious crime is only one of the many functions of a police force. Performance evaluation and productivity measurement for police demand a complex multifaceted perspective that, even in total, will fall short of what, ideally, we would wish to have. And this, among local government functions, is far from being the most serious problem. The ambiguities inherent in an effort to measure the output of a school system or a police force pale beside the problems of determining the results wrought by a social case worker or a psychiatric counselor.

Ambiguous performance measures make it difficult to measure program results but often they pose even more serious problems in communicating goals and objectives or performance expectations to those who do the work. It is very easy to establish understandable expectations for the performance of a refuse collection crew, but what does the productivity coordinator say to a police patrol or a psychiatrist?

While these problems are raised under the measurement rubric, it is clear that measurement is not the only problem. More basic is the absence in many areas of established relationships between input and output. The lack of means-ends or input-output relationships is coupled commonly with an absence of continuing scrutiny and adequate information and a widespread, typically uncritical acceptance of traditional professional operational norms.

This suggests that for many functions, a productivity program may eschew measurement problems for a scrutiny of process and input allocation—simplistically, a search for the equivalent of the man to hold the horses in the British gun crew. The focus would be on supporting and secondary functions and on those aspects of direct service that seem, on the face of the matter, to be unrelated to either the quality or quantity of program output.

The problem in these areas forces those who would increase productivity to step further back in the service production chain. The problem of determining the effectiveness of the services of a psychiatrist or a social worker or police officer would, on this reasoning, be put aside and effort concentrated on increasing proximate output or time spent in actual provision of services. For social workers, doctors, psychiatrists, counselors, and the like, a productivity program might seek to increase the proportion of patient or client contact time as a percentage of total time and/or to set minimum standards for the number of persons counseled or treated per average work week. For police units, one might attempt to maximize the proportion of time spent on patrol or in crime investigation and minimize the amount of desk duty, time spent in court, and similar duties. The assumption that hours not spent in direct service to the public are unproductive is subject, in varying degrees, to argument but, within limits, increasing direct-service hours is likely to represent an increase in productivity.

A closely related approach would improve the relationship of resource allocation to the configuration of the problem. For example, police deployment might be adjusted temporally and geographically to more nearly accord with the incidence of crime. This assumes that equal police patrols around the clock are inherently underproductive if crime is concentrated—as it typically is—in the evening hours. The reasoning is subject to verification in the eating of the pudding: a crime intensity pattern for police patrol allocations should result in either a reduction in crime rates, an increase in arrests, or both from what they would otherwise be.

There are some programs where existing program problems suggest that a concentration on output would not be appropriate. In these programs, the most important performance measure is the proportion of total services that are unnecessary. For example, a number of retrospective analyses have indicated that 20 percent or more of hospital admissions are unnecessary. If this is correct, a productivity program for a municipal hospital or medicaid program might better concentrate on more effective screening of patients before hospital admission than on improving the efficiency of the hospital. Similarly, quality control audits of public assistance case loads show that in many states 10 percent or more of the recipients are, in fact, ineligible and that even larger proportions are receiving payments in excess of their entitlements. Here, too, a reduction in the intake error rate would appear to be vastly more important than an effort, say, to increase the number of cases handled per staff member.

In a similar but broader vein, there is a more general question as to when the focus should be on efforts to reduce workload rather than on more efficient or more effective performance. The state of Oregon, by prohibiting disposable bottles and cans, almost certainly effected significant reductions in the workload of every refuse collection and waste disposal operation in the state. Tougher building codes and more aggressive action to remove abandoned structures would undoubtedly reduce the number of fires in many cities. Both are cases where costs are shifted from government to the private sector but, perhaps, reduced in aggregate.

The Milieu of Local Government

Some tens of thousands of times annually, the absence of businesslike methods in government is decried in the press and on television and radio. But government is not business, and there are many reasons why it cannot behave as though it were.

In the more competitive sectors of the economy, no business firm can long survive if it lags behind the productivity standards of the leading firms. Even in noncompetitive areas, any reduction in costs from higher productivity means, other things equal, increased profits to the enterprise. The pressure to improve productivity in business tends, consequently, to be sustained and significant.

Government is not immune to pressure for increased productivity. Citizen resistance to increased taxation is widespread and, moreover, the legal limitations on the local power to tax often create needs for expenditure reductions.

But neither the demand nor the need for productivity improvements is likely to be comparable to that in private industry.

The absence of direct competition is one factor. Another is the lack of performance standards and of data on the performance of other governments. Citizen expectations of local government are typically low, and citizens rarely have the information to either identify possible productivity-increasing changes or to demonstrate their feasibility.

Local government, furthermore, is a low-change system by design. A maze of procedural requirements on budgeting, on hiring and firing, on purchasing, and on contracting make any change from the modus operandi very difficult. New ideas must undergo the scrutiny of a city council and sometimes an independently elected comptroller as well as the overhead agencies such as budget and personnel. The civil service system and, frequently, employee unions add to the difficulties.

There is also rarely any significant investment in self-criticism, performance evaluation, or the development of new approaches. Changes must typically be developed from outside the organization or elicited from the organization by outsiders.

Ultimate accountability is to elected political officials, typically serving two- or four-year terms between elections. Managerial experience among them tends to be limited and, often, their experience in local government is no greater. Frequently the form of municipal government disperses executive responsibilities among many officials.

A city manager once remarked: "When an established program or activity runs into trouble, it is an act of God. When a new program fails, it is my fault." Innovations in local government involve real risks—of program failure, of raising politically influential opposition, and of causing strikes, slowdowns, or other problems of employee resistance.

The result is that, in local government, the cards are stacked against new ideas. There will rarely be strongly supportive forces in the community. The inertial drag of the system will make internal progress slow and difficult. The political risks are substantial.

Those who would improve productivity in local government must overcome these deficiencies. They must increase the political rewards and reduce the political risks of change. They must increase the likelihood that changes will be successful. They must establish a favorable climate for performance improvement with the public, the civil servants, and the city council. They must find means to either make the government systems responsive to the new needs or to subvert system constraints. They must, in other words, create artificially a milieu that is equivalent, in effect, to the role of profit and competition in the private economy.

The Stages of Innovation

The improvement of productivity in a municipal government agency requires innovation in an organization with unusually rigid rules and procedures and, ordinarily, little receptivity to new ideas. Innovation in this setting cannot take place unless a series of obstacles are surmounted and conditions met.

The requirements can be simply put:

1. Innovatory leadership willing to take the risks of a serious effort to improve performance.
2. Ideas on how productivity might be improved as well as the capacity to evaluate them and translate them into working plans.
3. The cooperation of the staff and employees of the organization.
4. Accommodation with external participants such as the city council, the unions, and interested community groups.
5. An adequate managerial capacity to implement the change.

This five-element scheme provides a structure for examining the productivity improvement process in various settings to assess the importance of the different elements as well as the means by which the necessary conditions were satisfied. Let us, first, develop each of the elements in greater detail:

Initiation

No productivity improvement or new idea can be put into effect unless someone is willing to make the effort to initiate it. The initiator may be the mayor, city manager, or department head or even a lower-level employee of a city agency. If the change is significant and visible at the citywide level, if it has opposition or if it involves potential political problems, it must have the support or tolerance of top political officials. The citywide productivity programs with which we are primarily concerned must be initiated by the mayor, the city manager or possibly the City Council. A program may be initiated because someone else— say an agency head, a consultant or a newspaper editor—suggested it, and it seemed like a good idea. The program may be started because of top-level dissatisfaction with agency performance, or it may come about because of citizen pressure to ameliorate problems in the performance of one or more agencies. A productivity program may arise from the experience of some other city or local government. It may come from the personal initiative of a mayor or city manager.

Why do innovations occur in some governments and not in others? Certainly the climate for innovation varies among governments and from one time to the next. Special opportunities and situations arise randomly. But the principal factor is likely to be the varied incidence of entrepreneurial and innovating characteristics among mayors and city managers.

Program Development

With the possible exception of the Stakhanovite approach, productivity improvement requires ideas on how it might be done and, eventually, the translation of those ideas into an operational program. There are significant differences of opinion on how difficult a job this is and how it should be done.

One approach depends on the experts—the management analysts, industrial engineers, systems analysts, and operations researchers—who are trained and experienced in analyzing organizations and processes. The experts are commonly outsiders to the organization, bringing with them not simply their expertise but also an external perspective. It can be argued that that perspective produces fresh insights into problems and that it is more important than expertise.

The alternative approach is based upon the belief that those best equipped to do the job are those long involved in the management of the subject operation and intimately familiar with them. This approach also places a high value on avoiding the disruption and conflict that the introduction of outside experts will frequently bring to an established organization.

A third possibility depends on the transfer of good ideas and approaches developed elsewhere. Among those who favor this approach, there are many differences in how the transfer of technique or technology is best done.

Internal Accommodation

The success of an innovation depends, in part, on the ability of the innovating manager to secure the minimum degree of acceptance by both the senior civil servants, who are the career managers of the organization, and the lower-level workers.

Some see accommodation as no great problem: "You tell them what to do and make sure they do it." Those at the other extreme see the civil service organization as insulated from effective disciplinary action and with a mind of its own; they must be wooed and won over to any idea that is to have a chance for survival.

There are several key questions: How important and difficult is the accommodation process? How is accommodation achieved? What kinds of inducements, incentives or managerial pressures are typically involved?

External Accommodation

One of the characteristics of government is the large number of actors external to an operating agency that are involved in key decisions. A major change in operations will frequently, perhaps usually, have aspects that require the approval of budget, personnel, perhaps the purchasing agency, the mayor and/or city manager, and, sometimes, the city council. Employee unions, where they exist, may pose more serious obstacles than any of the officials or units within government. Sometimes, citizens' groups have a strong interest in the way a service is performed and the political power to block changes if they oppose them.

Much is made of the obstacles to change in the bureaucratic net of local government outside the operating agency. However, it is difficult to analyze because the successful innovators make little of it, and the failures are rarely documented. Problems and solutions in dealing with the unions tend, fortunately, to be given far greater attention.

The variety of approaches to accommodation is endless. The immediate image of success is the shrewd negotiator, but there are successes among those who disdain negotiation or even discussion. There are cases of rational proposals, seemingly beneficial to both sides, which fail to be accepted. The arena of accommodation is, at a minimum, a field of great complexity.

Implementation

Many a good policy and program has failed in implementation. This occurs most often, perhaps, because of the great difficulty in imposing new duties on a staff heavily engaged in operations. Others have failed because of program defects undetected before implementation and others because of insufficient or inadequate managerial talent.

There are several key issues. To what extent does innovation require new organizational forms—such as project management organization or coordination—for implementation? What is the role of pretesting, training, or pilot projects?

This simple five-stage schema is a process model for which calibration is needed. Each stage may be regarded as an obstacle or hurdle to be overcome or evaded. We need a sense of the relative importance of the obstacles to productivity innovations posed by each stage of the process—with respect to any particular project in a specific community. We need to also know the range of variation among types of communities and kinds of projects.

Second, we need to identify, with respect to each of the five stages, the characteristics of solutions, the means by which the obstacles were overcome. The characteristics of failure are potentially equally important, perhaps more important, in determining both the most serious obstacles and the critical aspects of solution strategies.

The five stages of the schema are interrelated aspects of an integral process. The approach to any one aspect of the process has, accordingly, a potential impact on others. Strong and effective political leadership in the initiation phase may moderate the resistance and opposition to the effort, easing both internal and external accommodation. The use of "alien" experts for program development may, on the other hand, greatly increase the difficulty in securing the needed accommodation with agency staff and the employee unions. Similarly, an early understanding with employee unions on productivity improvement may provide the thrust to carry through the other aspects of the process.

These suggest critical or strategic factor theories of innovation. Such theories are particularly important because the local governments undertaking productivity programs have tended to focus on some particular aspect of the process as critical. The earliest programs began with a heavy emphasis on the buildup of expertise from in-house analytic staffs and contract research and consultation. In some later programs, the first step was a preliminary accommodation with the employee unions. There have also been efforts to develop programs based on work redesign by the employees themselves or on the talents of the senior civil service.

The five–stage model was used as the structure for inquiry and analysis for each of the eight programs reviewed in the chapters following as well as for the discussion of the key factors in successful productivity programs in Chapter 11.

Note

1. Solomon Fabricant estimates that between 1889 and 1964 output per man hour in the United States increased at an average annual rate of about 2.4 percent. He estimates that increases in tangible capital considered *without changes in the quality of labor or in efficiency* was responsible for only one-sixth of the productivity increase or about 0.4 percent per year. But Fabricant excludes from these calculations "the changing form the capital goods may take as a result of technological advance." His main concern, seemingly, is to lay to rest naive statements on the role of increasing capital investment in productivity. Since 1889, capital goods have, on the average, become twice as productive, i.e., capital, *per unit output*, has been reduced by half. At the same time, capital *per man hour of labor* has trebled. Ultimately, Fabricant apportions the responsibility for the 2.4 percent annual increase in productivity as follows: 0.5 percent from the improved quality of labor; 0.4 percent to the increased capital stock and the remainder (which Fabricant says is 1.7 percent!) to greater efficiency in the use of capital and labor. Solomon Fabricant, *A Primer on Productivity*, New York, Random House, 1969. See part 2, *Sources of Higher Productivity*.

2 Dallas

Dallas is America's eighth-largest city with a 1970 population of 844,401. It is, perhaps, symptomatic of Dallas' rapid growth after World War II that the Bureau of the Census and the Dallas Urban Planning Department differ by over 100,000 people in their estimates of Dallas' current population. The Census believes that the city's population has declined to just over 800,000, while the city's own planners estimate that population has continued to increase to well over 900,000.

Annexations have permitted Dallas to gradually extend its boundaries to cover an area of 340 square miles, roughly 10 percent more than the five boroughs of the City of New York. Large tracts within the city limits remain undeveloped. This substantial amount of land available for development provides the potential for very large future increases in population.

Dallas has all the problems of a new city—the need to provide the supporting facilities and services for its developing areas and to assimilate large numbers of newcomers to the city. At the same time, however, it is beginning to face problems and situations more common in the older cities of the east and midwest. The white middle class has shown an increasing preference for residence in the suburban areas outside the city's boundaries. Despite annexations, the proportion of blacks and Mexican-Americans in the city's population has increased and over 50 percent of the students in the Dallas school district (which does not cover the entire city) are from minority groups. A federal court has rejected the school district's desegregation plan and, presumably, a court-imposed busing plan is in prospect. There is a large middle-class black population but most of the members of the minority groups are poor or near poor.

Economic activities are also shifting to suburban locations. The new Dallas–Fort Worth Airport is well beyond the city's limits. The Dallas Cowboys no longer play in Dallas but in a stadium erected in suburban Irving. Manufacturing has become predominantly oriented toward suburban locations. The city's real property tax rate, $1.395 per $100 of assessed valuation with assessments at 75 percent of market value, is well above the property tax rates in most of the city's suburbs.

Dallas has a city manager form of government. Its city council of eleven was once elected at large, although eight of its members represented particular districts. This has been changed and the present council is the first in which the eight district members are actually elected by districts. The new system has substantially changed council membership, and the present council is, compared to its predecessors, less experienced in city government, more oriented toward district needs and problems and, probably, more conservative.

The Dallas Productivity Program

Dallas has no formal citywide program for performance and productivity improvement. Instead, an effective but unstructured productivity program functions largely through the city manager's continuing pressure on the operating agencies and through the efforts of the Office of Management Services (OMS) to identify opportunities for productivity improvement and assist the agencies in realizing them. The administration has, in addition, created a favorable environment for the more aggressive and innovative department managers; some significant productivity gains have, as a result, come from departmental initiative with little pressure from the manager's office or technical support from OMS.

There are wide variations in the breadth and quality of departmental performance. There are some departmental programs with very substantial accomplishments, strong continuing programs, and much promise for future productivity improvements. Others have done comparatively little.

Department of Building Services

One of the best is the Department of Building Services. Building Services was one of three departments created by a reorganization dividing the old Department of Public Works. Building Services has two principal internal divisions, one responsible for the design and construction of public buildings, and the second, with which we are primarily concerned, handling the maintenance, custody, and operation of public buildings.

Assistant Director M.W. Whitsitt, who heads the building maintenance and operation unit is, relatively speaking, a newcomer to the city government. Whitsitt has brought an analytic and imaginative cast of mind uncommon in the management of routine and tradition-bound government housekeeping functions. The results are impressive.

One example is the cleaning of public buildings. Four years ago it cost the city approximately $2.00 per square foot annually to clean the 300,000 square feet in the central complex including the police and courts building, the municipal building and the central library. Subsequent increases in the cost of labor and materials would have raised these costs to $2.50 per square foot or more but 1975 costs are, in fact, only 96¢ per square foot, a reduction of more than

60 percent below the cost of the 1972 operation in 1975 prices. Moreover, building cleanliness—a serious problem in 1972—has been markedly improved.

An in-depth analysis of the building cleaning operation was made shortly after the creation of the new department in October 1972. The analysis showed that cleaning practices and equipment were both antiquated and inefficient. Personnel needed to learn more effective cleaning practices; to do this, an academy was set up to provide two weeks of instruction in methods and equipment use for all cleaning staff and for all later additions to the cleaning staff. A plethora of different cleaning compounds was being used; materials and supplies consumed roughly 40 percent of the total budget. With standardization on a small number of cleaning items and heavy reliance on one multiuse superconcentrate cleaner, the cost of materials and supplies dropped to only 8 percent of the lower current budget. With the new methods, it was possible to reduce the staff by about 35 percent.

One of the more expensive aspects of the maintenance of public buildings is the waxing of vinyl tile flooring. Wax is expensive and requires substantial labor time both to apply and, later, to remove as it accumulates in less trafficked areas. The basic purpose is to prolong the life of the tile. A study concluded that it cost six times as much to preserve flooring through waxing as it would if waxing were eliminated and flooring replaced more frequently. The result was a "no wax" policy; instead the floors are polished with a buffer equipped with a spray detergent.

In some city operations, uniforms for maintenance personnel were provided by city contract with a uniform and laundry service at a cost of $2.03 per week. By simply providing four uniforms to each employee and a replacement uniform every six months, the city will be able to reduce its costs by 53.4 percent, or $7500 per year.

A Honeywell Delta 2000 system has been introduced to provide remote surveillance and control over city buildings twenty-four hours a day, seven days a week. The system is now handling heating and air conditioning control but will be extended to cover security and fire protection. It has already permitted the elimination of ten positions in the branch libraries and further reductions will be possible as the system is expanded to additional city buildings. The savings from the system should ultimately reach about $132,000 per year in salaries alone.

One of the most impressive accomplishments of the Building Services Department has been in its energy conservation program. The measurement of actual light levels against established standards for desk level lighting identified a general condition of overillumination in city offices. Whitsitt ordered the removal of redundant fixtures to reduce lighting to the desk level standard. In his own office, a single flush fluorescent ceiling light is flanked by three new ceiling panels marking the areas from which surplus fixtures were removed. Public area lighting was also reduced and offices darkened when not actually used.

The department staff reasoned that light and heat or air-conditioning for public buildings were being supplied for a two-shift operation, one during the day when the regular business of the city was transacted, a second at night when the custodial force went to work to clean the building. The second shift could be eliminated if it were feasible to clean the buildings during the day while offices were actually in use. The Department finally decided on a 10:30 a.m. to 7:30 p.m. shift for the cleaning force, which provided 2.5 hours after the normal working day to tackle those areas not accessible to cleaners during working hours. The new system proved feasible and resulted in a substantial saving in energy. Unexpectedly, the cleaners were also more productive during the daytime permitting a reduction in the size of the cleaning force required. Morale also improved as nearly all the cleaning force enjoyed the shift to daytime work and the association with the city's 'regular' employees.

The Department had previously discovered that city buildings were heated or air-conditioned to maintain comfortable working temperatures twenty-four hours a day. To reduce energy use, the cooling and heating equipment was, instead, turned down at night and turned on again at 5:00 a.m. to restore the temperature to comfortable levels by the beginning of the working day. With the temperature monitoring and equipment control capacities of the Honeywell Delta system, it was possible to determine for each building the time actually required to cool or heat to working temperature levels. It proved feasible as a result to put the equipment back to work only an hour or less before the start of the working day in most buildings. With the custodial employees on daytime duty, the provision of heat or air-conditioning and lighting could be limited to twelve hours of the twenty-four hour day.

The department is now closely examining the effectiveness and efficiency of air-conditioning equipment proposed for city purchase as well as the systems already in use in the city. Whitsitt's staff has been instructed to review air-conditioning needs in every case where they are called on to repair equipment that has broken down. One of the first, a system of large roof installed condensers, proved to have redundant capacity; the defunct unit could be removed and its functions served by connecting its ducts with a neighboring unit. Another check disclosed a defunct unit that had not even been reported; it proved to be devoted solely to the cooling of a rarely used parts storage room.

The reductions in energy use were massive. The large city building on Mockingbird Lane functions with 55 percent fewer kilowatt-hours than were used before the conservation program began. Building Services is applying citywide new standards not just on desk level lighting and equipment operation, but on total kilowatt requirements and kilowatt-hour usage per square foot of floor space for different common types of space usage. Now Building Services is turning its attention to the use of solar energy. The first effort will provide hot water and a part of the space heating and air-conditioning requirements for a fire station; in the second phase, hopefully with the aid of a federal grant, solar heating will supply part of the requirements for a community center. The costs are high, and at least the second project would be infeasible without the federal funding. In the longer run, Building Services believes standardization will lower solar energy costs. In the meantime, Dallas is getting a head start in using an energy source that will be increasingly important in the future.

The building maintenance group is also involved in the design process for new buildings to help assure that design emphasizes low maintenance and low energy use. One interesting aspect of this process is the Department's experimental furniture landscape. Manufacturers of various modular integrated office furniture configurations, complete with partitions and storage units, have loaned units to the city that are being tested for use in the new Municipal Building. The Municipal building is being constructed with a minimum of fixed internal partitions to increase flexibility in handling the inevitable changes in space needs over the life of the building. The 'landscape' furniture is a means of maximizing this flexibility, permitting variations in layout at minimum time and expense.

Building Services has done all this without a staff unit for program and operations analysis. Now, they see opportunities and needs for efforts that outrun the part-time capacity of the operating staff. The department requested and received approval for the addition of three industrial engineers in the department's 1975–1976 budget—but priorities dictated their assignment to the work of an energy conservation committee.

Department of Streets and Sanitation

The Department of Streets and Sanitation was, like the Department of Building Services, created from the 1972 division of the responsibilities of the former Department of Public Works. John Teipel who heads the new department had carried essentially the same responsibilities as an Assistant Director of the old department, with the exception of the Traffic Control Division which was added to the department on October 1, 1975.

Assistant Director Morris Bishop has introduced a series of changes designed to increase the productivity of garbage and trash collection. Collection had previously been performed by three-person compactor truck crews—two loaders and a driver. The department examined the possibility of shifting to one-person collection following the Phoenix approach. They decided, however, that Dallas' predominantly alley collection would be best handled by two-person crews using modified cab trucks, which allow the driver to load from one side of the alley and the loader from the other. Three-person crews were retained for downtown collection and one-person trucks used for curbside collection in residential areas without alleys. The impact of the reduction in most crews was eased by upgrading forty-eight workers to the position of Leadman, a working supervisor. The changes permitted a reduction in the collection work force from 861 to 663 and an annual savings to the city in 1975 prices of about $1.3 million.

A more revolutionary change was the decision to put the sanitation workers on a weekly work schedule of 4 ten-hour days. The change has been successful Most sanitation workers prefer the four-day work week and no complaints have been received. The shift was crucial because it made possible a reduction in the number of trucks required from 210 to 140. With each member of the collection force reporting on only four of the six working days, the number of workers working on any given day is only two-thirds of the number reporting on the traditional work week of 5 eight-hour days. The same number of collection man-hours would, consequently, require only two-thirds as many trucks.

Reportedly, the sanitation workers have been able to work the long day with-out evidence of appreciably greater fatigue. Thirty-six of the surplus trucks have been disposed of but the remaining thirty-four are being held, at least temporari-ly, to assure an adequate number of spares for trucks out of service for repairs. The cost of replacing the present sanitation fleet will be $1.2 million less—the amount the seventy collection trucks would have cost. The one-time savings will, of course, be largely offset by the costs of faster depreciation and replacement of the trucks. The main advantage seen by the Department's management is a more rapid turnover and, hence, a younger and more modern truck fleet.

The change is not without its problems. The maintenance workload of the Equipment Services Department has increased substantially due to more intense use of the trucks. Moreover, trucks are more difficult to service since Sunday is the only day they are not in use.

The department is now using a device called the rotoboom for uncontainer-ized collections. The radio equipped rotoboom mechanizes the pickup of loose trash and miscellaneous bulk items left for collection. The material picked up by the rotoboom is dropped in large open body trucks. When the truck is full, it takes its load to a landfill or transfer station and another truck takes its place to be loaded.

A transfer station now in operation has greatly reduced truck mileage in travel to the landfill. Plans for a recycling/transfer station promise to further reduce collection costs.

Streets and Sanitation is also responsible for street maintenance and repair. The department has been concerned with the problem of flooding and the need for early and continuous monitoring of changes in water level to assure that crews are properly deployed at the right time to the areas where they are needed. This need has been met by placing water level sensors at critical points in the flood plains with the information transmitted to a single central point.

The Water Utilities Department

The Dallas Water Utilities Department (DWUD) and its Director, Henry J. Graeser, have been highly esteemed in Dallas. Graeser earned a national reputa-tion for advances in water quality control and local regard for his aggressive and

effective efforts to secure for Dallas the water rights necessary to supply its growing population. Budget analyses, however, indicated that the DWUD required a
larger staff per million gallons of water delivered, per capita population, and per
connection than any of a group of other municipal water systems examined. On
this basis, Graeser was persuaded to engage a management consultant to undertake an in-depth management analysis of the department.

The Dallas-based management consultant firm of Lifson, Wilson, Ferguson
and Winick, Inc. (LWFW) was selected to do the job. LWFW recommended the
establishment of eleven departmental task forces to examine various management problems within the department. Six of the task forces had been set up by
May 1975, and two of the six had completed their assignments. In addition, long
term planning and industrial engineering staffs were set up in the department at
the recommendation of LWFW. The management analysis of the department's
operations was done cooperatively by LWFW, the task forces, and the new industrial engineering unit.

The management analysis effort cost the department $66,000 in consultant
fees during the first year, $176,000 in the second year, and continuing costs for
additional staff of $85,000 annually beginning in the third year. By the third
year, 1974–1975, the resultant management improvements were saving the department over $1 million per year, about 4 percent of the department's $25.9
million budget. If the task forces still to report or still to be organized prove
equally effective, savings will be significantly increased in the future.

The Metering Activities Task Force was one of the first started. It recommended an integration of the department's dispersed functions concerned with
meters. In addition, work management analysis led to improved productivity in
meter reading and inspection. Under the new system, the metering division required $250,000 less per year to perform the same functions. In addition, the
new plan also resulted in greater responsiveness and more effective control.

A task force also examined the department's commercial division. Procedures were standardized, methods improved and work simplified wherever possible. Forecasts of work volume were developed. Each individual task was
analyzed to develop reasonable work performance standards. A staff scheduling
model was developed to assure efficient work flow. A program of cross-training
was introduced to assure adequate coverage of all aspects of the work process. A
reporting system was installed to better monitor performance and labor cost on
an ongoing basis. The resulting savings were $75,000 annually. A similar work
management approach to Accounting and Finance saved another $43,000 per
year.

The District Pilot Study Task Force examined the work of the blue collar
repair and maintenance work force with the aid of the consultants from LWFW
and the department's own industrial engineers. They concentrated on three particular areas: fire hydrant maintenance; the repair of street cuts; and back hoe
use. The task force and its supporting staff reviewed job tickets, examined opera-

tions in the field, discussed methods with workers and supervisors and made extensive use of time-lapse photography. The use of the camera was carefully explained to the workers and was done with their agreement.

On the recommendation of the task force, the operation was reorganized on a geographic instead of a functional basis. This reduced travel time, cut back the number of supervisors required, improved the balancing of workload among crews, and increased the capacity to provide special skills and equipment where needed. Individual operations were also reorganized. For example, two-person crews replaced the old five-person pavement cut repair crews; under the new scheme, concrete was provided by leased concrete batch trucks instead of by a crew-run hand mixer. Productivity in fire hydrant maintenance was increased by separating routine maintenance from major repair. The total savings effected by these changes amounted to $186,000 per year.

The District Pilot Study task force also combined four district operations into two. This has so far resulted in the elimination of sixty-nine positions for an annual saving of $494,000.

The Department's new industrial engineering staff is beginning to examine other areas. Ed Samuels, who heads the combined planning industrial engineering group, is especially interested in information storage and retrieval. A promising analysis of the installation of new mains and connections has been temporarily shelved until new bond funds make it possible to continue the basic activity.

The Police Department

There is much going on in other departments to improve productivity and performance. The Police Department, for example, was able to eliminate thirty non-uniformed positions at an annual saving of approximately $210,000, as a result of recommendations made in study by LWFW. The department has, for some time, made extensive use of civilians and uniformed public service officers where they can be substituted for higher-paid sworn police officers.

Dallas has one of the first computerized police dispatch systems and has introduced police officer expediters to assure prompt attention to emergency calls and permit the screening of low priority requests that do not require an immediate response. Under a Law Enforcement Assistance Act grant, the Department is engaged with the Hazeltine Corporation in a large research and development effort to develop an integrated automatic patrol car locator system with a computer-aided dispatch system. In the first phase, the system will cover about one-fourth of the city. Dallas has also received one of the very large LEAA impact grants—about $20 million—designed to so increase the level of police protection as to produce, hopefully, measurable impacts on crime rate.

The Fire Department

The Fire Department has greatly increased the sophistication of its approach to deployment. It began with the use of the Public Technology Incorporated fire station locator model. The model proved too unwieldly for the Dallas problem but it led to a detailed analysis of deployment with other techniques. One result was that all four of the new fire stations provided in the last city bond issue will be manned by the transfer of existing fire companies and, contrary to initial expectation, no new companies will be required, thus saving over $600,000 per year.

A computer simulation of ambulance response was the basis for the design of the citywide ambulance system in the fire department with two to three fewer ambulances than planned and with response times as low or lower than specified. Ambulance calls and service rapidly outran the projected volume resulting in severe workload pressure. The workload was, however, concentrated in a few companies and the simulation model showed that the conventional addition of new units would do little to relieve the most hard-pressed units. Relief is being provided from staff in the same fire house as well as through peak period part-time units.

Other Projects

The Office of Management Services is now working on the implementation of the recommendations of a consultant study of the city's financial system. The first steps will involve the simplification of city purchasing.

A project now underway in the Department of Traffic Control is attempting, through statistical analysis, to develop a systematic approach to the maintenance of traffic signals. Early results include decisions to relocate certain signals with apparent high vulnerability to traffic accidents, to provide more training for personnel and to introduce performance standards for maintenance personnel. Signal light bulbs are now being replaced on a systematic routine basis rather than after burnout. Equipment with high frequency malfunction is being replaced.

The Initiating Nudge

It is clear that Dallas has been successful in creating in many of the agencies of its city government a climate conducive to productivity improving innovations. The critical factors in the development of this climate are more difficult to discern than in most other cities because of the virtual absence of formal citywide programs to obtain that result. There is not a formal productivity program, no citywide work measurement program and no planning-programming-budgeting system.

Assistant City Manager James Favour, who has responsibility for budget and the central administrative service agencies, sees the post–World War II development of the city government in terms of a succession of major waves. The first came after World War II when Dallas recruited an unusually young and competent management group that introduced many innovations in the city government. Many of this group remained as department heads through the 1960s. There were many variations among them but, as a group, they became, predictably, more conservative and less innovative with time. Below them in the hierarchy were younger men eager to take over and introduce a more aggressive managerial posture.

A second overlapping wave came from Erik Jonsson who served as Mayor of Dallas from 1967 to 1971. Jonsson was President of Texas Instruments, a relatively young high-technology firm built on a heavy investment in research and development. Jonsson came from an environment where research and innovation were critical to success, and he tried to create a comparable environment in the city government. The Jonsson regime produced a milieu favorable to innovation, which still persists in the city government.

George Schrader became City Manager in 1973 after serving for six years as Assistant City Manager. Unlike his predecessor as manager, his career had been outside the Dallas city government; he had been city manager of suburban Mesquite immediately before his appointment as Dallas' Assistant City Manager.

Schrader had significant opportunities to bring new leadership to the fore in the city's departments because the post–World War II department chiefs were gradually retiring. One significant success came from the decision to divide the old Department of Public Works into three departments after the retirement of its long-time head. This made it possible to "unleash" the old department's three assistant directors on the problems with which they were most familiar; I have already recounted the subsequent accomplishments achieved in Streets and Sanitation and in Building Services.

Schrader also elected to build a strong centralized structure of common services. Building Services has gradually taken on citywide responsibilities for both the maintenance and operation and the design and construction of city buildings. A new Department of Data Services was created. The maintenance and control of all motorized equipment was assigned to a new Department of Equipment Services. Favour places great importance on this approach in strengthening central control of the agencies and in bringing an analytic perspective to some of the city's important problems.

The actual initiatives from city hall have taken the form of "nudges"—some subtle and gentle, others more forceful—to move the department heads toward improved performance. Schrader and Favour made it clear to the new heads of

Streets and Sanitation and of Building Services, when those departments were created in 1972, that they expected action in the right direction. The management analysis effort in the Water Utilities Department was initially urged by City Hall on a department head who has since been an enthusiastic supporter. Higher raises for police than for other city employees were tied to a commitment by the police chief to effect reductions on civilian jobs in the department. Schrader refused to release bond issues funds for new fire houses until the fire department provided something more than a routine conventional justification. Currently, pay increases for department heads are tied to performance—chiefly the ability to effect productivity gains and make savings within their budgets.

Other actions help. The extension of Building Services' turf to all city buildings will expand the scale to which that department's analytic approach is applied. The recent merger of Traffic Control into Streets and Sanitation will provide new opportunities for an integrated approach to the management of city streets and extend the innovatory approach of Streets and Sanitation to a new area.

The budget process in the Office of Management Services is important in identifying cases, as it did in the case of Water Utilities. The Office's two industrial engineers also provide a capability for deeper involvement.

Schrader sees the occupational disease of city managers as a kind of tunnel vision focussing almost exclusively on the problem of expenditure control to keep spending within the range of available revenues. He is trying to break out of this narrow perspective—to recognize the possibilities, for example, of increasing revenues through new revenue sources or through efforts to build existing revenue bases. He recognizes, too, that expenditure control per se assures neither increases in productivity nor the maintenance of program effectiveness and quality.

Programs and Ideas

The work of the Office of Management Services has been at the heart of the Dallas productivity improvement effort. The Office has played a key role as problem identifiers, peddlers of good management techniques, coordinators and overseers of agency studies, and performers of analysis. Most of the program and operations analyses performed in Dallas have either been done by OMS or have had substantial participation by OMS staff.

The present Office of Management Services was created in 1969, under the current Assistant City Manager James Favour, by merging Management Services, as then organized, with the Budget Office, The thrust, even before the merger, was to establish an analytical staff not typical of city government. Dean Vanderbilt, the current OMS director, had been recruited, fresh out of M.I.T., with a Ph.D. in Computer Sciences, to head the premerger Management Services unit.

He built there a staff with education and background in city planning, business administration, and engineering.

The Office of Management Services added two industrial engineers to its staff several years ago for the purpose of aiding productivity improvement actions. Nearly all the earliest productivity improvements were initiated by the Office of Management Services, and a high OMS involvement has continued. The Water Utilities project, the Traffic Control study, and a major analysis of the Health Department were all OMS-initiated projects. For example, the Water Utilities project was initiated as a result of an OMS study; OMS industrial engineer William McNary spent a year on the project. Dean Vanderbilt coordinated the work of the consultant and served as a member of the Implementation Task Force. The Fire Department station location and ambulance studies were performed in large part by OMS, chiefly by industrial engineer John Moren.

Management consultants have played an important and sometimes a crucial role. The LWFW study of the Water Utilities Department, for example, was critically important in providing external and presumably objective validation for the city hall position that managerial reform was necessary; no staff agency could have easily served the same function. One suspects that the trimming of civilian positions in the Police Department was, similarly, more smoothly effected through the recommendations of a consultant than would have been possible had the action been taken as the result of budget review.

There are small analytic staffs in several city agencies. The Director of Streets and Sanitation has a group of administrative assistants who have assumed some of the responsibilities for the evaluation of operations and the development of new approaches. Water Utilities has a three-person industrial engineering staff plus a small planning group. Both Police and Fire have analytic staffs oriented primarily toward computer usage and information needs. Building Services has the three new positions now devoted to energy analyses.

To these resources must be added the skills available in the centralized service agencies. The computer and information systems staff in the Office of Data Services is especially important. The managerial information and reporting system is very good. Quarterly department reports include activity and productivity indicators as well as financial performance against targets. The reports also include Action Center data on departmental response to citizen service requests and current citizen ratings of departmental service delivery. Obviously, the reporting system provides strong support for the efforts to improve the effectiveness and efficiency of city performance.

The city has also had more than usual good fortune with a handful of administrators who have themselves contributed innovative ideas and provided a ready market for other ideas. John Teipel in Streets and Sanitation and M.W. Whitsitt in Building Services are prime examples. In Water Utilities, ideas for performance improvement were sought and obtained from both foremen and workers.

Technology transfer has had a place as well. The fire house study began with the use of the fire station locator model developed by Public Technology Incorporated, and the findings of the Rand studies of alarm response in New York and other cities were also used. The shift to two-person sanitation crews was made after a review of Phoenix's one-person crew and a decision that it was not appropriate to the Dallas situation. The rotoboom used in bulk collections was a designed-in-Dallas application of a commercially available technology.

This undoubtedly understates the role of technology transfer. The city's managerial cadre are professionals in their own areas; most of them are aware in varying degrees of what is being done elsewhere and of new equipment and methodology becoming available.

Productivity-Generated Tensions within the City Government

In those cities with an elected executive mayor, the primary tension in a change-oriented administration tends to develop between politically appointed commissioners and the department's senior civil service. In Dallas' city manager form of government, most of the department heads are careerists who have risen through the ranks of the department. Careerist leadership tends, even when significant change is being introduced, to have a high degree of acceptance among subordinates. By the same token, the careerist department head is, in general, likely to be more sensitive to the views of his associates and less inclined to introduce changes to which there might be significant internal opposition. One result is that the locus of change-caused tension tends to shift upward to the relationship between department heads and the city manager, his staff, and staff agencies.

This seems to be the case in Dallas. Improvements in the less innovative departments seem to depend in large measure on the manager's willingness and capacity to cajole, persuade, and demand action by the department head. The discussion of Water Utilities and Fire above provides some indication of the character of this tension in Dallas. The end results appear to reflect a tendency toward mutual accommodation. The city manager typically gets some progress but at a slower rate than he would like. The manager's role may be almost as important in easing the way for more aggressive and innovative department heads.

The relationship between the city's management and its rank-and-file employees is necessarily more inchoate. Schrader believes that he has a responsibility to represent legitimate employee concerns before the city council. He made a strong case, for example, in the final deliberations on the 1975–1976 budget that the budget should not be balanced by trimming a moderate provision for employee pay increases.

Indeed, there seems in Dallas to be a genuine concern for employees and their attitudes in the city government. No employees have been laid off as a result of productivity improvements. The ten-hour day, four-day week was introduced in Sanitation only after it was clear that it was favored by most employees. Employee participation in the Water Utilities management improvement effort is another example.

Dallas has conducted an employee opinion survey designed by consultants Vincent Flowers and Charles Hughes. The questionnaire does not deal directly with questions of employee productivity but it covers in twenty questions key issues in employee job satisfaction. Replies were received from 9000 of the city's roughly 12,000 employees. John W. Cutsinger of the Personnel Department has had the replies tabulated in numerous forms by department, by organization within each department organizational unit, and separately for management personnel. The significance of the results is now being explored in several departments through an organization development process.

To the superficial observer, the survey results do not indicate serious employee attitude problems. The strongest and most widely held negative views concerned the lack of cooperation among work groups and the absence of adequate information on the performance of the employee's own work group. Nonetheless, the matter is being elaborately and patiently pursued. In one department, an identification of specific situations or complaints related to the opinions expressed in the survey were solicited through interviews with a sample of employees; then, the departmental work force was resurveyed for opinions on those specifics. Task groups of employees and supervisors are, with the assistance of organization development experts, attempting to reach a consensus on the nature of employee relation problems within the department. The effort has deliberately focussed on problem definition rather than solutions in the belief that the former is the more important first-stage objective.

City Manager Schrader has taken the survey to heart. He has been impressed with the need to communicate more effectively with employees, for example so that they are aware of important developments in their own departments before they read about them in the newspapers. Hughes and Flower have also convinced him, from the replies to a different set of questions dealing with employee attitudes toward authority, that he should play a more visible leadership role with respect to city employees.

The gains, if any, from this process to date are minor. It is important today as an indication of the city government's recognition of the importance of employee attitudes.

The World Outside

Local governments in Texas are not now authorized to bargain collectively with employee unions. A recent state law, however, permits bargaining if it has been approved by popular referendum in the affected jurisdiction. Dallas voters have once rejected collective bargaining, but there is little doubt that the issue will come before them again in the near future.

In the meantime, employee unions are not powerful even in an informal sense. Police and fire fighters are both organized as local associations rather than as locals in international unions. The fire union has pressed toward parity with the police and the city has been responsive to the extent of taking one step in that direction. Neither union has raised any issue of significance for productivity.

The city-operated public transportation program was previously a private enterprise with unionized employees; the employee union has continued under city operation. A local of the American Federation of State, County and Municipal Employees counts a few hundred of the city's other employees as members. There are no other unions.

The absence of unions gives the city management in Dallas flexibility in work organization and method of the kind that has long since vanished in the unionized large cities of the northeast and the midwest. No one believes that this situation is likely to change very suddenly. But it seems equally clear that Dallas sees the spectre of New York and San Francisco in its future and that it is not going to create a climate conducive to militant unionism. The city will be responsive to employee attitudes and will maintain adequate compensation levels at least partially on the theory that an ounce of prevention is worth a pound of cure.

The city council has, until its action on the 1975-1976 budget, tended to direct its attention to the broad policy issues of the budget leaving the details to the city manager. This council and its predecessors have had a strong interest in economy and expenditure control. It has given the city manager the support required for his efforts to increase productivity, neither taking the initiative nor placing obstacles in the way of the manager's approach.

Productivity improvement in Dallas as elsewhere has attracted little attention or interest from the voters or the general public. This is probably because there have been few significant changes in the way services have been delivered to the general public save the extension of hours for garbage collection.

The Dallas Citizen Survey

The Dallas City Profile Survey has been carried out annually by the Office of Management Services since 1973 as part of the federally-assisted comprehensive planning process. The survey has been designed with unusual care. City departments were solicited for questions to which they would like answering. Experience with other city citizen surveys was reviewed. Professional assistance was used in questionnaire design, sample design, and survey techniques. The cost for the 1975 survey was $50,000.

The survey includes: an interviewer evaluation of housing conditions, significant detail on the demographic and economic characteristics of respondents, and, of course, citizen responses on experience with and attitudes toward various city services and programs. The sample is designed to provide statistically valid data for major city neighborhoods as well as the city as a whole.

Mark Wassenich of the Office of Management Services reports that the city council was surprised by the size of the deteriorated housing stock and the numerous complaints about neighborhood appearance and deteriorated buildings. He attributes to the survey results the decision by the City Council to proceed with a number of housing improvement programs with general revenue sharing funds rather than wait the additional year for Community Development funds. This was a marked departure from the previous policy of restricting housing programs to the availability of federal grants for that purpose. The housing issue is, however, probably the only instance where the survey data have influenced council action.

The city manager established a special task force to investigate the handling of citizen complaints and requests as a result of the survey finding that two-fifths of the citizens did not receive a satisfactory response.

The survey data has provided more balanced data in some areas. For example, complaint volume had identified Traffic Control as a serious problem but the survey showed high citizen rating for that service. The survey has also contributed to planning efforts, notably the Community Development Plan.

It seems clear, however, that the Citizen Profile, to date, has had very limited impact on city policies and programs. There are real dilemmas. Under what circumstances, for example, should citizen attitudes overrule the judgment of professional traffic engineers on signal location? To what extent are unfavorable minority attitudes toward police simply a reflection of higher crime and arrest rates among minority groups than among whites? If the sanitation chief argues that the reported proportion of missed collections is inevitable at current funding levels, should more funds be provided to reduce missed collections?

Changes in public attitudes between surveys may prove to be the most useful survey data but, even here, the implications for action may be obscure. The 1975 survey, for example, showed a significant drop but a still high rating for the fire service. Who knows what caused the drop or what can remedy the situation? To take another change, how does one explain an increase in crime coupled with a sharp decline in the fear of crime?

The potentially valuable behavioral data, such as the 1975 questions on library use and users, could result in an effort to promote library use by poor people or, on the other hand, a decision to improve the quality of service to middle-class clients.

Almost certainly, data usefulness will increase with time, experience, and the buildup of time series data on changing attitudes.

Management and Implementation

The conception and development of productivity improvements in Dallas have never been far from operations management. Managers have been closely involved in nearly all the developments, thereby contributing a heavy emphasis upon the practical feasibility of proposed changes. At the same time, the Office of Management Services with its superior technical skills in the managerial disciplines has typically kept a close involvement through the implementation period. OMS Director Vanderbilt has been project director on many of the larger endeavors. These two factors provide the best explanation for the general absence of significant problems in the implementation of change proposals.

In some instances, notably in Building Services, any doubts have been resolved by testing new approaches on a pilot basis before moving to general application. There has been little use of project management systems or other scheduling and control systems to assure prompt implementation.

There are other reasons why implementation has posed no special problems. Most of the productivity improvements have taken place in well-managed departments and the improvements have been understood, accepted and, in fact, typically instigated by department managers. Although Dallas is the nation's eighth-largest city, the scale of operations within city departments has not passed the point that would jeopardize managerial comprehension and control. Perhaps, it is also important that work force attitudes toward change have not been negative or hostile.

An Overview

The productivity program in Dallas falls more within the internal discipline of the executive branch of the city government than do the productivity programs of most other cities. It has, unlike Detroit, Nassau County, or New York, no complex problem of negotiating productivity increases with strong employee unions. Unlike its counterparts in Phoenix, Milwaukee, or Palo Alto, the City Council in Dallas is not deeply involved in the details of the productivity improvement program. The City Manager has, consequently, a relatively free hand in shaping the productivity improvement effort so long, of course, as he remains within limits dictated by the political sensitivities of the community and the City Council.

The productivity strategy in Dallas has been unstructured, opportunistic, pragmatic, and adaptive rather than systematic and comprehensive. The city has "picked its spots," concentrating its productivity efforts on opportunities with a high potential payoff and low departmental resistance. Two of the big winners—Streets and Sanitation and Building Services—required little more than moral support for departmental management. The third—the Water Utilities Department—was dependent on a substantial investment for consultants and the time of central office staff. In the Fire and Police Departments, where resistance to outside direction is traditionally strong, the City Manager has not grasped the nettle; instead, he has exploited his opportunities for bargaining on incremental programs and funding, such as salary increases for police and funds for more fire houses.

The initiatives have come largely from the Office of Management Services or from the Manager's Office. OMS has, in addition, been the major source of expert support. This is likely to change with the successful experience in Streets and Sanitation, Building Services, and Water Utilities and with the approval of industrial engineering staff for the latter two agencies.

Dallas has enhanced its opportunities for productivity improvements by an unusually active reorganization program. Beginning with the breakup of the large Department of Public Works, the city has moved toward smaller, more homogenous departments with single or closely interrelated missions. This has provided opportunities for managerial changes and for increased attention to neglected areas within the larger departments.

Consistent with this approach, the supporting services, usually given short shrift in the substantive departments, have been consolidated in central service departments—Data Services, Equipment Services, and Building Services—where they can be given consistent professional attention. At the same time, the Office of Management Services has been strengthened by new staff skills and by the application of a broad mission concept linking budget functions with planning, management analysis, and technical assistance to the operating agencies.

The city has given far greater recognition than most to the need to explore the attitudes of both its employees and its citizens. These efforts do not seem, to date, to have made a substantial contribution to policy making but there is every reason to expect that they will do so increasingly in the future. The follow-up of the employee attitude survey with elaborate organization development approaches seems particularly promising.

The basic strategy has worked well for Dallas. Opportunities for substantial productivity gains have been exploited with central staff of minimum size. It has maintained a high ratio of productivity savings to the investment required to produce them, largely because it has been selective rather than comprehensive.

A basis for further progress has been established by the new staffs in Water and Building Services and by the transfer of Traffic Control to Streets and Sanitation. More problematical is the extent to which the present approach will prove adequate in stimulating change in the remaining agencies of the government. One would guess that future progress will depend on the investment of more OMS staff time in problem diagnosis and agency education—a function that can be performed to only a limited degree with available staff.

Dean Vanderbilt, the Director of Management Services, has a somewhat different perspective. He has concluded that a budget agency's adversary position with respect to the operating agencies greatly limits the use of budget staff to assist agencies in problem solving. This made the industrial engineers on his staff less useful than he had hoped. He contrasts this situation with Dallas' unusually effective utilization of consultants. The experience indicates that where problems have been identified and where the agency can be persuaded to act, the actual analysis can be done more effectively by consultants.

3 Detroit[a]

Detroit, with a population of 1.3 millions, is America's fifth-largest city. Only New York, Chicago, Los Angeles, and Philadelphia are larger. The others are urban centers of extraordinary economic diversity but, in Detroit, despite more diversity than is usually recognized, the automobile remains undisputed king. Detroit may, in fact, well be the largest town in the world so dominated by a single industry.

With all of the ups and downs of the economy, automobile manufacture was, for perhaps half a century, the most important and powerful growth industry in the American economy. The automobile made Detroit, and it did so largely after the first World War. Detroit is, much more than the other large cities of the east and midwest, a product of the twentieth century with a low density pattern of development resembling that of Los Angeles rather than Chicago, Philadelphia, or Cleveland.

The automobile worker has been long the elite of industrial workers ever since Henry Ford raised the pay of his workers to an incredible five dollars a day in 1915. The auto worker's high position has been extended and maintained since unionization and the growth of the United Automobile Workers. When Detroit has been flush and jobs abundant, prospective workers have come in droves. The city's huge role in World War II production brought thousands to the city including large numbers of both Appalachian whites and Southern blacks. Some of the migrants returned when the good times ended, but many stayed and more came on later surges of industry prosperity.

Detroit's three-quarter century romance with the automobile has left it with three important characteristics today. First, it is the model, the very prototype of a union town. The employees of its government are more organized and its unions more aggressive and militant than anywhere except New York. Second, the migrants have made it a city with a black majority, the largest city in the country of which this is true. Racial relations are a continuing and important problem as is the high concentration of poverty among the black population.

---

[a] My review of the Detroit Productivity Center was greatly aided by access to the evaluation report on the Center by Professor Robert DauffenBach of the University of Illinois.

Lastly, Detroit's economy follows the cycle of the automobile industry with few other basic industries to dampen its impact on either the upside or the downside.

These alone would give the city government a hatful of problems. Detroit faces, in addition, its decline in relationship to its own suburbs. The impact on Detroit has been pronounced, probably greater than in most eastern and mid-western cities. The city's population, which twenty years ago was approaching 2 millions, has fallen by a third to its current level of 1.3 million. The classic central city syndrome of declining resources and increasing problems is already well advanced.

Detroit is a city with severe fiscal problems. Budget pressures led to reductions in the city's work force from 23,677 in July 1974 to 18,403 in June 1976. The 1976-1977 fiscal year began with the discharge of 913 police officers, a sixth of the force, as the first step in the elimination of a $103.3 million budget gap.

The Productivity Program

The origins of the Detroit productivity program can be traced back to the pioneering effort at productivity bargaining in 1973. That effort resulted in a contract with the city's refuse collectors providing for incentive payments for performance exceeding specified efficiency and quality standards. At the time, the contract seemed to represent a major breakthrough in achieving managerial productivity objectives in a strongly unionized city. That effort (which is more fully discussed in Chapter 10) did result in measurable gains for the city and somewhat less certain benefits for the collectors. Ultimately, the union refused to continue the arrangement in the new contract signed in 1974 but, in the fall of 1973, the productivity bargain still could be counted a success.

After Coleman Young's election as mayor in 1973, he set up meetings for himself and his staff with the department heads of the outgoing administration of Mayor Gribbs. One of the latter was Peter Jason, the Director of Labor Relations. The new mayor and Jason hit it off from the beginning, partly perhaps because of Young's own background in labor relations.

Jason voiced his opinion that if the Mayor wanted to improve the performance of city agencies he would have to start doing something about it then. He couldn't wait for the expiration of city labor contracts three years hence. Jason spoke of the work Andy Giovanetti, a young graduate student, had done in his thesis on Detroit's refuse collection operation. Giovanetti later worked for the city where he was instrumental in the development of the productivity incentive payment system negotiated with the sanitation workers. Jason thought the city needed to develop an analytical capacity with more staff like Giovanetti. The Mayor liked the idea.

Daniel Dozier of Young's staff, who had been involved in these conversations, developed the ideas into a proposal for a Productivity Center for which Ford Foundation funding was requested. When the Foundation approved, the center was on its way.

The Detroit Productivity Center (DPC) was set up in the Office of the Mayor in the summer of 1974 with initial funding of $150,000 from the City of Detroit and $75,000 from the Ford Foundation. The Center had positions for ten professionals, about half of which were filled by civil servants transferred from other agencies and half by contract consultants. There were, in addition, three professional service trainees employed from federal funds under the Comprehensive Employment and Training Act (CETA).

The Center's first Director was John M. Cox, who served in that capacity from September 1974 until July 1975. Cox is an M.B.A. and an industrial engineer with extensive experience in industry and other government organizations and as a consultant manager. Cox was replaced by Ollie McKinney, an economist and career civil servant, then acting director of Manpower and previously Deputy Director of Planning. The new director engaged as his deputy Daniel Dozier, the mayoral assistant who had written the original grant proposal and who was responsible for liaison with the center; Dozier left city employment in March 1976.

The Center reports directly to the Office of the Mayor without formal ties to either the Bureau of the Budget or the Department of Finance. Its independence was an issue at the time of its establishment and not finally resolved until November 1974. Reportedly, the budget director, the finance director, and the director of Data Processing have not been strongly supportive of the Center.

Cox's plans for the Center involved an extensive organizational structure. Two committees were established to work with and assist the operations of the Center. The first is the Mayor's Management Advisory Committee (MMAC), which Cox patterned after a State of Michigan Governor's Committee on Expenditure Management with which he had once worked. The membership of MMAC was drawn from business, union, and academic leaders in the Detroit community. The committee was cochaired by Wayne State University's Vice-President for Urban Affairs and the Regional Director of the United Automobile Workers. The committee included such members as the deans of Engineering at the University of Detroit, Oakland University, and Wayne State University, Chrysler's manager of Systems Planning, the manager of Operations Planning and Technical Services of the Michigan Consolidated Gas Company, Chevrolet's director of Research and Training, Ford's manager of Operations Research, as well as many senior officials of the AFL-CIO and the United Automobile Workers. The committee clearly had superb technical credentials in management analysis in addition to its broad business-labor-university representation.

MMAC was intended to provide policy advice and guidance on the use of the Center's resources. A second group, drawn from MMAC membership, the Committee on Management Effectiveness in Government (COMEG) was a technical task force of productivity specialists from area businesses, designed as a conveyance mechanism to bring private sector technology to the city. COMEG members are supposed to work closely with the departments on implementation of productivity improvement efforts and the establishment of the management development program.

The Cox productivity program blueprint also called for program coordination through productivity representatives in each department; some fifty such representatives were appointed. In addition, Productivity Improvement Committees were created in May 1975 in most departments. The committees generally included union and management personnel from the department plus representatives from labor relations, MMAC, the Productivity Center, and middle management. The deputy department director served, in each case, as chairman of the committee. The committees were barely underway when Cox was replaced by McKinney, and most have not met since that time.

The Productivity Center was designed as a service organization. It was intended to provide resources needed by the departments in developing productivity improvements and, of course, to encourage the departments to think about productivity. The Center had limited "muscle," and it was not designed to force productivity changes on the departments. The DPC assignments are determined by the Center's ability to sell the heads of the various operating agencies and, occasionally by the Office of the Mayor; presumably in areas of high mayoral priority the mayor will exercise whatever muscle is necessary to bring around reluctant department heads.

The Productivity Center was to function in three different ways. The first, productivity coordination, is essentially system development. The DPC planned to work with the departmental productivity improvement committees, train the departmental coordinators in industrial engineering and management science techniques, and assist the departments in the establishment of output units, time targets, and productivity indices.

Special staff studies, the second thrust of the DPC effort, are designed to achieve specific productivity improvements. These could be major studies, short-term limited projects, the development of advice on technology and best practice for the departments, or the evaluation studies done before any major DPC resource commitment is made.

A third category, special projects, was to cover those activities that cross departmental lines, such as the proposed development of a City Procedures Manual, centralized control over consulting contracts, and a centralized materials management system. However, the projects of this character proposed by the Center were not approved by the mayor's office and were, instead, referred to the Finance Department for action.

Productivity Improvement Projects

By the winter of 1975-1976, the Detroit Productivity Center was staffed and had initiated ten major productivity improvement projects as well as a number of lesser projects.

The Fire Department Apparatus Shop Project was one of the first projects to be begun by the Center. The apparatus shop is the central repair facility for all the equipment of the Detroit Fire Department including the Emergency Medical Service. The basic problem leading to the Fire Department's interest in a DPC analysis of the situation was the high proportion of first-line equipment (less than twenty-years old) usually out of service for repairs.

The source of the problem was identified as inadequate inventory and preventive maintenance systems and the lack of labor performance controls. In addition, short-term operating information was inadequate for the proper management of the repair facility.

To help resolve these problems, the DPC staff developed the Service Information Control System with Inventory, Repair Performance and Vehicle Reporting subsystems. The system will use a system of work order, labor tickets, and the like for off-site computer processing and analysis. A variety of periodic management reports will be provided including: performance summaries by type of repair; overall summaries of shop performance; a weekly report on backlog status; inventory status reports; and vehicle status reports identifying all labor and materials use by vehicle and summaries by vehicle type and year. Labor performance targets will be established for most maintenance and repair tasks and documented in a manual. Finally, a physical inventory was conducted and all obsolete parts disposed of preparatory to the establishment of a data base for the inventory module of the Service Information Control System.

The Recreation Department Forestry Project was also begun in the early days of the Productivity Center. The Forestry Division is responsible for the trimming of healthy trees and removal of dead and diseased trees from the city streets. Part of that responsibility is contracted out to private firms. A study showed that trees were removed by private contractors at one-third the unit cost of city operations.

The mayor's office rejected a recommendation by the Center's engineers that a substantial additional part of the service be contracted out to private contractors. The Productivity Center then conducted a work sampling effort that indicated that productivity could be doubled and developed measures to achieve that objective. The project will have no effect on the city budget since the service is financed by state grants.

The president of the union representing the employees involved cooperated with the initial work of the Productivity Center. He saw productivity improvement as a necessary step to prevent the eventual contracting out of the activity.

He helped by identifying the adverse effects on productivity of the use of trucks too small to carry a full crew and the shortage of trimming equipment and saws resulting from snafus in equipment repair.

The DPC staff assigned to the project established labor performance standards for crews and a performance monitoring system. Increased supervision was recommended as well. A new equipment replacement policy was proposed to deal with the problem of equipment out of service for repairs. The recommendations also called for some additional shifts of work to private contractors.

While DPC staff members were measuring and reporting productivity for a sample pilot crew, productivity increased by 30 percent. The director of the Department was enthusiastic about the project and interested in going forward with the recommendations. However, she resigned after employee complaints to the Mayor's Office led to what she regarded as constraints on her managerial authority. Her successor also supported the productivity improvement effort and directed his staff to proceed with it. The effort languished in the absence of effective follow-up. Eventually, the DPC engineer dropped the project believing his time could be more profitably spent elsewhere. There is currently no effort to implement the DPC recommendations.

The Russell Ferry Garage Project is also in the Department of Recreation. The garage is responsible for the repair of the department's special equipment ranging from aerial towers to mowers and sprayers; all automotive repairs, even on such equipment, are done at another garage.

The record of the repair facility has been unsatisfactory with respect to both the cost of repairs and the time equipment is kept out of service. An aerial tower, for example, averages two months a year in the Russell Ferry garage and another month in the automotive repair facility, with aggregate annual repair costs of $3,000. Repairs on some $200 saws have run as high as $100.

The DPC designed a system of labor standards and management controls. It included a job coding manual with time estimates for the most frequently done repairs, the use of work orders and labor tickets with estimated and actual repair times, and management reports summarizing performance by foreman, employee, and type of repair. The completed system has been tested but not implemented.

The Vehicle Management Division Project in the Environmental Protection and Maintenance Department also involves a repair facility. The Division manages eight different garages at seven locations, servicing 4,000 vehicles including 1,600 police vehicles, 850 sanitation packers, 600 specialty vehicles and 950 other passenger vehicles. Many city vehicles were tied up for long periods of time for repairs; garage operations were visibly sloppy. Although the operation had an annual budget of $15 million, there were no on-going productivity measures or enforcement of labor controls and standards.

The recipe for improved operation included a computerized management information system as well as labor and job standards and a scheduling system.

In addition, recommended physical improvements are being made in the garages to improve traffic and work flow and to provide a better working environment. The work force has been expanded to aid a smooth flow of current work and to start a preventive maintenance program, but eventually, staff reductions will be possible as productivity increases. More efficient operations should also permit a reduction in requirements for city vehicles.

The Inventory Control Project in the Department of Transportation started in May 1975 calls for the development of a computerized control system for the inventory of parts for the city's 980 busses and a small number of other vehicles. There were 30,000 parts in four garages. Inventory record and control was manual, and more than half the parts in inventory were obsolete. Many coaches, on the other hand, operated without needed repairs because of the absence of the required parts. Moreover, the manual system was extremely costly to operate.

The Payroll System for bus drivers in the Department of Transportation would, under DPC recommendations, be automated on a mini-computer. Standard shifts and times would be maintained for each driver. Exceptions for overtime, switched routes, vacation, sick leave, and the like would be inputted by a clerk for each pay period. This project was initiated in 1976 as an offshoot of other projects within the department.

A Repair Facility Labor Performance System is to be installed in the bus repair garages of the Department of Transportation. The initial DPC work sampling in April 1975 showed that only half of the time accounted for was productive time and that work done during productive time was at half the productivity of the rates specified in the department's job repair manual. This yields an average productivity rate of about one-fourth the specified standards. One-fifth to one-fourth of the busses were out of service for repair at any one time. As a result, scheduled routes were sometimes missed and far more was expended on repair than should be necessary.

The DPC engineers planned to install a computerized management information system, using a minicomputer, to create a repair history for every bus and a work performance history for every employee and type of job. Plans also included a preventive maintenance program and a work scheduling system.

A survey of the Water and Sewage Department was initiated at the request of the Water Board. The Water Board's president, in a letter to the mayor, cited the disappearance of $60,000 worth of copper pipe, poor inventory control and security, and high payments for mileage and overtime.

The DPC survey in July 1975 identified a need for widespread managerial changes with substantial potential impact on revenues and expenditures. Labor standards for vehicle and water line repair, improved repair and replacement policies, as well as more advanced technology for water meters, automated inventory control, and some organizational changes would be required to do this. The department asked DPC to conduct an operational audit and provided

$14,000 for that purpose. The audit identified the areas where improvement was needed and DPC was negotiating in mid-1976 for projects to design the needed changes. By this time, however, DPC no longer had the industrial engineering staff to do the job, and top management in the Water Department was skeptical of DPC's competence.

DPC also developed recommendations in early 1975 for the reorganization of the Operations Analysis Staff in the Environmental Protection and Management Department. The staff was supposed to be the in-house technical and analytical staff for the EPMD Director but, actually 85 percent of staff time (more than twenty employees) was used for the preparation of daily solid waste operating summaries and other clerical tasks. Little time was left for analysis of any kind or for work on other EPMD activities.

The DPC proposed that most of the present employees be reassigned to the department's operating divisions and that clerical-administrative responsibilities be transferred with them. The staff would be reconstituted with higher professional titles. The department agreed to these recommendations but has taken no action to implement them.

The Phone-In System Project in the Purchasing Department came about as a result of the failure of an attempted improvement in agency requisition procedures begun without DPC involvement. A system for phoning-in requisitions was introduced to cut delays in procuring equipment and supplies. The phone-in system complicated the purchase process with increased errors and actually added to the average time required to fill requisitions.

DPC proposed to eliminate the Phone-In system, the extra phones, and costly transcription equipment. This recommendation was implemented in early 1976. For the longer term, more changes were indicated. DPC expected that its further recommendations would involve massive computerization and telecommunications. The Center was, however, apparently stepping on someone's toes and was pulled off the project by the Mayor's office.

This group of projects represents less deliberate selection by DPC than the opportunities afforded by the more cooperative agencies. Each project also required prior approval by the Mayor's office.

Heavy concentration on vehicle and equipment repair projects is especially interesting in this light. These were almost certainly advantageous projects for the DPC, inasmuch as they were amenable to straightforward application of management and industrial engineering techniques.

The projects did not, in the main, represent newly discovered problems. In at least four of the projects, there were prior consultant studies with recommendations that were never implemented. DPC's special advantage in these cases was the capacity to evaluate and update the old studies, to monitor and assist in implementation.

The NSF Purchasing Project

The Detroit Productivity Center initiated in collaboration with Wayne State University on October 15, 1975, a project financed by a $164,000 grant from the National Science Foundation to develop and test productivity measurements for municipal purchasing. This is a fifteen-month project with John M. Cox, former DPC director, as project manager. It involves a search of the relevant literature, a questionnaire survey of purchasing functions in other states, cities, and counties, and in-depth studies of purchasing in eight selected state and local governments.

The effort is intended to define factors and systems with respect to productivity measurement of purchasing and related functions. Those factors and systems will be pilot tested in Detroit. The results are being disseminated to other cities in bulletins, fact sheets, and reports.

The NSF project represents an expansion of about 40 percent over the basic Center program. It permits the Center to participate in applied research on one of the basic problems of productivity programs.

Expertise

The basic DPC concept called for in-house consulting capacity. From the beginning, staff for the Productivity Center was drawn from two groups. The first were those with expertise in management and the methodology of work analysis—MBA's, industrial engineers, operations researchers, and computer systems analysts. Individuals with such expertise were hired as contractor consultants. At the end of the first program year, the Center Director and five staff members had been drawn from this category.

The second group were civil servants drawn from various other agencies of the city government. At the end of the first year, there were four professionals in this category plus an additional three financed from CETA funds. None had significant credentials in quantitative analysis, but the Center conducted training sessions in analytic techniques for them and encouraged them to take courses that would add to their capacities.

The mixed group, in these proportions, proved effective. The civil servants were effective, partially because they were familiar with the city government. Moreover, they had back-up support from the experts on the staff in any problem that did require a more sophisticated analytic approach.

In the year following the replacement of Cox by McKinney, there were drastic changes in the staff of the Center. All but one of the original group of engineers and analysts hired as contract consultants left the Center and were not replaced. Recruitment concentrated on civil servants, none of whom were industrial engineers or management scientists. Although the City increased the Center's budget from $150,000 in the 1974–1975 fiscal year to $285,000 in 1975–1976, the size of the staff actually declined.

McKinney emphasizes the need for civil service staffing as a means of assuring the continuity of the Center into another mayoral administration. He believes that the Center's career staff is of very high quality. Two have Master of Business Administration degrees, another a Master of Industrial Psychology, and a fourth, an M.A. in Political Science. Four of the remaining five are enrolled in master's degree programs while the fifth is taking work in accounting and computer sciences. Three of the nine had been manpower planners, one a purchasing agent and another a budget analyst. An even distribution by race and sex was sought and obtained; there are four blacks, two of them female, and five whites including two women.

The education and experience of the career staff clearly has relevance for the work of the Center. There is, however, no indication that the career staff has the technical skills in industrial engineering and operations research lost by the departure of the contract consultants. That technical expertise has certainly been drastically reduced by the changes.

The Productivity Center is now the Productivity and Management Division of the mayor's office, and McKinney is both director of the Division and executive assistant to the Mayor. The new organization underlines the vastly better connections with the mayor's office resulting from McKinney's appointment. The staffing changes within the center have had a parallel effect by expanding a civil service staff with less specialized expertise but with more knowledge of the city government and the machinations of its bureaucracy.

In retrospect, it seems apparent that Cox and his small group of industrial engineers and management analysts were highly vulnerable. They were all outsiders to city government and politics as well as new additions to the payroll in a government that had laid off thousands of civil servants. Cox's technocratic concept of the Center was viable only so long as it had top-level support. That support was, seemingly, ambiguous during Cox's tenure and unlikely to survive his departure.

Mayor's Management Advisory Committee

Despite its high technical and leadership credentials, the Mayor's Management Advisory Committee found it difficult to establish a useful role for itself in the city's productivity program. Professor DauffenBach, in his evaluation report, notes that as late as August 1975, the minutes of the Committee's meeting show members still asking: "What are we here for?" The mayor never met with the Committee or translated his general charge to the Committee into specific missions. The Committee, to a large extent, was required to develop its own role.

The Committee has made two useful concrete contributions. First, its Subcommittee on Data Collection and Productivity Enhancement critiqued the Productivity Center's plan to collect output data from the operating agencies. The subcommittee suggested that this function be performed by Finance or Budget. They also pointed out the limitations of such output data without corresponding input data; the proportion of DPC's limited resources required to audit the data and provide technical assistance to the agencies; the desirability of looking first at systems in other cities; the need to explore the use of more sophisticated EDP equipment; and the problems inherent in combining DPC's service mission with the incompatible function of monitoring and evaluating agency performance.

A second Committee contribution was the development of a priority decision grid for evaluating potential projects. The grid took into account a variety of factors such as payback, probability of successful execution, the suitability of DPC's resources for the particular problem, public opinion, and the special opportunities afforded by concurrent changes in program service level.

A potentially more important role for the Committee seems in process of development. The Committee was exploring the possible usefulness of a program of seminars on productivity for city officials. They elected to examine this problem in the specific context of one agency, the Detroit General Hospital (DGH). In discussions with many of the hospital's supervisory staff, the Committee members discovered a host of managerial and productivity problems, including the lack of systems planning for the new hospital facility scheduled to open in 1978. Ultimately, the Committee elected with the agreement of the hospital to survey eight DGH systems and, in one area, Nurse Staffing and Scheduling, to go beyond the survey stage to perform an analysis of the system. The Committee developed a proposal for the creation of a Hospital Management Engineering or Operations Research Group within DGH or, possibly, outside DGH to service other health facilities in addition to the hospital. DPC Director McKinney has voiced exception to the creation of such a Management Engineering Group.

At this stage, the DGH project is a possible model for orienting the Committee's future work toward specific agencies. An alternative, with some similarities, is to increase the involvement of the Committee's members in projects being carried out by DPC staff.

The Results

The Center has had significant success in persuading some of the operating agencies in the city to use its services. Fire, Transportation, Environmental Protection and Maintenance, Water, and Recreation have all become significant clients of the Center. It is not easy, in any setting, to achieve voluntary entry for outsiders likely to be disruptive and perhaps eventually critical of existing agency arrangements. The feat is the more impressive inasmuch as it was done without any strong pressure on the agencies by the mayor. On the other hand, there has been no involvement in most other agencies, a situation the Center is likely to correct only with marked and visible success on its current projects. (The Center was given specific instructions by the mayor's office to stay out of the Police Department.)

The failure of the Center has been in implementation. Cox estimated in his June 1975 report to the Ford Foundation that DPC projects would yield savings of $1.5 million in the 1975–1976 fiscal year. None of these savings were, in fact, achieved.

DauffenBach, in his draft evaluation report of March 1976, wrote:

... The actual practice of implementing productivity improvement designs has proved cumbersome. So cumbersome, in fact, that none of the major project designs is installed and operational. The blame for poor implementation performance rests on all parties associated with a given major project activity. This includes not only operating agency personnel such as the Forestry Department people and the DPC, but also people in finance and budget, who have been known on several occasions to engage in foot dragging, in my view, on purchase requisitions coming out of DPC.[1]

DauffenBach may, in fact, understate the problem. In truth, there seems to have been little serious interest in advancing projects into implementation.

The program carried out by the Center has departed rather sharply from initial expectation in several respects. Nearly all the work performed by DPC has been in the area of special staff studies. The productivity coordination function—the training and development of departmental staff assigned to Improvement Committees and the establishment of targets, output, and productivity measures—was initiated in the Center's first year but has received little subsequent attention. Similarly, comparatively little work has been done on interagency programs, such as the City Procedures Manual. The first of these is probably most important, because it indicates the failure to develop supporting skills and operations in the agencies.

At the same time, there are strong indications that the internal management of the Center has deteriorated. From August 1975 when McKinney took over from Cox until June 1976, not a single new project of any significance was initiated. An April 25, 1976 article in the *Detroit Free Press* by William J. Mitchell reports complaints by various employees on the absence of technical direction, the lack of any effort on the part of the director to keep informed on staff activity and the failure to "unleash" Center staff on projects that need doing. McKinney is quoted as emphasizing his role as a "policeman" over agency performance; at the same time, he argues the case for caution in moving recommendations into implementation.

The original grant application to the Ford Foundation envisaged substantial involvement by employee unions. This involvement has not yet developed, perhaps because the projects to date have not affected unions with high sensitivities on the workload issue, or, perhaps, because none of the projects has been implemented so far.

The departmental productivity improvement committees were intended to be the vehicle for union involvement in specific projects. The inactivity of most of these committees has consequently reduced the extent of union involvement. One significant exception has been the productivity committee in the Department of Housing, which has continued to meet to identify and discuss departmental productivity programs.

The abandonment of the initial emphasis on the development of an in-house staff with high expertise suggests a different future mode of operation. Nearly a year after Cox's replacement by McKinney, however, no new strategy had emerged. A Productivity Center can function with a staff with limited skills in industrial engineering and like disciplines but only with a far different approach. If such a staff were to continue to concentrate its attention on industrial engineering type problems, it could do so only with extensive use of project consultants.

The drift and delay in focusing the work of the Mayor's Management Advisory Committee, the failure to move completed designs into implementation, the limited agency coverage of the program, and some other aspects of the Center's experience to date are symptomatic of an absence of strong top-level support for and direction of the program to date. Professor DauffenBach mentions the mayor's seemingly detached role as a significant problem. The Center is Mayor Young's creation, and he has found city funds to support it in an increasingly tight budget. Yet, the visible support from the mayor's office has been tempered and the Mayor's personal involvement limited. The radical changes in city operations such a Center should eventually produce are simply not feasible without the forceful backing of the chief executive.

Future Prospects

The Center's prospects are not promising. It has won a significant degree of acceptance among a few of the city's operating agencies. It carried out analyses and developed productivity improvement designs of professional quality. It has successfully enlisted the participation of the top technical and managerial talents of the Detroit business, union, and university communities. But it has, as yet, made no entry on the "bottom line."

The failure to move its projects into execution and the decline in the professional quality of its staff are all ominous signs. The key factor is the extent to which the mayor will support an aggressive and effective productivity program.

Note

1. Robert C. DauffenBach, "An Evaluation of the Detroit Productivity Center," A Report to the Ford Foundation, August 1976.

4 Milwaukee

Milwaukee had a 1975 population of 669,022 according to a special census, indicating a decline of 48,350 or 7 percent since the decennial census five years earlier. The city is less than half as old as Boston and New York but, in American terms, it is an old city with the problems of old cities. It is wrestling with the problems of suburbanization of both the middle class and industry and with the post–World War II influx of low-income blacks. Milwaukee, unlike many other large cities, remains, visibly and statistically, an industrial city and a markedly brawnier town than, say, San Francisco, Boston, Atlanta, Phoenix, and other cities in the same size range.

Milwaukee is different even from other industrial cities in the unusual ethnic distribution of its population. Like nearly all the Great Lakes cities from Buffalo to the west, it has a large Polish population. However, only St. Louis and Cincinnati competed with Milwaukee in attraction for the nineteenth and early-twentieth century German immigrant. The strong German imprint on the city remains today not just in its famous breweries and restaurants but many believe in a population that has placed a high value on cleanliness, order, efficiency, and prudence in both its government and community. Amidst the decay and deterioration of our industrial cities, Milwaukee as portrayed in a recent *New York Times* article, "remains livable."

Long before World War II, Milwaukee acquired the reputation among those concerned with municipal government as one of the best-managed large cities in America. Among the older large cities of the northeast and midwest, it has an almost unique history of honest government. The pattern of graft and corruption common in many cities and appearing intermittently in most others has been almost unknown in Milwaukee. The city's bonds have long held the highest underwriter's rating, AAA.

Milwaukee is also unusual in the stability of its government. The turmoil in urban America in the mid-1960's took a savage toll among big city mayors. Among them, Henry W. Maier of Milwaukee is the only survivor. In Milwaukee, the long mayoral tenure is common. Maier's fifteen years as mayor, Frank Zeidler's twelve years and Daniel W. Hoan's twenty-four years account for fifty-one of the past sixty years of Milwaukee government.

53

In an administration as long lived as Maier's, the mayor and many of his appointees tend, from long experience, to become far more knowledgeable about city government than the political leadership of most American cities. The gap in understanding and perspective between civil servants and politicians tends to narrow. Radical changes in policy become less likely but, on the other hand, it becomes possible to provide the sustained support needed for long-term changes in government. At the same time, short-term political expediency tends to be less important in municipal policy making. All this seems, in varying degrees, to be true of Milwaukee.

Milwaukee has an elected executive mayor form of government. The powers of the mayor fall short of New York and Detroit, but they are substantially greater than those in the weak mayor charters, such as Los Angeles. The mayor shares power not only with the Common Council but also with the independently elected officials—the city attorney, the city comptroller, and the city treasurer—who are members of the powerful Board of Estimates. The Board also includes the mayor, the president of the Common Council, the five members of the Common Council's Committee on Finance and Personnel and the commissioner of public works (who is appointed by the mayor). The Board plays the dominant role in budget administration. The director of the Bureau of Budget and Management Analysis reports not to the mayor but to the Board.

The Initiation of Milwaukee's Productivity Program

They used to tell the tale in Boston of the innocent young newcomer who admired the hat of a lady of very proper Bostonian lineage and had the temerity to ask her where she had purchased it, to which the Boston lady icily replied, "Here, young lady, we don't *buy* hats. We *have* them." Milwaukee's productivity program is very nearly a case of the same kind. The city has had a productivity improvement program for nearly as long as anyone can remember.

The formal beginning of the program goes back to 1950. It began with a four-person management analysis unit in the Budget Bureau created initially to carry out the recommendations made by Griffenhagen and Associates after a review of all city departments. The responsibilities of the unit were gradually extended over the years to cover special management studies, review of vacant positions, record and forms control, review of data service applications, space utilization review, and staff support for the Council's Special Committee on Organization and Methods.

Milwaukee's productivity program does not have that name. Rather, it is an integral part of the budget process and so regarded by the staff of the Bureau of Budget and Management Analysis. The present effort is the result of twenty-five years of evolutionary development during which the budget and budgetary processes, as well as management analysis, have been greatly strengthened.

Milwaukee's budget is a modified performance budget; a more appropriate description might be a program performance budget. Since 1963, the budget has included for each appropriation the number of "units" of work performed or services provided and the cost index per unit. In 1975, the number of employee hours and the number of hours per unit were added to provide a measure less distorted by inflation. The units used vary, depending on the program, from direct and comprehensive workload measures to various indirect indicators of need or work. The effect of this approach is to bring performance and productivity issues to the surface where they will demand the attention of agency heads the budget reviewers, the mayor, the Board of Estimates, and the Common Council.

Since 1964, the performance information in the budget has been supplemented by an annual report, *Operating Improvements and Efficiencies Effectuated by the City of Milwaukee.* This is a compilation of reports prepared by each agency head. Needless to say, this reinforces the pressure to direct agency attention to productivity questions.

Milwaukee uses not only the annual budget process but also the full range of traditional tools of municipal budget administration. No vacant position (with some exceptions) can be filled without budget study, and the Bureau regards this as an important means of reducing staff in areas of low productivity. Space utilization review, forms control, and data service applications are all used to the same basic end.

The Bureau's Division of Management Analysis is responsible for management studies of various city programs. In 1974, the bureau listed a total of 172 reports completed, including both management analysis and budget research reports as well as budget information releases. Not all these deal with productivity issues nor do all of them result from special studies. Yet, a high proportion of them are productivity related.

The studies performed by the Bureau are undertaken with the approval and, often, at the instigation of the Board of Estimates. In fact, the Bureau will typically request a Common Council resolution before initiating a major study. Usually, the implementation of the recommendations of a completed study will require action by the Board of Estimates and the Common Council. This process might be regarded as limiting the free rein of the Director of Budget and Management Analysis. It has, on the other hand, offsetting advantages in the education of political participants in the uses of research and the opportunities for improvement in operations. It also should produce a very realistic research agenda limited largely to projects that the Board and Council regard as both important and actionable.

A large part of what has happened in Milwaukee must be attributed to the leadership of the Bureau of Budget and Management Analysis. Edwin C. Whitney has spent most of his working life in the Bureau and has been its director since 1958. It is obvious that Whitney has developed an extraordinary reputation for integrity and competence with both agency heads and the members of the Board of Estimates and the Common Council. The respect with which Whitney is held has clearly contributed to his ability to develop and apply over a period of seventeen years a rigorous and systematic approach to the control of public expenditures. Walter Simko, the Bureau's assistant director, has been with the Bureau almost as long as Whitney as has Marion J. Kammerer, who heads the Management Analysis Division.

After two decades of working together in the city's budget, the threesome knows nearly everything about the city government, its agencies and programs, about the Board of Estimates, the Common Council, and the political temper of the city and about working with each other. This is not unusual among the best of long-time senior civil servants. What is rare about Whitney, Simko, and Kammerer is that long service seems to have neither dulled nor slowed their efforts to improve the performance of city government.

Skills for Analysis and Program Development

Most of the management analysis incident to productivity improvements has been carried out by the Bureau of Budget and Management Analysis. The Division of Management Analysis on which most of the workload falls consists of only eight professionals, who are engaged for a quarter of the year or more in the reviews required in the preparation of the annual budget. The entire professional staff of the Bureau numbers only fifteen.

Few of the staff have strong training or background in industrial engineering, systems analysis, operations research, or other analytic methodological disciplines. Whitney describes his staff as including "persons with education and training in such things as engineering, statistics, accounting, marketing, economics, and even sociology and nursing." A number of the staff have master's degrees in public administration.

Marion Kammerer comments that new recruits "are hired for their potential and trained on the job." Whitney argues for recruiting staff on the basis of "certain personal attributes rather than work specialities." Those attributes include a dedication to economical and effective government, curiosity, stubbornness and determination, verbal and writing communication skills, accuracy, truthfulness and objectivity, and a willingness to continue learning. He points out the important role of further training and education in the acquisition by his staff of more specialized work-oriented skills.

There are no agency staffs devoted to program and operations analysis. The agency contributions to analysis and to program development come from the time of personnel with other responsibilities, most commonly from those with managerial duties.

Milwaukee's investment in analytical staff is clearly modest. This is the result of neither penury nor accident but rather an expression of Ed Whitney's philosophy. Whitney ridicules the recipe of 5 analysts for every 1000 city employees contained in *So, Mr. Mayor You Want to Increase Productivity*, a publication of the National Commission on Productivity and Work Quality as "one of the best ways to ruin a productivity program." He argues against decentralizing analytic staff to the operating agencies where "productivity invariably ends up by being one of the lesser duties of the department head, shunted aside for items the department head considers more important." Rather, a productivity staff belongs in an agency where it has "the backing of top executive or legislative personnel," is not distracted by extraneous administrative duties and "is in the best possible position to translate productivity increases into budgetary savings." Under usual circumstances, of course, the preferred locale would be the bureau of the budget.

Milwaukee also uses outside consultants. Touche Ross was engaged for work on municipal equipment management, H.B. Maynard on water works management, Price Waterhouse on work measurement in the Bureau of Engineering, Gage-Babcock on Fire Department deployment, and PRC, Public Management, Inc., on management analysis of the police department. The University of Wisconsin-Milwaukee reviewed a Bureau study of code inspection activities. The University has also been involved in training activities through the City Personnel Department and some special economic studies for the Department of City Development.

Whitney emphasizes the supplementary role of consultants and the heavy investment of internal staff time required to properly use consultants. Internal staff is needed for the careful design of the contract and work plan and to supervise the implementation of the consultant contract.

Milwaukee has been associated with Public Technology, Incorporated (PTI) on two projects. The PTI fire house locator model has been used and, currently, PTI is working with the city on a Municipal Equipment Management Program.

The Achievements of the Productivity Program

The Bureau of Sanitation

The *pièce de résistance* of the Milwaukee productivity program is, without question, the 1971 reorganization of refuse collection under the Bureau of Sanitation. The annual savings in terms of reductions in city cash outlay were $3.8

million in 1974 prices. Staff allocated to refuse collection and disposal was cut
by 471 positions.

The Bureau of Budget and Management Analysis had pointed up the potential for cost reduction in studies dating back twenty-five years and had advocated
the reorganization for years without success. Whitney comments that "while the
advantages were apparent, the departmental personalities involved, tradition and
union opposition combined to frustrate the effort."

Milwaukee had two refuse collection operations. The first, the Bureau of
Street Sanitation, collected noncombustible refuse approximately sixteen times
per year, and disposed of it in land fills. Historically, noncombustible refuse
meant the ashes from coal-burning furnaces. Local ordinance required householders to deposit ashes in concrete ash boxes built on the alley side of the lot;
the collection crews emptied the boxes by shoveling out their contents. The
Bureau was organized by ward and was traditionally highly responsive to coun-
cilmen. It was not an efficient organization.

The Bureau of Garbage Collection and Disposal collected combustible refuse, chiefly garbage and paper, forty-eight times per year or about once a week
for disposal in the city incinerators. The Bureau was organized by administrative
districts and generally regarded as more efficient and less political than the Bureau of Street Sanitation. The incinerator work force was organized as a separate
union; it was an area of serious concern to city officials in terms of both employee work practices and union behavior.

With oil and gas rapidly replacing coal for space heating and an influx of
newcomers who did not distinguish between combustible and noncombustible
refuse, there was an increasingly strong case for a combined collection. However,
to do this, it would be necessary to resolve several troubling issues. First, the existing city incinerators did not have adequate capacity to handle the combined
collections and, at the same time, the city's land fills were approaching exhaus-
tion. Second, the political popularity of the Bureau of Street Sanitation not
only made it difficult to secure the elimination of that Bureau but also suggested
that the price for consolidation might be acceptance of the inefficient ward organization for the merged operation. Third, the collection techniques of Street
Sanitation were literally set in concrete—in over 25,000 concrete ash boxes into
which refuse would continue to be dumped, regardless of rules, and which could
be emptied only by shoveling.

The beginning of the end came with the arrival of federal and state air pollution emission standards. The incinerators were old and expensive to operate and
could meet clean air standards only with a very heavy investment in pollution
control gear. The exploration of possible alternatives uncovered the possibility
of contracting out total responsibility for disposal, including trucking refuse from
city transfer stations to out-of-city contractor-operated landfills. Moreover the
troublesome incinerator work force and a union suspected of questionable prac-

tices made the contract approach especially attractive to city officials. The decision was made to go ahead with contract disposal. The difficult districting issue was resolved by substituting for the original four-district plan a three-district scheme that put the Polish and German southside in a single district.

The City Council adopted the plan in December 1970, creating the new Bureau of Sanitation on January 1, 1971 by merging the old Bureau of Street Sanitation into the old Bureau of Garbage Collection and Disposal. The city fathers maneuvered successfully to get the management they needed to head the new bureau, selecting Howard Thompson, an assistant superintendent of Garbage Collection and Disposal, as the first Director.

The Council ordnance provided for the continuation of ash box and basement collection until June 1972. In the interim, a federal employment grant became available which could be used for the work force necessary to demolish and cart away the 25,000 remaining ash boxes without cost to householders. Hardship service was continued after June 1972 for households with coal furnaces, but this required the services of only a single collection crew.

With refuse disposal by contract and a new combined 48 times a year collection, Thompson cut the work force from 1187 to 770 and reduced the number of truck drivers assigned by the Municipal Equipment Bureau from 223 to 169 with, of course, a comparable reduction in the number of trucks used.

Other changes came with the new management. Better scheduling reduced overtime by over $200,000 annually. Insert spreaders and sensor controls have eliminated the need for a helper on salt spreaders at a saving of $80,000 a year. A safety program cut departmental costs resulting from employee injuries by about $40,000 annually. Two-way radios eliminated headquarters check-in and check-out, saving the equivalent of seven crews and $250,000 a year.

More changes are in prospect. The city has contracted with American Can to build and run a recycling plant to handle all the city's refuse. This will cost the city more money than contract disposal through landfill. It is basically a response to citizen pressure for recycling, but it may be a more reliable means of disposal in the future. Thompson has announced his intention of reducing the number of loaders per truck from three to two; the union has challenged his right to do this, and the issue is in abeyance pending arbitration.

Even in the largest American cities, a change that both improves the quality of service and saves nearly $4 million annually is a rare event. It is, by any measure, an impressive managerial performance. Yet, Thompson believes there is still substantial room for improvement. The two-person loader crew standard is not in force. The Bureau is still using some excessively small and obsolete equipment including some sixteen yard trucks. Over the longer run, there will be more thinking about possible alternatives to the expensive backyard pickup system with its heavy labor requirements.

The Water Distribution Division

The Bureau of Budget and Management Analysis completed a study of water distribution operations at the request of the Commissioner of Public Works in June 1973. The study was a devastating indictment of the management of the Water Distribution Division. The Budget group concluded that it was taking twice as long as necessary to repair water main breaks with unnecessary delays occurring at virtually every stage of the complex process.

Field investigation was slow partially because the pair of investigators working the second and third shifts continued to double up on the investigation of every reported break, partially because reliance on manual closing of main water gate valves took too long. Trenching crews reported to the site more than two hours on the average after they were advised of the break. In what sounds like a comic routine, they went to the site pulling the work shanty on a trailer, then sat and waited while the truck returned for the compressor needed to operate the pneumatic hammers. Despite an oversize crew, only one man worked with the jack hammer to open the pavement. Excavation would typically be delayed because the back hoe did not arrive when needed. Four-and-a-half-cubic-yard trucks were used though most trenches were half again to double that size; consequently, work would be stopped in mid-course while the truck left to be emptied. More delays would arise because a specialized caulking crew was needed to actually make the repair.

The study recommended new leadership for the division and a new structure of management systems. The city engaged the management consulting firm of H.B. Maynard to do a more detailed analysis, which, when completed, verified the findings of the budget study and expanded on them.

A new top management position was created over the distribution division and some organizational changes effected. The specialized crew system was eliminated with new general repair crews trained to handle all aspects of water main repair. Crew sizes were reduced. Locator techniques were systematized. The repair staff was cut from 133 to 98, but all jobs were retained for one year, and specialists continued for that period to earn premium pay.

The employee union objected to the reductions but received little support from the leadership of the citywide union. The Council elected to proceed with the recommended changes despite the opposition. The ultimate savings to the city will be approximately $500,000 annually.

Important earlier changes were also made in the Water Bureau. The Riverside and Northside Pumping Stations were automated some years ago, and approximately fifty-five positions were eliminated by attrition in each plant.

Department of Buildings

Prior to 1969, code inspections of existing structures were carried out by five different city departments. Housing code inspections were carried out by sanitation inspectors in the Department of Health. Building inspection was the responsibility of Building Inspection and Safety Engineering. Fire prevention inspections were done by the twenty-five-person fire prevention bureau in the Fire Department. Sprinkler systems and water wastage were the domain of specialized inspectors from the Water Department, but plumbing inspections were done by the Bureau of Plumbing Inspection in the Department of Public Works.

A study by the Bureau of Budget and Management Analysis recommended that the five functions be consolidated into the Department of Building Inspection and that generalist inspectors be cross-trained to do all maintenance type inspections. The mayor wanted a second perspective and asked the Center for Advanced Study in Organization Science of the University of Wisconsin-Milwaukee to review the problem. The university research team supported the findings of the Bureau study.

The Council accepted the consolidation scheme despite strong union opposition from the fire fighters. There was some concern with the adequacy of the administrative capacity of the Department of Buildings Inspection to oversee the implementation of the consolidated system. This was resolved by the mayor's appointment of Alex P. LeGrand, one of his assistants, as special deputy inspector of Buildings. LeGrand carried out the merger and was appointed inspector of Buildings a short time later. He was able to eliminate twenty-two positions by attrition at an annual savings of at least $270,000.

LeGrand believes that the largest benefits from the consolidation came not from the reduced number of inspectors but from the development of systematic enforcement procedures covering violations of all basic codes.

Plumbing, electrical, and construction inspections of buildings under construction were also brought together in the department but not integrated. There have been gains there as well from better coordination in scheduling inspections and from a closer interrelation among the specialized inspectors.

Six years after the event, the fire fighters union was still contesting the consolidation. It managed to get legislation through one house in the State Legislature to require the State Department of Labor, Industry and Human Relations to appoint the Fire Chief as its deputy for Fire Prevention Inspections. The department presently has the option of appointing either the Inspector of Buildings or the Fire Chief as its deputy for this purpose, and annual state payments of some $230,000 to the city depend on the certification of this deputy.

When the legislation was blocked in the other house, the fire fighters were able to get the State Department of Industry, Labor and Human Relations to take their option of removing the deputyship from the Inspector of Buildings and bestowing it on the Fire Chief, thus requiring that state-aided fire inspections be limited to those certified by the Fire Chief and thus, presumably, to those inspections actually done by the Fire Department. Hearings have been held on the City's request to reconsider the action.

Other Productivity Improvements

These are not garden variety productivity improvements, especially since two of them required the merger of operations from separate agencies. Whitney describes "major reorganizations such as the combining of departments or sections thereof to be one of the most challenging, time consuming, obstacle ridden courses you will ever pursue . . . [and] . . . it can be the most profitable in tax saving, resource utilization and service to the public."

Milwaukee has effected a number of such reorganizations. The Sealer of Weights and Measures was merged into the Health Department to form a consumer protection service. The Bureau of Community Development, which maintained property ownership lists, was integrated with the Tax Department. The old bureaus of Street Construction and Maintenance were reorganized into a new Bureau of Street and Sewer Maintenance with all construction assigned to the city engineer.

Another such reorganization has been proposed. The Bureau of Budget and Management Analysis has recommended, in a recent report, the consolidation in a bureau of the Department of Public Works of the responsibility for the maintenance, custody and operation of city buildings and structures now being provided in twelve different city agencies. The report estimates that the merger would yield savings of $150,000 annually.

A comprehensive management audit of the Bureau of Municipal Equipment in 1971 by the Touche Ross consulting firm recommended changes in inventory control, improvements in fleet maintenance records and fleet utilization, and the establishment of maintenance mechanic work standards. The department head, Mr. Louis Miller, has used the recommendations as a guideline to increase the productivity from less than 70 percent of standard to more than 90 percent of standard. During the period 1971–1974, thirty-five positions were reduced by attrition at a final annual saving of at least $400,000.

The city has also achieved very significant budgetary savings from the introduction of new equipment and new technologies. The annual reports on *Operating Improvements and Efficiencies Effectuated by the City of Milwaukee* for the past three years identify a number of such savings:

1. The Bureau of Engineers in the Department of Public Works saved $325,000 in 1974 from a new system of using television to examine sewers for points of clear water infiltration and then sealing the leaks with a spraying technique from inside the sewer.

2. Electric pumps automatically activated by high storm water levels were installed at twenty-nine locations in 1974 at a cost of $167,000 but will save over $50,000 annually by eliminating the need to dispatch emergency crews with portable pumps.

3. Sanitation was able to eliminate six jobs and save $64,000 annually by introducing larger twenty-five-yard packer trucks for some of its bulk collec-

tions. Other significant savings, already mentioned, have come from two-way radios and sensor-controlled salt spreaders.

4. The Bureau of Traffic Engineering and Electrical Services will save $21,000 annually from the use of a pneumatic mole to install PVC pipe crossings under paved roads. The Bureau is also saving $16,000 annually by more extensive use of epoxy-encapsulated transformer units in lieu of cast iron case units.

5. The Police Department has increased revenue by $1 million annually as a result of the computerization of warrant preparation and the addition of a Special Warrant Division.

6. A new harbor crane for container lifting will increase revenues by $20,000 annually and save $10,000 in contract costs for stevedores.

7. The substitution of low-pressure gas-fired boilers for high-pressure coal-fired boilers has led to substantial savings in various agencies—now totalling about $155,760 annually.

Some of the savings achieved in Milwaukee are unusual in a productivity program:

1. An extensive manpower planning program reduced the number of temporary employees used but extended the work season; the reduction in seasonal layoffs will save the city an estimated $150,000 annually in unemployment compensation costs.

2. The city is saving $15,000 annually as a result of negotiations under which the state agreed to finance the cost of electricity for traffic signals adjacent to freeway ramps.

3. Stopping city meat inspection, a state responsibility, saved $43,000 annually and another $139,000 annually was saved by eliminating milk inspection.

4. The city also eliminated the Fire Department arson squads on grounds that arson investigation is a state function.

The contracting out of some services to private industry has also been used to reduce costs or improve performance. Among the services contracted out are:

Refuse disposal.

The Bureau of Engineers TV examination of sewers and spraying technique for sealing.

Laundry for the health department at a net savings of $60,000 per year from the elimination of six positions.

Bookbinding, saving an estimated $40,000 to $80,000 per year depending on the actual degree of implementation and rate of attrition.

Custodial work in some city buildings beginning with the museum and gradually expanding to other city buildings.

Better control of overtime for police officers testifying in court reduced costs by $62,000 annually beginning in 1972. A new simplified parking citation with a return envelope increased revenues from parking fines by $300,000 per year.

Milwaukee has, like some other cities, been able to reduce costs and increase the return to the city by a number of actions to improve cash management and investment practices. It has achieved more than usual benefits from space utilization review—$188,000 in annual savings from a single 1973 move. They have done well on computers; savings are reported from computerization, from centralizing computer responsibilities, and from substituting purchase for lease. The steady elimination of vacant positions in areas with excess staffing adds up to significant totals. Gasoline conservation has contributed appreciable savings.

The Bureau of Budget and Management Analysis estimates that savings from efficiencies introduced in 1974 will amount to $1,530,000 annually and that increased revenues will be well over $400,000 per year. The 1973 program resulted in annual savings of $1.3 million and revenue increases of more than $350,000 annually. In 1972, the comparable annual savings were $1.1 million and the revenue increases $950,000.

Resistance to Change

There has sometimes been opposition to proposed changes among senior staff of the affected organization. It has probably contributed to delays—for example in getting the refuse collection plan accepted—but seems not to have been a serious problem once the decision was made. It is noteworthy, however, that in all three cases discussed in detail—building inspection, sanitation and water distribution— the city administration made a significant effort to assure that the reorganized activity had new, competent, and sympathetic leadership.

The attitude of the department head has probably been the most important factor. The DPW Commissioner, Herbert A. Goetsch, has, for example, clearly been a strong supporter of the effort to improve performance. It is not surprising that the most successful department in effecting productivity improvements has been the Department of Public Works.

Resistance to change is, in any event, an oversimplification. Even very conservative agencies must adapt, in some way, to some external changes beyond their control. Often, this provides opportunities for top management to sell a different approach. The Fire Department in Milwaukee provides a good example.

In 1963, the city was faced with a costly reduction in the fire fighters' work week from sixty-three to fifty-six hours. The city was helpless in arguing against the Fire Department's contention that the city's fire insurance rating would drop if it did anything else except add more fire fighters. Gage-Babcock was hired and did an excellent job refuting many of the Fire Department's contentions. While the total report was never implemented, the report forced the Department to come in with alternative recommendations that saved the City $520,000 annually. Through the relocation of two stations and the reassignment of companies, the Department was able to eliminate four stations, six companies, and two battalions without significant reduction in operating efficiency.

Several years ago, fire force needs were again being pressed. Gage-Babcock did an update of the 1963 study and the PTI station locator model was used to analyze deployment. A special subcommittee of the Organization and Methods Committee augmented by other representatives (including the fire fighters' union) used the PTI program to develop plans for the Organization and Methods Committee. The plans gave alternative locations for 28-30-33-35-38-40 stations. At the time of the study, the City had thirty-three stations. The plan selected by the Committee and passed by the Council called for thirty-five stations—two new ones and the relocation of five existing ones. This was done only after assurances by the Fire Chief that he could do it without any additional personnel or equipment.

The central role of the Board of Estimates in both the initiation of studies and action on their recommendations seems to have prevented the development of the strong differences between the mayor and council that are likely in cities with a more conventional division of legislative and executive responsibilities.

Citizen attitudes have been very important in some instances. It appears, for example, that the popularity of the Bureau of Street Sanitation made the Board and the Council reluctant to approve a consolidation until the circumstances made it ripe and then only under a plan that promised to minimize any adverse citizen reaction. The water distribution study, on the other hand, had its genesis in citizen complaints. Complaints of rooming-house owners, tavern keepers, and other regarding duplication of inspections were a part of the impetus for the consolidation of building maintenance inspections.

Wisconsin law provides for collective bargaining by local government employees. And, in Milwaukee, the unions are strong and aggressive. Ed Whitney, in an address to the Municipal Finance Officers Association on productivity, said, "Unions can be a constant problem. Someday in the not-too-distant future it must be determined whether management or the unions control the destinies of our cities. If we do not fight for strong management rights in our labor negotiations we will find ourselves helpless."

The unions have opposed a number of productivity improvements including: the consolidation of refuse collection, contracting for refuse disposal, integration of building inspections, the reorganization of the water distribution division and two-person refuse collection crews. The last named is in arbitration, but all the others have been implemented without strikes, serious job action, or the payment of any productivity bonus. Yet, the changes involved substantial reductions in staff and increases in average employee workload. Sanitation alone cut total staff by about 40 percent and totally eliminated the employees of one union (the incinerator workers).

These cases are not unrepresentative. There is not a single case of any significant improvement in productivity that has been approved by the city council and then killed by union action. An arbitrator's decision did prevent the contracting of custodial service at the Fire-Police Academy. This does not mean that the unions are impotent. Union resistance was, for example, one of the factors in the long delay in getting approval for the consolidation of refuse collection. The union similarly helped delay for two years the introduction of contract bookbinding in the library. There are undoubtedly other issues that union opposition has made too hot to handle. The absence, for example, in three years' reports on operating efficiencies of any action significantly impacting the working life of fire fighters or police officers probably reflects, in part, the reluctance at the departmental level or above to take on the strong police and fire unions.

Reductions have ordinarily been effected in a manner designed to minimize potential employee and union grievances. Cuts have been usually carried out by attrition. Time has been allowed for reassignment to other jobs. Red line rates have temporarily maintained the salaries of overqualified employees in their new assignments.

The unions seem, as Ed Whitney suggested, to be "a constant problem," a matter of concern in any action that affects workload, working conditions, or staffing. Yet, the unions appear to have tolerated the ultimate right of the city to exercise its managerial prerogatives to make productivity improvements.

There are not now any workload or staffing restrictions in city labor contracts. The city once had a minimum staffing requirement in the contract with the fire fighters. It was removed by an arbitrator at a price in increased wages.

Management and Implementation

Milwaukee has been able to implement proposed productivity improvements without serious managerial setbacks. This reflects not so much the absence of deficiencies in the quality of management as it does the capacity to remedy those deficiencies. Note that managerial changes were made in each of three major productivity-improving changes discussed earlier.

The mayor recognized the administrative weakness of the Department of Buildings Inspection and appointed new leadership to oversee the implementation of the consolidated code inspection. Similarly, the administration installed a new management team at the top of the Bureau of Sanitation and refused the easier option of drifting into a seniority-based selection. The study team reviewing the water distribution division placed the highest priority on the creation of a new managerial position to be filled by recruitment outside the distribution division.

Top management appears to be a thin and lean layer in most of the operating bureaus and departments of city government. For example, Sanitation Superintendent Howard Thompson, recounts how his ability to implement consolidated refuse collection was seriously jeopardized by the sudden death of his assistant superintendent and resolved only by both a good replacement and the agreement of Budget and Management Analysis to approve a third top-management slot for an administrative assistant.

In the absence of any significant managerial staff support in the agencies, the effectiveness of implementation depends primarily on the managerial savvy and perceptiveness of the top managers.

Milwaukee approaches management and implementation with much the same common sense, down-to-earth thinking it applies to program analysis. Manpower is tight, and there are few unnecessary frills. The management and monitoring of changes in an area as major as refuse collection and disposal is done with a minimum of staff and with simple straightforward methods. There is no routine use, for example, of project management or other scheduling systems for this purpose. Unless and until the need for more elaborate approaches is clearly demonstrated, Milwaukee will almost certainly continue with its current methods.

Milwaukee's style runs closer to the philosophy of Sergeant Friday of the old Dragnet radio-TV drama: "All we want are the facts, ma'am." The Bureau of Budget and Management Analysis study team was clearly appalled by a water distribution management that functioned without the facts and without apparent interest in the facts about its own operations—and the study report consequently calls for workload forecasting, work force planning and scheduling, and the information system to support them. Thompson's requested administrative assistant was crucial, in part, because he needed someone who could assemble, analyze, and follow the "numbers" on the bureau's performance during the implementation of the consolidated collection.

The Budget and Management Analysis staff follows the implementation of productivity improving changes. The Bureau has an obvious stake in seeing that estimated savings are actually realized. The record in doing so has been surprisingly good. One certain result is to keep the attention of agency management focused on the changes and the results it is designed to produce.

Milwaukee's success in carrying out large complex changes must, however, be attributed, in the main, to competent and innovative managers like Howard Thompson and Alex LeGrand. The big changes are understandably small in number and are concentrated in a handful of agencies, most of them bureaus in the Department of Public Works.

Ed Whitney notes that nearly all changes proposed have met with initial department resistance and, as a result, nearly all of them took too long to achieve acceptance and be carried out. However, the administration has, apparently, not had to nurse many major changes through agencies with weak or nonsupportive management, because few such changes have been initiated by such agencies or forced upon them. At the same time, the patience, persistence, and persuasion of

Whitney and company have often managed to either turn around the resisters—or, sometimes, outlast them.

Unlike the major reorganizations and restructuring of work processes, smaller incremental productivity improvements are scattered throughout the government. There are typically 300 or so improvements of this character reported annually. Most of them create few demands for managerial effort beyond initiation. Some, such as better space utilization and the elimination of redundant vacant positions, seemingly reveal the long arm of Budget and Management Analysis. Many are related to acquisition of new and better equipment. Once decided on, most of these require only "check list management" to make sure they are not forgotten.

The Department of Public Works occupies such an important role in Milwaukee's productivity improvements that it deserves some special attention. The Department is, in truth, what might elsewhere be called a superagency. It includes bureaus, such as water, sanitation, and sewers, that might in many other cities be separate departments. Commissioner Goetsch is, consequently, the equivalent of a group executive or the head of a conglomerate with a perspective detached from the details of highly specialized operation. He has had no personal involvement in the long development of the modus operandi of, say, the water bureau and hence no reason to be defensive or insular about the proposals to change the system. This broader perspective is undoubtedly strengthened by Goetsch's participation in overall city policy as a member of the Board of Estimates. The point of all this is to suggest that institutional as well as personal characteristics are important in his supportive position toward innovation.

An Overview

Milwaukee's sustained twenty-five-year effort in management improvement is almost certainly unique among the nation's larger cities in its longevity and in the magnitude of the results achieved from a relatively small investment.

In most cities, management analysis is still struggling for acceptance and vulnerable to the doubts of the sceptics. Milwaukee is long past such insecurities and able to provide persuasive evidence that a soundly conceived management analysis and improvement program can pay its keep many times over, year after year. Indeed, the Milwaukee experience would suggest that some large part of the potential for management improvement can only be achieved with a long-term effort. The sustained and effective effort in Milwaukee built credibility for management analysis and educated political leadership to its uses. It has meant that the city was ready when those problem areas long proscribed by political, union, or management objections finally became ripe for solution.

In most cities, critical analysis of performance is a relatively new function, an operation carried out by new people on the works of the established career administrators and professionals of the civil service. Under the circumstances, resistance and hostility are not difficult to understand. Milwaukee departs sharply from this pattern. Here, management analysis has long been institutionalized as an integral aspect of the budget process and carried out under the leadership of established careerists. Clearly this reflects, in part, a degree of continuity in key personnel that few other cities are likely to duplicate.

The conservatism of Milwaukee government pervades nearly every aspect of its management analysis and productivity improvement effort. A management analysis staff of four was an impressive commitment to an untested idea in 1950; after twenty-five successful years, an increase to only eight would appear to fall short by any measure of both need and opportunity in a government the size of Milwaukee's. The seemingly strict policy of centralizing analytic talent cannot but have foreclosed action in some problems that an agency head would tackle on his own but not through Budget and Management Analysis.

One wonders why it should take so long—twenty years or more—to rationalize the known inefficiencies of refuse collection or to uncover the long managerial neglect in water distribution operations. There are comparable questions on investment policy. If sensor controls on half the salt spreaders save $60,000 a year, why were not all the spreaders so equipped? Given the high labor costs incident to operating undersize collection trucks, why does the city still use some such trucks? There is even a question as to the apparent absence of any major failures in the twenty-five-year history of management analysis; one would expect any moderately aggressive effort in managerial reform to occasionally fall flat on its face.

The answer to most of these questions is that management analysis has adapted to the style, the philosophy, the *weltanschaung* of Milwaukee government. The management analysis division may be too small to take on the full menu of city management problems, but it is large enough to analyze nearly all of the issues on which the Board of Estimates and the Common Council want and will apply solutions. As a small staff, it can communicate and carry credibility with both Board and Council in a way that would be impossible for a large staff, a staff dispersed among the agencies, or a staff drawn from more esoteric disciplines. If the Council moves slowly, it is because it fits their judgment of what they *can* do, given constituent and union attitudes.

Lastly, one maintains a tight and prudent budget and enforces a standard of scarcity on public expenditures by being tight and prudent with everything and, especially, with the budget bureau. Proposals for management analysts, new garbage trucks, and sensors for salt spreaders must all be tested against the cynic's standard that no idea is more than half right.

The proof of Milwaukee's pudding is in the eating. Management analysis has survived twenty-five effective years, because it adapted successfully to the realities of city politics and government.

5 Nassau County

Long Island stretches 150 miles from the East River that separates it from Manhattan to Montauk Point at its eastern end. New York City's boroughs of Brooklyn and Queens cover 178 square miles at the western tip of the island, in which 4.5 million people, over half the population of the city, live. The eastern two thirds of the island is Suffolk, still New York State's most productive agricultural county, and a major resort area with ocean beaches extending from Fire Island to the Hamptons and a roughly parallel shoreline on Long Island Sound; it is now rapidly suburbanizing. Between Queens and Suffolk is Nassau County with 1.4 million inhabitants in its 289 square miles and some of the characteristics of each of its very different neighbors. The county has about the same area as Phoenix, Arizona but is twice as densely populated. It is slightly smaller in area than New York City and about one-fifth as densely settled.

Nassau is both very old and very new. Its first settlers came before New York was English and within the first quarter century after the Pilgrims landed at Plymouth. The seal of the Town of Hempstead carries the date, 1644 and that of the Town of Oyster Bay, 1653. George Washington was there briefly fighting and losing the Battle of Long Island before retreating to Brooklyn Heights and then to the hills of northern Manhattan. With its flat and fertile land and long growing season, Nassau was long a major farming area. The north shore with its many coves and bays has for years provided estates and vacation homes for the city's well-to-do, including one president—Theodore Roosevelt—whose family home, Sagamore, is in Oyster Bay.

Today, Nassau is far more new than old. Its present population is three and one-half times its 1940 census of 407,000. In the first decade after World War II, the Levitt brothers and other builders converted hundreds of square miles of potato farms in the southern half of the county into subdivisions. Before the end of the 1960s, the huge development effort in which hundreds of thousands of houses, innumerable shopping centers and schools, hundreds of miles of roads, and scores of factories and warehouses had been built was nearing its end. Under present town and village zoning, the county is virtually 100 percent developed and the development pressure has moved east to Suffolk.

Three-fifths of the county's labor force now work in the county. The Census Bureau has recognized the declining dependence on the city by establishing Nassau-Suffolk as a separate metropolitan area. Yet, the symbiotic relationship with the city continues. About 200,000 commuters still travel to New York daily, and thousands of city dwellers work in the county. In summer, Jones Beach is Coney Island for the city's middle class and indeed for anyone with an automobile. Geography intensifies the relationship. There is no land route to any place off the island that does not go through New York City and Suffolk's Islip airport is, at best, a limited and, for most, more distant alternative to New York's John F. Kennedy and LaGuardia airports.

Nassau has the highest median family income of all counties in the greater New York area and among the highest of all American counties. In the 1970 Census, it ranked first among New York State counties in median income, in percent of families with incomes over $15,000, and in the percent of its workers in white-collar occupations. It had the smallest proportion of families with incomes below poverty levels.

Nassau has a modern county government charter with an elected county executive. It retains, as its legislature a Board of Supervisors made up of the supervisors of its three towns and the mayors of its two cities. The next tier of government includes the three towns—Hempstead, North Hempstead, and Oyster Bay—and two cities—Long Beach and Glen Cove. Within the towns, there are sixty-four villages. The public schools are the responsibility of fifty-seven separate school districts. Completing the picture are 195 special districts.

The State Comptroller reported for 1973 (the last year for which all data are available) that the aggregate expenditures of all local governments within the county totalled $1.8 billion, divided as follows: county, $743.5 million; cities, $23.0 million; towns, $201.2 million; villages, $89.2 million; school districts, $716.3 million; and fire districts, $10.1 million. The county government accounted for 41.8 percent of total expenditures and 70.4 percent of the total excluding the school districts. The total expenditure figure includes both debt service and capital outlay; only $476.1 million of the county expenditure of $743.5 million were devoted to current operations.

Nassau County had 23,338 employees in 1974, nearly double the number a decade earlier. It was spending $250.1 million on labor costs (somewhat less in the 1973 figures above).

The Multi-Municipal Productivity Project

The Multi-Municipal Productivity Project was the brainchild of Vincent J. Macri, then Executive Assistant to the County Executive. Macri's basic notion was that a governmental productivity program should be developed cooperatively and jointly by government and its employee unions. This cooperation would be built on a government commitment to share the benefits of such a program with its employees.

The Multi-Municipal Productivity Project was announced in November 1972, but Macri had been putting together the necessary ingredients and developing the approach for nearly a year. During the course of that year, he had convinced Ralph G. Caso, Nassau's County Executive, to undertake the program and to do so on the cooperative government-union basis he had proposed. He secured the support and commitment of President Irving Flaumenbaum of the Civil Service Employees' Association, the union representing the vast majority of the employees of both the county government and the governments of the county's three towns. Finally, he had persuaded the supervisors of the three towns to participate, thus extending the project to cover four separate governments rather than limiting it to the county government.

This was a remarkable accomplishment, a tribute to the attractiveness of Macri's basic idea and to his own persuasive abilities. It was made easier by the dominance of a single employees union and by an interlocking system of government under which the County Board of Supervisors consisted of the chief elected officials of the three towns and two cities in the county.

Macri was equally effective in securing outside funding support for various aspects of the process of productivity improvement. The support included $220,000 from the U.S. Department of Labor and the National Commission on Productivity and Work Quality to assist the productivity bargaining process through the development of prototype cases of productivity improvement, of a management-labor liaison structure in the operating agencies and of a productivity incentive scheme for employees. The Ford Foundation contributed $150,000 for the demographic analysis and survey of employee attitudes and opinions, and $54,500 came from the New York State Office of Local Government using Federal Intergovernmental Personnel Act funds to conduct job specification and salary level surveys among the four governments, to assess possible job specification changes resulting from the impact of productivity improvements, and to assess the related need for employee training. These funds provided financing for the Productivity Project Staff, for consultant groups from Cornell's School of Industrial Relations and C.W. Post College of Long Island University and for the engagement of Dr. Dina Paul to develop, administer, and analyze the results of the employee attitude survey.

No reviewer of the project's literature could miss Macri's talent, flair and, perhaps, weakness for the grand design. The structure and even the concepts of most municipal productivity improvement programs have tended to evolve with experience. This is not so in Nassau. Instead, the Multi-Municipal Productivity Project emerged in almost fully developed detail, springing forth full-blown like Athena from the brow of Zeus.

The overall governance of the project was vested in a Voting Team on which were represented the chief elected officials of the county and the three towns and the counterpart officials of the Civil Service Employees' Association. With four government votes and four union votes, there was an equal sharing of authority over the project. The four governments were divided into 168 micro-study units (later reduced to 125), in each of which a management representative and a labor representative were to be designated. The two representatives would jointly have responsibility for initiating a productivity improvement effort (PIE) and for developing a Productivity Improvement Plan (PIP). These efforts and plans would require the approval of both labor and management representatives and of the Voting Team as well.

The project was designed to proceed in two stages. During the first year, 1973, productivity improvement efforts would be initiated in eight microstudy units and carried out primarily through work by the Productivity Project Staff. During the second year, 1974, an attempt would be made to initiate PIEs in all of the microstudy units of the four governments.

In the second year program, the labor-management team in each of the micro study units would be expected to develop its own ideas for productivity improvement, carrying out such analysis and program design as were required with the staff and resources available within the unit. The central Project Staff and its consultants would be available for limited technical assistance.

The technical support available from the consultants and the Productivity Project Staff was very limited. There were only four consultants, an industrial engineer, an economist, a statistician and a labor relations expert. By explicit design, the Productivity Project Staff included no one with productivity program experience or training in industrial engineering or systems analysis. Macri's intent, in so doing, was "to prove that economies of scale would be greatest if few consultants and many employees were mobilized to bring about improvement."

The central Productivity Project staff had, in addition to the work on the PIEs, its own agenda of preparation for the introduction of productivity provisions in the collective bargaining contracts that would be negotiated for the two-year period beginning January 1, 1975. The preparation included an effort to develop common language on the many existing aspects of the four contracts, the development of an acceptable means of measuring productivity, and the design of a system for distributing to employees a share in the productivity gains.

Another element of the project, the Attitudinal Program, was also the responsibility of the central staff. It involved opinion surveys, the collection of demographic data, and a concurrent productivity educational effort. This effort, financed by the Ford Foundation, was designed to determine potential employee receptivity to productivity changes, to identify problem areas and priorities for improvement, to learn what inducements might be helpful in obtaining effective employee cooperation and participation in a productivity program, and lastly to compare findings over time, especially possible change in employee attitudes after the implementation of productivity improvement efforts.

Employee Attitude Survey

One component of the Multi-Municipal Productivity Project was an unusually extensive and sophisticated effort to determine employee attitudes. There were three components: (1) an initial general survey of employee attitudes conducted in September 1973; (2) postintervention surveys of employee attitudes in the eight microstudy units for which PIEs were initiated in the first program-year; and (3) a second general survey of employees identical in design to the first but conducted early in 1975.

The first general survey involved a random sample of 1766 employees, roughly a tenth of the CSEA membership in the four governments. The sample was stratified by income level and functional category; it included 380 job classifications within four broad occupational categories from unskilled to professional. The survey provided data on the demographic characteristics of the work force as well as data on employee attitudes.

The demographic data from the first survey showed a county work force with a high average age and a tendency toward relatively brief tenure. Sixty-seven percent of the employees were forty-years-old or older; 44 percent were fifty or older. The average tenure in government employment was between five and six years; only 28 percent of the employees had served longer than ten years, and a mere 6 percent longer than twenty years

Of the employees, 80 percent had completed high school and 24 percent had completed college; nearly half of the college graduates had attended graduate or professional school. Yet, only 3 percent of the employees held professional positions and only 7 percent were in managerial jobs. One-fifth of the employees were unskilled manual workers and another 15 percent were skilled manual workers. Clerical employees accounted for 21 percent and skilled, nonmanual workers for 33 percent of the work force.

Of all employees, 26 percent earned salaries of less than $8,000 per year and only 6 percent earned $17,000 or more. Many of the lower-paid employees were women who accounted for 39 percent of the entire work force. Among male employees, 15 percent earned less than $8,000 and 9 percent $17,000 or more. These data place government employees in a relatively low economic position among the county's population. Fewer than a tenth of the males employed by government had salaries large enough—without a working wife or supplementary income—to place them above the median family income in the county. Median male earnings for government employees in 1973 were less than the median for all males over sixteen reported by the Census for 1969. The difference must be regarded as a source of tension.

The survey showed the vast majority of county and two employees well satisfied with supervision and their coworkers and only slightly less satisfied with their work. The majority of both male and female employees, on the other hand, indicated low satisfaction with promotion opportunities. Pay was the other area of signficant dissatisfaction particularly for men—with three-eighths indicating low satisfaction and only 14.9 percent high satisfaction.

Dissatisfaction with salary was concentrated heavily among males earning less than $11,000 a year. For both sexes, satisfaction tended to increase with salary but women were happier at lower salaries; the satisfaction profile for women earning less than $8000 is almost identical to that for men earning $11,000–$13,999. The most dissatisfied employees were also those in the younger age groups, those with the shortest job tenure and those in jobs with the lowest skill level. The same group also shows markedly greater dissatisfaction with work. An independent measure of alienation produced parallel results with roughly half the employees with salaries under $8000 and about two-fifths of those in the $8000–$10,999 bracket showing high alienation.

Favorable attitudes toward innovation were prevalent among male employees in all age categories under fifty but declined steadily with age among female employees. On the other hand, favorable attitudes toward innovation rose with salary level, but more sharply for women than for men.

Of the men, 51 percent picked pay as the first or second choice among job incentives and nearly as many, 48 percent, selected job security as first or second choice. For women, pay was also the highest priority, but ranked as first or second choice by only 38 percent; challenging work was close behind, selected by 36 percent of the women compared to only 19 percent of the men. Curiously, promotion opportunities, which figured so strongly in employee dissatisfaction, were placed first or second as a job incentive by only 21 percent of the men and 13 percent of the women. With regard to the possible benefits of a productivity program, two-thirds of the men and one-half the women thought they would be better off if a salary increase depended on improving their own performance.

There has been a spate of employee attitude surveys in local government over the last several years. The Nassau County survey is one of the most interesting and potentially useful of these. It is potentially useful not because it suggests solutions but because it seems to have delineated with uncommon sharpness the major problem areas within the work force.

The 1975 general employee survey produced responses that generally followed the results of the first survey, two years earlier. There were a few differences:

Job security became a more important objective for a larger proportion of employees, ranked equally with pay by men and above both pay and challenging work by women.

The vast majority of both men and women in the second survey demonstrated an understanding of "productivity," whereas less than 10 percent of the 1973 respondents showed any basic knowledge of the concept.

Dissatisfaction with pay was even greater in the second survey than in the first.

The postintervention surveys in the microstudy units with first year PIES indicated that employee attitudes can change rapidly with changes in working conditions and workloads. These findings are discussed below as part of the summary of the results of the first-year productivity improvement effort.

Baking the First PIEs

The eight microstudy units selected as pilot projects in 1973 were all proposed by department heads in response to a November 1972 request for such proposals. It is clear that the enthusiasm of the department heads varied, some suggesting projects on their own initiative, others being persuaded by the Project Staff to do so. All the projects had the special advantage of some significant degree of top-level departmental support. They had the second advantage of the expertise available from the Project Staff and the two consulting groups. All the projects proved successful, some with significant qualifications.

Building Custodial Services, Town of Hempstead

The Commissioner of Hempstead's General Services Department suggested a project dealing with a number of building operation and maintenance issues. Custodial services were ultimately selected from among these. The decision had the strong support of the union, which saw the project as an opportunity to press for the initiation of group team cleaning. Group team cleaning was, in fact, initiated on a trial basis, implemented by the labor representative as soon as the Commissioner had formally approved the project.

Implementation was not smooth, probably chiefly because the cleaning crews were not briefed in detail on the changes before they were introduced. This was corrected. During the test period, absenteeism dropped by 7.3 percent and productivity increased by 19 percent as reflected in the increased assignment of work force to less frequent maintenance chores. Surveys taken before and after the effort showed an increase in favorable employee attitudes toward productivity and satisfaction with pay but a reduction in the percentage of employees indicating high satisfaction with supervision. Building cleanliness was reportedly improved.

Purchase and Supply, Nassau County

The Commissioner of the Department of General Services proposed a study of
the constituent Division of Purchase and Supply for two reasons: (1) the need
to act on a recent report by outside consultants, and (2) the general dissatisfaction with purchasing among user agencies, documented by replies to a questionnaire sent to all county departments. The Deputy Commissioner in charge of
purchasing was interested in a system to improve work flow and identified
the typing pool as a special problem. That emphasis raised some likelihood of
friction, since one of the two union representatives assigned to the project was a
CSEA Vice President, who also happened to be supervisor of the typing pool.

The effort was directed at reducing the throughput time for handling purchase requisitions. An analysis of a sample of requisitions showed an average
throughput time of 19.1 days in purchasing and a total throughput time of
33.1 days, the remainder being spent in offices of Budget and the Comptroller.
The plan proposed by the project staff succeeded in reducing the time in purchasing from 19.1 days to 16.1 days.

The recommendations were developed by the Project Staff and their consultants, who had little success in inducing inputs from either labor or management representatives. Not surprisingly the recommendations were accepted
only after substantial modification. The staff had recommended eliminating
duplicate approvals of requisitions under $500 but the Deputy Commissioner
objected strongly to delegating that authority to his Director of Purchasing
and Contract Administration. A transfer of two typists to the buying section
was vigorously opposed by the head of the clerical administrative unit and, as
a result, modified to provide for the transfer of a single clerk to maintain logs.
A single word processing unit was purchased, rather than two that had been
recommended. The Commissioner's modified acceptance was further made
conditional on changes proposed for Budget's handling of the requisitions;
the Budget Director initially agreed but, later, under pressure from his staff,
withdrew his approval.

The modified scheme was ultimately implemented without the Budget
component. It met with many problems. The project staff reports that supervision within the Purchasing unit was nonexistent, leaving employees free to
ignore the new procedures. The effort was rescued only by the intervention of
the Productivity Project Director with department management and by the
introduction of feedback and performance measurement reports. The Productivity Project Staff report concluded: "The lack of a strong, effective managerial
unit bodes ill for the probability of lasting change within the division."

Probation Department, Nassau County

The Probation Department had already engaged IBM to do a feasibility study
of technological possibilities in a departmental stenographic pool. The Produc-

tivity Project Staff was brought in to help evaluate the IBM proposals and establish the productivity impact of the new machinery on the department.

The central element of the project was the introduction of magnetic card typewriters and the training of employees in their operation. The project almost foundered on Budget's unwillingness to provide funds for the typewriters without a commitment to staff savings and the department head's equally adamant refusal to accept any staff reduction. The Project Staff "had serious problems in achieving these approvals" but succeeded in doing so.

During the test period, the system produced savings at an annual rate of about $14,000 with an eventual potential of about $200,000. Employee attitudes underwent a marked improvement with more favorable views of their equipment, the productivity program, and supervision. NBC featured the improvement in its March 1975 documentary, "Trimming Fat City," and achievement awards were presented to both management and labor representatives involved. The system is being expanded to other stenographic operations in the Department.

Medical Center Emergency Room

The Emergency Room of the Nassau County Medical Center was selected as a result of informal discussions between the Project Director and the Superintendent of the Medical Center and after months of preparatory work by the staff and the Voting Team. The effort was aimed at reducing throughput time, the average time between patient entry and discharge.

The productivity improvement plan called for: (1) variation in staffing by shift to provide more staff during peak hours and fewer during the low-activity periods; (2) use of a triage nurse to separate out nonemergency cases (60 percent of total); and (3) a walk-in clinic for nonemergency patients. The Project Staff found the emergency room was not under the control of any single department of the hospital, and changes could be implemented only after successful negotiations with several different parties. No agreement was possible without an understanding that the changes would remain in effect only during the test period. The walk-in clinic could be staffed only three days a week instead of five. The triage nurse would be required to back-up regular emergency room nurses. Patient throughput time was, despite the plan modification, cut back from an average of 110 minutes to 86 minutes. After the test, the emergency room returned to its prior modus operandi.

The project was hampered by the preoccupation of Medical Center personnel with plans for their coming relocation to a new building. In addition, the Nursing Department believed that available staff were not sufficient to staff the proposed system.

After the relocation of the emergency room, the head of the Medical Department and the Emergency Room reviewed the results of the effort to see if it could be replicated in the new facility. The physical structure of the new

building introduced new problems and required additional staff to provide
the same service. Despite the problems, the walk-in clinic was continued and
eventually put on a five-day-a-week basis. Newly hired nurses were put on shifts
in a pattern more nearly approximating patient demand, and one of the new
nurses was assigned to triage duty.

The employee survey indicated that employees felt that the changes had
made their situation worse than before. Understaffing continued to be a major
souce of complaints.

Early in 1975, the Emergency Room productivity increases were featured
on an NBC documentary about productivity.

Department of Social Services, Nassau County

The Commissioner of Social Services mentioned several possible areas for a
productivity improvement effort in his original proposal. Because of a workload
dispute in the Recertification Unit, both management and labor representatives
strongly recommended that that unit be selected. The union was convinced that
an objective outsider would find the staff workload excessive. The job of the
Recertification Unit is to reexamine the status of all public assistance recipients
yearly.

The ideas for change in the Recertification Unit came from the Productivity
Project Staff but they represented an adaptation of a system already in use in one
of the unit's satellite offices. The plan was based on a task allocation study and
required a reorganization consolidating in-house and field examiners into integrated units. When the plan was presented, the Project Staff discovered that the
department had developed its own plan, a defective one in the view of the
Project Staff. The department finally agreed to give the project plan a three-
month test.

An increase of 19.8 percent in case completions per examiner per month
demonstrated the utility of the new approach. Further experience and additional
innovations have increased that gain subsequently. Yet, the project staff reported over six months later that top management in the department remained
skeptical of the plan. The resurvey of employee attitudes showed an increase in
alienation, a decrease in favorable attitudes toward both work and satisfaction
with promotion opportunities. Not all the change in attitude is attributable to
the new system; some is clearly due to rising caseload and increasingly burdensome requirements imposed by the state.

Department of Public Works, Nassau County

The productivity improvement effort in the Road Maintenance Division of the
Department of Public Works was initiated by the department's commissioner,

largely as a result of budgetary pressure. An identifiable labor-management team worked on the project with the project staff. Most of the staff recommendations were developed with the aid of the labor-management group, and all but three of the recommendations were accepted by the commissioner. Labor attitudes did not change significantly. A productivity gain of 10 percent was achieved.

Sanitation, Town of Oyster Bay

The Town Supervisor proposed the study; the local union president also encouraged the staff to undertake it. Labor unrest, soaring overtime costs, and high absenteeism were the problems of greatest concern to the supervisor. The unrest was largely among refuse collection crews and related to inequalities among routes. There were also problems from the large number of trucks out of service and the effect on the ability of crews to meet their daily work schedule.

The maintenance shop was selected for analysis. The management and labor representatives functioned separately with the project staff. The support and availability of top departmental staff was a critical factor.

The project staff developed an inventory control system and recommended a night shift for mechanics to carry out a preventive maintenance program and to assure that all trucks would be ready for operation in the morning.

The plan succeeded in cutting by 5 percent the number of vehicles experiencing three or more breakdowns. The average number of repairs and the number of trucks out of service were both reduced by 13 percent. In addition, overtime was sharply cut. The improvements continued after the completion of the project, and further improvements are being made by the department.

Building Department, Town of Hempstead

This productivity improvement effort in the complaint section of the Building Department was suggested by the Commissioner. The Project Staff worked separately with the Deputy Commissioner, who was the management liaison and the shop steward representing the CSEA. Management took an active role in reviewing recommendations, but the union representative merely wished to be kept informed.

The project staff recommended an increase in the inspector time in office chiefly to help screen out the "no violation" cases (51 percent of the total) for which an inspection should often not be necessary. The proposal for clerical scheduling of inspectors developed from interviews with the inspectors. Training sessions were necessary to introduce both inspectors and clerks to the change in operations.

As a result of the effort, the number of cases closed per year was increased by 12 percent, the number of no violation cases was cut by 13 percent, and the number of inspections per complaint was reduced by 18 percent. Employee attitudes toward the changes were favorable. The changes have remained in effect.

The changes produced no related change in the number of inspections per man day, which remained constant. The commissioner had elected not to use inspections per man day as a measure of productivity, believing that it "would be an inflammatory issue which the staff did not wish to pursue at that time."

The Second Year in the Kitchen

The goal of the second-year plan was to achieve participation from every municipal department and to institutionalize productivity improvement procedures in the departments. In January 1974, four hundred departmental management and labor representatives were given a two-day training sessions at C.W. Post College of Long Island University. The training program covered data collection, output definition, productivity measurements, and systems analysis.

The central project staff was divided into two groups. One general staff advisor was assigned to each of the four governments as liaison and to help generate proposals. The second group, called Productivity Improvement Effort advisors were assigned to provide expertise in each of seven functional areas of government.

As a result of the workshops, thirteen PIE proposals were received in February and March. The number was not sufficient "to satisfy bargaining requirements." The county executive and the chief deputy county executive sent out memoranda in February and March to all department heads setting a 10 percent productivity improvement goal for each department, laying out guidelines for productivity improvement efforts. As a result forty additional PIEs were submitted in April, May, June, and July. During August and September, project staff members visited all department heads in the county and the towns and generated another forty-two proposals. The total number of second-year PIEs finally reached 109, of which 10 were rejected as not meeting the criteria.

The ninety-nine surviving PIEs have been classified in several ways. They included eight filing system projects, seven involving forms revision, thirteen paper flow projects, two based on inventory control, twenty-four technology projects, seventeen depending on a rescheduling of activities, eight requiring staff redeployment, eleven more using task reassignment, and nine involving employee training.

The ninety-nine projects were a very heterogeneous group. Most but not all of them seem to have been completed. Most are small projects typically with modest impacts on the effectiveness or efficiency of service. Some of the more significant are the following:

1. A centralized work order system in purchasing in Oyster Bay will reduce personnel needs in the user agencies by about thirty-five positions.

2. The computerization of 100,000 student transcripts at Nassau Community College will save $21,000 to $33,000 in its first full year, with a possible doubling of savings in the future if extended to cover all transcript-related transactions.

3. Mosquito inspector productivity in the county Department of Public Works was increased by 15.9 percent and fuel consumption reduced by 9 percent by redrawing inspection areas and scheduling inspections to minimize travel time.

4. The county Motor Vehicle Bureau utilized a rotational cross-training program and a redeployment of personnel to better handle peak demand. Average throughput time was cut by 15.5 percent despite a 5.5 percent increase in transactions. Overtime was cut by 23.5 percent.

5. A computerized system for issuance of sewer permits will save $75,000 annually in personnel costs in the county Department of Public Works.

6. An Automated Material Inventory System in the Department of Public Works made it possible to identify and sell $32,680 in obsolete stock held in inventory.

7. A new superstriper for painting highway center stripes permits three persons to do the work previously requiring twelve.

8. North Hempstead, by shifting the town incinerator from a seven-day to a five-day week will save the salary of eight to ten workers, decrease absenteeism, and eliminate overtime.

9. The county Department of Public Health will save nearly one-and-a-half man-years in inspection by curtailing nonproductive inspections to establishments opening after working hours or closed one or two days a week; by eliminating inspections of stores selling only packaged food; and by reducing inspections of food premises rated excellent or good and increasing inspection frequency for fair and poor establishments.

Some of the PIEs omitted from this list may conceivably prove more important when productivity impact estimates are available.

The ninety-nine projects as a whole have the flavor of what might be called the government list syndrome. A governmentwide call for productivity improvements: (1) induced some new productivity improvement efforts, (2) brought forth under the productivity rubric already underway or decided-on projects initiated quite independently of PIE, and (3) led some agencies to submit in the guise of PIE evidence that they were already very productive. Despite the qualifications, the list is impressive in the numbers and range of genuine improvement projects. It is, on the other hand, of minor significance in terms of

the aggregate dollar value of the increases in productivity or effectiveness that
have been realized or are expected.

Measuring Productivity

If employees were to share in productivity generated savings—as had been
agreed from the beginning of the project—it would be necessary to develop and
obtain concurrence on a method for measuring productivity for this purpose.
The early productivity bargaining contracts in Flint, Detroit, and Orange,
California posed limited measurement problems inasmuch as the contracts
applied in each case to a single service. Nassau's governmentwide scheme would
be more difficult and considerable attention was consequently devoted to the
measurement problem.

A measurement formula was developed and widely propagated relatively
early in the project. The formula was as follows:

$$P = 100E\sqrt{(c^2 + s^2)d}$$

where E represented efficiency expressed as an index of efficiency in a prior
base period. The other independent variables were consistency (c), user satisfaction (s), and employee dependability (d).

Statisticians excepted, one could probably count on one's fingers the
number of county employees who understood this formulation. It had the
additional disadvantage of not being readily quantifiable. This approach was
extant during most of the project's history, but there is no indication that it
provoked any serious discussion outside the project staff and their consultants.

The second productivity measurement formulation simply identified the
improvement factor as the labor cost per unit in the base period divided by the
labor cost per unit in the present or reference period. Costs would be deflated
to reflect inflation and, where appropriate, adjusted to cover relevant capital
costs. The improvement factor multiplied by the total labor budget would
determine total productivity gains in dollars; the pool for distribution to employees would be half that amount.

The Project Report to the U.S. Department of Labor identified seven
categories of productivity "units" among the PIEs (the number of PIEs in each
category is shown in parenthesis):

1. cost savings (20)
2. manhours saved (35)
3. physical units (9)
4. throughput time (14)
5. down time (3)

6. additional revenue (7)
7. miscellaneous (16)

The measurement issue in Nassau County was, in fact, two issues: first, how to measure the value of increases in productivity and, second, how to determine what part of that increase should properly go into the pool for employee sharing. The second issue was not treated; it was assumed that the benefits of all productivity improvements should be shared.

If the purpose of the program was, as stated, to reduce the county budget by cost savings and cost avoidance, the amounts proposed to be shared should, logically, have been limited to realized savings in expenditures. This certainly fitted the Caso plan to pare the work force by attrition. A program of incentive payments for performance quality improvements without budgetary savings may make sense, but it ought to be recognized for what it is, namely a decision to invest funds, perhaps from productivity savings, in improvements in program quality.

A much more limiting line might well be taken. For example, is it appropriate or necessary to include *all* productivity savings in the base for employee sharing? The superstriper, for example, is a case of capital substitution apparently demanding no more in worker performance. Should, then, half the savings be paid to labor? Would the union otherwise attempt to block increased mechanization? Or is it intended to be a means of stimulating worker initiative in proposing productivity improvements?

The use of some of these output measures produces some rather odd results. Throughput time is a good example. One case is the hospital emergency room PIE, where the reduction in average patient throughput from 110 minutes to 86 minutes is treated as a 21.8 percent gain in output. That percentage applied to the initial payroll of $366,300 yields $79,853 as the calculated value of the productivity gain; after deduction of the increase in payroll of $43,333, the net gain is $36,520. The PIE involved no increase in number of patients, no reduction in staff, and no savings to the county.

Even in more routine cases, the application of the formula is questionable. For example, the superstriper purchased by the Department of Public Works permitted the reassignment of twelve of the fifteen men assigned to striping, probably reducing striping costs by four-fifths of the initial $120,000 annual payroll. The Project calculation applies a productivity improvement gain of nearly 400 percent to the $120,000 payroll for an estimated dollar 'gain' of $463,040 offset by a $16,000 increase in salaries! These are nonsense calculations. It is difficult to believe they could survive if anyone were taking the numbers seriously enough to read and review them. If amounts so calculated were used—as planned—to determine the productivity benefits to be paid employees, a large and successful productivity program might lead the county to bankruptcy.

The Unions

Fourteen thousand of Nassau County's twenty-two thousand employees are members of the Civil Service Employees' Association. The CSEA occupies a similarly dominant position among the employees of the county's three town governments. The only other union with which the county bargains is the Patrolmen's Benevolent Association representing the county's police.

Under New York State's Taylor Act, government employee unions must be taken seriously. Local governments must bargain with them, and disagreements may be carried through impasse proceedings and ultimately to the local legislature for resolution. To the protections of state labor law, CSEA adds its own strong position as the representative of the majority of the employees of the second largest local government in the state.

The CSEA has never gone out on strike against the county. Its collective bargaining agreements (unlike those of the PBA) contain no direct or indirect limitations of employee workload.

Yet, no one seems inclined to doubt the union's importance. Cheek by jowl with New York City, those in Nassau County have before them the potentially contagious example of the city's more militant and aggressive unions. The quieter relationship between the county and the CSEA reflects, to some substantial extent, the fact that most of the county's employees have been able to obtain pay levels competitive with their city counterparts without resort to more muscular tactics.

CSEA leadership is an important factor. Irving Flaumenbaum, the union president, is widely regarded as an unusually constructive labor leader. He has been progressive and understanding of the problems of management, preferring cooperative approaches to more aggressive adversary positions. These attitudes are clearly reflected in the role played by Flaumenbaum and the union in the development of the Multi-Municipal Productivity Program.

In the typical municipal productivity program, the employee unions have been potential obstacles to productivity improvements that city management has developed and proposes to implement. The accounts of union relationships are concerned, hence, with adversary relationships reflecting the relative power of the contestants and strategies for negotiating with the union or for dealing with the union problem. The Nassau County experience is wholly outside this frame.

The Multi-Municipal Productivity Program was conceived from the outset as a joint government-union program at every level, in which labor would share in whatever benefits the program produced. Discussions with the leadership of the Civil Service Employees Association began well before the public announcement of the program. The union leaders went on record as supporting the program at the time it was originally announced and at many subsequent occasions.

The union leaders in the county government and in each of the three towns were members of the governing Voting Team from the beginning, and had the same number of votes as the government representatives. The plan provided for every productivity improvement effort to be a joint project governed by a management representative and a union representative in each of the 125 microunits or government operations covered. Union representatives in the microunits were frequently indifferent about the productivity efforts, but they were given an opportunity for participation seemingly on almost any basis they found desirable. Notably, in the development of the second year program, the Project Staff would not accept for consideration by the Voting Team any proposed PIE that had not been endorsed by both the management representative and the labor representative in the particular unit.

In the PIEs that were actually undertaken, there is little evidence of defensive union behavior or obstructionism. The labor representatives seem to have typically accepted the results of the efforts, even where they involved more work on the part of the employees and even where the attitude surveys indicated significant employee discontent with the changes. Management acceptance of at least those changes developed by the project staff seems to have been a far more difficult problem. It is possible, indeed quite probable in some instances, that neither management nor the unions were interested in taking on projects that would produce results to which the union would have strong objections.

The supportive position of the union leadership was a direct result of the proposal initially presented to them and supported throughout the first two-and-a-half years of the project by the project staff and its director. That proposal called for a guarantee that no civil servant would be fired as a result of the productivity program and that any manpower savings would be realized through employee attrition; this removed, for the union leadership, the threat of the most serious possible adverse repercussion. On the positive side, the plan as consistently advanced called for a fifty-fifty sharing in any savings or improvements achieved by the program.

The intent was to include this provision or some alternate developed from bargaining in the labor contracts between the CSEA and the four separate governments. The productivity program was, however, developed too late to be reflected in the bargaining process in 1972 for the contracts covering the 1973 and 1974 years. Rather, language was included in all four contracts committing both labor and management to a joint effort to develop a productivity provision for the next contract. Expiration dates were conformed in all four contracts so that they would expire at the end of 1974. During 1974, new two-year contracts would be bargained, presumably including productivity provisions.

The project staff and its consultants devoted considerable attention during 1973 and 1974 to formulae for measuring the benefits from productivity improvements and for distributing those benefits between labor and management.

Early in 1974, the staff conducted a three-day practice bargaining session with the Voting Team. These sessions covered questions such as the use of master contract provisions applicable to all four municipalities, initial discussions of the payout issue, and the identification of systemwide approaches to increasing productivity.

Subsequently, the project staff developed the Productivity Benefit Improvement Fund (PBI) concept. Under this approach, the labor share of productivity benefits would be placed in a trust fund, where it would earn interest and would be withdrawable by the individual beneficiary on resignation, retirement, or, of course, death. There would be a four-year moratorium on withdrawals. Then each employee with at least one full year of service would share equally in the PBI for each year. The trust fund concept meant that the payments would not be regarded as additional salary and wage income on which the governments would have to make added contributions to retirement funds. The PBI was a disadvantage to the employee preferring a current payout but had the advantage of deferring taxation for those who would have put the money into savings had they received the cash on a current basis.

County Executive Caso and CSEA President Flaumenbaum agreed in the 1975 negotiations to a planned reduction in the county work force by attrition. Over a four year period, 1975 through 1978, the work force would be reduced by slightly less than 10 percent or approximately 1500 employees. Flaumenbaum accepted the PBI with a county payment of $400 per employee to be made in the first year.

Bargaining between the CSEA and the county reached an impasse on the basic provision of the contract, the percentage increase to be provided in salaries and wages over the two-year contract period. The impasse went to a fact-finding panel that included the provision for PBI in its recommendations along with 9.5 percent and 9 percent increases in the two contract years over and above normal 5 percent increments. The County Executive rejected the fact finders' salary recommendations as beyond the county's fiscal capacity.

Under the New York State Taylor Law, this automatically passed the matter on to the County Board of Supervisors for determination. The County Executive's recommendations to the Board included provision for an appropriation for PBI equal to 1 percent of salaries. The Board approved a contract at a substantially lower general pay increase than recommended by the fact finders but without provision for PBI. The Board stated its view that employees preferred cash on the line. They made reference to a tax law issue and to the current national economic condition and also indicated that they did not believe employees needed incentives to be productive.

The project staff interviewed the Voting Team members using a standard set of questions to better understand the reasons for the rejection. The management Voting Team members included representatives of the town supervisors who sat on the Board of Supervisors. The management team members felt that productivity had played a minimal role in bargaining. The negotiating teams were not well informed on productivity, and there was some skepticism about including productivity in the collective bargaining. It was also a management proposal rather than a labor demand and, hence, expendable if necessary to help meet demands for current cash increases.

Labor favored PBI and confirmed the management view that it was never really an issue in negotiations. They suggested that PBI was developed too late in the negotiating process. The union representatives also made clear their own preference for current salary increases over the deferred PBI, if it came to a choice.

The project staff believed that the county might have provided for PBI if it had been included in the town contracts negotiated earlier. They found throughout an underlying reluctance to include productivity incentives in a wage contract.

The town supervisors who, as members of the County Board of Supervisors, rejected the Productivity Benefit Improvement Fund had, two years earlier, agreed to bring their town governments into the Multi-Municipal Productivity Project. For two years, their representatives were members of the Project Voting Team. The PBI concept, although developed in detail later, was part of the project plan from the beginning and, as such, implicitly accepted by the supervisors.

Macri believes that the supervisors never really understood or were interested in the productivity projects. "They thought I was a PR man while really I was trying to behave like an industrial engineer."

A final point on the supervisors' attitudes. The supervisors certainly must have been aware that Caso's strong support of the plan was not shared by some of his principal subordinates. In addition, as the early PIEs showed, middle-management personnel in the operating agencies were often hostile and resistant. There is little doubt that this dissidence at high and middle levels made it easier for the Board to act negatively on PBI.

Collective bargaining was a new issue for the Supervisors. The Board of Supervisors is required to act on a collective bargaining contract only if the County Executive fails to reach agreement with the union. This had never happened before, and the Board's action in March 1975 was its maiden voyage into labor relations.

Death and Rebirth?

The Multi-Municipal Productivity Project is dead. Macri resigned after the Board of Supervisors rejected the collective bargaining contract provision for a Productivity Benefit Improvement Fund. Macri did not leave quietly; he was publicly critical of the Board and its negative action, obviously feeling betrayed by their failure to approve a program representing the culmination of a two-year effort conducted by him with the seeming cooperation of the supervisors. In Nassau County's Executive Offices Building, the view is that Macri's actions polarized the controversy and made it impossible to continue the project with the hope of an eventual accommodation with the Board of Supervisors.

Less than a year after the Board's action, the Productivity Project Staff was virtually eliminated—down to three survivors from a peak complement of sixteen. The development of PIEs and PIPs has ceased. Work continues only on the last stages of an Intergovernmental Personnel Act project to develop a directory of training needs for the county and the three towns and a referral guide to county services for citizens.

There is a new Director of Productivity and Administrative Analysis, Dr. Justin R. Renz, an economist with ten years experience in the county government, serving most recently as Assistant Director of the Budget. Renz concedes the demise of the Multi-Municipal Productivity Project but emphasizes that this does not mean the end of a productivity improvement program in Nassau County.

The new vehicle for change is the Commission on Priorities set up by County Executive Caso. The Commission includes the county executive, the three deputy county executives, the executive assistant to the county executive, the director of the planning commission, and Dr. Renz. It has four subcommittees: The Economy; Children and Youth Services; Services to the Aging; and Adult Services and Taxpayer Support; the subcommittees include both citizen members and county officials.

The key document is the first report of the Subcommittee on the economy issued in December 1975. The report centers around a projection to 1985 of the county's population composition, of its economy, and of the county government budget. The message is clear; Nassau's period of growth is over. The county's population has stabilized but is changing in composition. The number of children and youth is dropping sharply while the aged are increasing. Young adults are leaving the county to find housing they can afford. The economy is growing more slowly and becoming more service-oriented to match the demands of the changing population.

The county budget is a principal concern. The subcommittee estimates that a continuation of existing pressures will tend to push the operating budget upward from less than $600 million in 1975 to $1.6 billion by 1985. The already heavy burden on the taxpayer would be very substantially increased. The subcommittee calls for a reexamination of priorities and needs in terms of the changing population and for an effort to increase productivity and effectiveness to help control expenditures.

Renz has proposed to the Commission a set of recommendations to carry out the Commission's charge "to recommend such policies and priorities as will realistically reflect the differing needs of the County in the decade ahead and the taxpayers' ability to meet them." The proposals include:

1. organization studies to be initiated by senior administrative personnel for each demographic age group to develop concrete suggestions for appropriate structural changes in existing service delivery systems.

2. a mandated service study. An examination will be made of all expenditures mandated by federal and state requirements to determine the extent to which the county can legally reduce expenditures in these areas; this study has already been initiated by the county attorney.

3. a wage and salary study to be carried out by departmental personnel officers, Civil Service Commission members and, probably, management consultants to develop alternatives to the existing graded salary plan to lower automatic growth in personnel costs and to provide a basis for rewarding outstanding personnel and penalizing poor performance.

4. managerial training for supervisory personnel.

5. manual systems studies. Management analysts and industrial engineers would be recruited or trained to review all the county government's nonautomated paper flow processes.

There are no current plans for any substantial expansion of the Office of Productivity and Administrative Analysis. A plan has been agreed on to assign six administrative analysts from the operating agencies to the Office for training and a subsequent four months to begin to analyze some of the major opportunities for productivity improvement. Renz will, in addition, eventually replace the few behaviorists remaining from the Macri staff with industrial engineers and others of like skills, but his total approved permanent staff will remain at the current level of six positions.

One additional input will be an evaluation of the PIEs carried out under the prior Productivity Project. This will be done by Robert B. McKersie, Dean of The New York State School of Industrial and Labor Relations at Cornell.

Productivity Déjà Vu

In the many reports of Nassau's Multi-Municipal Productivity Program, there is no mention of the county budget agency or budget process. The absence is especially curious given Nassau's leadership in applying the Planning-Programming Budgeting System to local government in the heyday of PPBS in the late 1960s. PPB and productivity programs are, by no means, the same thing; there is, however, a significant overlap and, moreover, the two are strongly mutually supporting. In Phoenix and New York City, for example, the two efforts are both managed by the budget agency in close day-to-day interrelation.

Nassau's productivity program was organized outside the budget agency simply because Vincent Macri was outside the budget agency. According to Macri, the budget director and the first deputy county executive were both skeptical and nonsupportive of the effort. With the backing of the county executive as well as the cooperation of the union leadership, Macri was able to proceed without budget cooperation.

Perhaps more important, PPB was dead. The history of its birth, development, and demise is an important addition to an understanding of the problems of the later productivity program.

In August 1965, President Lyndon Johnson directed federal agencies to initiate the development of the Planning-Programming-Budgeting System pioneered by the Department of Defense under Secretary Robert McNamara. Barely five months later, County Executive Eugene H. Nickerson directed the beginning of a similar effort in the Nassau County government. Under the overall management of Deputy County Executive Ward Wright, the county proceeded over the next four years to develop a comprehensive and systematic structure for PPB. A detailed program structure was designed for the budget, and an unusually elaborate set of performance measures or criteria were developed for every program. A management information system provided three levels of output reporting on a monthly basis. Agencies were instructed in the use of cost-effectiveness techniques and in making multiyear projections.

The project had significant external support. Nassau was one of the five counties selected for inclusion in the federally supported George Washington University "5-5-5" project (so-called because it included five cities, five counties and five states). The County received grants from the Ford Foundation in 1967 and from the Department of Housing and Urban Development in 1969 to assist in the development of the system. Full implementation was achieved by January 1970—and the system was abandoned three-and-a-half years later concurrently with Macri's unrelated first steps towrad the development of a productivity program.

The Management Information System developed to support PPB in Nassau County required a substantial continuing effort in both the operating agencies and the budget bureau. It coupled relatively frequent reporting (monthly) with a large number of different measures. These characteristics made the system potentially especially useful to a productivity program. The budget agency was not staffed to provide the auditing of the work reports necessary to assure accuracy, to clarify work definitions, nor to improve the system. Hence, the MIS faced problems that suggested the need to either add staff or to tailor the system down to fit the capacity of the staff to manage it. Instead, the MIS was dropped.

The fundamental reason was a change in administration. Eugene H. Nickerson, a Democrat, retired as county executive at the end of 1970 and was succeeded by Republican Ralph G. Caso, the presiding supervisor of the Town of Hempstead. A new chief executive of a different political party meant, of course, a virtually complete turnover in the leadership of the staff units and agencies in the county's executive offices and very substantial changes in personnel at lower levels. The consequent loss in continuity and the introduction of new people with different perspectives was conducive to drastic change. And, in American local government, nothing is easier to discard than those practices and programs clearly identified as the work of a predecessor of the other political party.

An Overview

Vincent Macri regards the Multi-Municipal Productivity Project as a *succes d'estime* and an advance in the state-of-the-art. He believes that the project:

1. demonstrated that productivity improvement can be accomplished by rank-and-file employees;
2. developed effective training materials for line personnel;
3. produced through its survey a perceptive insight into employee attitudes;
4. identified key obstacles to productivity improvement;
5. Anticipated more recent trends in productivity improvement efforts, such as the emphasis on attrition as a healthy means of trimming government expenditures.

This is, with modest qualifications, a valid perspective of the project. By March 1975 when the collective bargaining contract was before the Board of Supervisors, a significant record of accomplishment had been achieved under the project.

The Multi-Municipal Productivity Project did not survive because it never achieved the support necessary for its survival—a not uncommon fate for new ventures in government. The failure of a project so strongly supported by the elected chief executive and the dominant union chief may, however, be unique.

The rejection of PBI arose, first, from the sheer happenstance that, for the first time, the union and the county executive could not agree on a contract. However, the proposal before the Board of Supervisors provided few obvious attractions to either politicians or labor leaders. With the county board certain to provide for a settlement well below both the union demand the fact finders' recommendations, there was obvious pressure to maximize the impact of the settlement on current paychecks. To incur a current expenditure of 1 percent of salaries for a benefit employees would not receive for four years seems poor political arithmetic, inherently vulnerable under the circumstances. The proposal posed substantially more difficult issues of choice and credibility than would the more conservative concept of paying employee shares from realized savings.

Had the impasse with the Board been either avoided or successfully passed, it is likely that the project would have remained at risk. The productivity measurement and sharing formulation had never been seriously dealt with as an issue. A program that was successful in terms of its own measurement formula would raise serious questions as to its desirability as public policy. The county executive, the budget director and the Board of Supervisors would, almost inevitably, become disillusioned with a system that paid off on productivity improvements that did not generate the budgetary savings necessary to make the payments. There might also be concern over payments for genuine productivity savings that were generated by managerial action and imposed no incremental burden on labor.

One acquires little sense of what was necessary to achieve labor cooperation. Fifty percent sharing and a pretentious, unfeasible productivity measurement formula come as parts of the project beginnings. There is no indication that anyone argued for lower sharing proportions or for a narrower definition of productivity improvements. Indeed, there is no evidence that these issues were negotiated or even seriously addressed.

These are formal characteristics of the project. Beneath the surface, the project was in greater trouble because it did not achieve the support of middle management, the senior civil servants in the county agencies. The opposition of this group was quite evident in the initial PIEs and Macri's Ford Foundation report identifies them as "antagonists or inhibitors" of the project. This is not surprising. Productivity innovations raised questions as to their prior stewardship and undermined or diluted their own managerial authority. There was no special effort to win their support by either cajolery or inducements.

Macri's own conclusions are to the point:

It was truly an exploratory project and, as is well known, explorers sometimes bring back bad news. The worst news to report is that until public awareness of the cost of operating local government is heightened, and until elected officials, political leaders and top management perceive incentives, and are better educated in the business of more effectively and efficiently operating government, the future of large-scale productivity improvement efforts is bleak.

In the tight and political environment of local government in the northeast, few would argue with this gloomy assessment.

Justin Renz is optimistic about the prospects for productivity improvement efforts in Nassau County. He sees County Executive Caso as still strongly oriented toward that objective despite the collapse of the Multi-Municipal Productivity Project. The Commission on Priorities is beginning to add a new ingredient —necessity. The Commission is, according to Renz, introducing a new realism into top-level thinking about county government, and the problems of Nassau's big neighbor have undoubtedly contributed to that attitude.

Renz believes expenditure control through program choices and productivity improvement is now recognized as essential. The publication of the expenditure projection in the report of the Subcommittee on the Economy is illustrative. A few years back, such estimates would have been regarded as a political liability; today, they may contribute to the necessary public understanding of the problem.

Without Justin Renz's optimism, one could easily be skeptical, even cynical about the prospects. Tiwce within a decade, the county has made a major commitment of energy to the improvement of performance and productivity and, each time, it has ultimately dismantled the new machinery. Currently, there is no likelihood that the county will commit the staff and resources required for an effort commensurate with the magnitude of the problem. Despite the county executive's support, increases in expenditures for that purpose are not regarded as feasible when large lay-offs of employees are a definite possibility. The Office of Productivity and Administrative Analysis will be staffed, not to do the job, but rather to, at best, make a significant beginning.

Justin Renz disagrees:

... the reduction in productivity staff should not be treated as a retrenchment or a withdrawal of Nassau's commitment to productivity improvement. On the contrary, the program's transferral to the Office of Productivity and Management Analysis, under the direction of an experienced economist, trained in using the tools of analysis, argues for a continuing commitment directed along pragmatic rather than conceptual lines. The activities of the Commission on Priorities, actively chaired by the County Executive himself which directly involves management to a degree not achieved under the Multi-Municipal Productivity Improvement Project also argues for a continuing and perhaps heightened commitment in this area.

If the Office of Productivity and Administrative Analysis is able to pick targets with high potential yield, finds responsive department heads, and has the county executive's backing when it needs it, it could make gradual but important progress. Whether or not it will make such progress is subject to question. The experience in Nassau County to date suggests that the odds are with the skeptics.

6 New York

In scale, breadth, and complexity, the city of New York stands by itself, a different order of magnitude than any other local government in America. It has a population two-and-one-half times that of Chicago, triple that of Los Angeles, and ten-to-fifteen times that of the more typical great city. This is only one of the factors.

Nowhere else in the United States except the District of Columbia are such a large proportion of governmental functions integrated in one local government. New York is one of only five cities among those with populations over 500,000 that do not share responsibility for local governance with a county government. It is even more unusual in the inclusion of the public schools within its budget and its government. It also embraces a hospital system with some 15,000 beds in nineteen different facilities and the third-largest public university system in America.

Moreover, density and complexity require functions unnecessary in smaller cities and complicate the performance of the most routine services. It has major managerial problems simply because of the scale of its operations, and the same scale has precluded any widespread coherent understanding of city government among even its educated citizens.

The giant is ponderous and slow-moving, because the extraordinary effort required to make it anything else has rarely been forthcoming. The system frustrates its managers and drives its employees and citizens to organize against it. The dialogue in politics and labor relations tends to be conducted at levels many decibels above federal noise standards because participants believe otherwise they will not be heard or, if heard, no one will believe they really mean it. The rhetoric of public debate is frequently shrill and destructive and sometimes vicious.

The city's politics are almost entirely the politics of distribution or redistribution. Neighborhoods fight the closing of police precinct stations, reductions in refuse collection frequency, or the opening of a drug abuse center. Employees fight for more money, for more benefits, and against increased workload or reduced staff. The increments, on the other hand, are virtually uncontested. No matter how questionable, a new $200 million hospital, a $100

97

million campus for a new college, 1500 more sanitationmen, 100 additional
budget analysts, or 20-year pensions for teachers has, in the past, produced no
significant objections from either politicians or citizens save those with allega-
tions of special injury, With all the procedural restrictions of state law and city
charter, the mayor's authority for day-to-day management is unmatched in
America; so long as he does not run afoul of any political constituency, he
can add and delete positions, adjust salaries, obtain the creation of new civil
service titles, and even create new agencies.

The development and implementation of public policy in New York is, as
a result, something apart from local government in all the rest of America. The
very existence of a productivity program in New York represents a defiance of
all the natural forces of the governmental system. A citywide comprehensive
program would embrace hundreds of productivity projects. Every major agency
in the New York City government has, for example, more employees than the
entire municipal government in Dallas, Phoenix, or Milwaukee. The process of
decision, development, and negotiation of a productivity program in any one of
these agencies can be as complex as the development of a citywide program
elsewhere.

The Productivity Program

The New York City Productivity Program was announced by Mayor John V.
Lindsay in August 1972. It was the first such effort to be called a productivity
program, and, as befits New York, it is by far the largest. Deputy Mayor Edward
K. Hamilton described it as "a 225-page statement of work objectives and units
of measure keyed to a specific timetable with quarterly subtargets, . . . the first
comprehensive set of objective measures of administrative accomplishment in
all large-scale program areas which any major government has made available for
public scrutiny and comment."[1]

The August 1972 program inauguration was, in fact, both a statement of
improvements already effected and a prospectus for improvements to come. It
announced accomplishments and established objectives for the nine administrations or super agencies, four departments—police, fire, corrections, and consumers affairs—the new model cities administration, and for certain citywide
programs. It included all the operating agencies subject to the mayor's direction
but did not cover the quasi-independent Boards of Education and of Higher
Education or the offices of independently elected officials. The quasi-independent Health and Hospitals Corporation was included, but the Off-Track Betting
Corporation was omitted.

The program was a mixed bag. Some goals were true productivity objectives calling for increased output in relationship to input. Others were performance objectives such as reductions in backlogs, improvements in quality

of service, adherence to schedules, or the inauguration of some new program or activity. In some cases, definition and measurement were feasible; in others, there were significant ambiguities. With all its limitations and its heterogeneity, the productivity program was impressive in its scope, in the real accomplishments already achieved, and in its goals for future action. It established the basis for a new pattern of accountability of commissioners and administrators to the mayor on an agenda that did, in fact, incorporate many of the mayor's objectives.

There were wide variations in the quality of the program from agency to agency. Indeed, in his first quarterly review memorandum to the mayor, which was released to the press, Hamilton roundly criticized the performance of the Housing and Development Administration and the Transportation Administration in failing to meet goals. This violates the usually accepted rules of top government administrators against washing dirty linen in public and provided apparent confirmation of the serious intentions of both Lindsay and Hamilton.

Hamilton classified the projects to be carried out under the productivity program in four separate categories:

Where output is easily measurable—e.g., the number of tons of refuse collected per sanitation truck shift—to reduce the unit cost and improve the responsiveness of city operations.

Where output is very hard to measure, e.g., in providing police or fire protection—to improve the deployment of resources so as to maximize the probability that our resources will be available at the time and place they are needed most.

To improve the organization and processing procedures of government, particularly through imaginative use of computers.

To develop new technological devices and approaches—e.g., the development of plasticized rapid water for firefighting—to make the best possible use of every, increasingly expensive city employee.[2]

Each of these categories was illustrated by examples that cast some considerable light on the program.

Reduce Unit Costs and Improve Responsiveness

Rat Control. Premises inspected increased from 6.1 to 20.1 per man-day and cost per inspection was cut from $9.10 to $2.74. Exterminations per man-day increased from 2.25 to 11.1, and unit cost was reduced from $22.50 to $4.89. Man-days per ton of refuse removed were reduced from 8.95 to 1.56 and cost per ton was cut from $179 to $31.

Park Cleaning. Workers were shifted from permanent work stations to mobile, three-person crews with a daily schedule and an estimated number of hours required to complete the work. Complaints decreased sharply and output doubled.

Street Patching. The average productive hours of repair crews had been only 37 percent due to excessively large crews and driver restrictions on asphalt delivery. Resurfacing increased from 350 miles to 700 miles despite a 250-person reduction in the work force.

Sanitation Vehicle Maintenance. The introduction of a new district garage system, preventive maintenance, improved parts inventory and delivery, new operating procedures, and imposition of private industry productivity standards reduced the number of vehicles out of service from 38 percent to 11 percent. (The new productivity standards nearly doubled output per mechanic.)

Improving Deployment

Fire Response. The traditional three-engine, two-ladder response was scrapped in favor of a probability-based adaptive response system. A High Fire Concentration System to increase manning in peak periods failed to secure union approval.

Police Dispatch. The SPRINT computerized dispatch system permits 87 percent of the 20,000 calls per day to be answered within 15 seconds, 95 percent within 30 seconds or less.

Sanitation Deployment. A new "chart" or work schedule introduced with union approval put 17 percent more workers on duty on Monday and 8 percent more on Tuesday—the days when workload was heaviest—with comparable reductions in end-of-week staffing.

Improving Government Organization and Procedures

Capital Construction. A Capital Construction Information System was introduced to schedule and monitor progress on 2,300 construction projects. The time required to plan and construct a building was approximately halved and contract awards increased from $250 million in 1966–1967 to about $900 million in 1971–1972.

Fund Control. A new system for vendor payment reduced departmental processing time from 58.4 to 11.2 days, total processing time from 90 to 35 days. It realized dollar savings as well.

Use of Computers. Many new systems were introduced, including those in the Off-Track Betting Corporation and the Parking Violations Bureau.

Technological Innovation

Principal accomplishments in the department of technology are the development of methadone as a heroin substitute and of polymerized "rapid water" for fire fighting.

Hamilton's sampler gives a good sense of the range in kinds of productivity projects, but it omits a few of the more significant projects. For example, in refuse collection, average tons per truck-shift were increased without change in crew size or equipment from 8.4 tons in June 1969 to 10.3 tons in June 1973, an increase of 22.6 percent. Missed collections dropped from 10 percent to 0 percent, night collections from 15 percent to 4 percent. Savings in labor time from 1970–1971 were estimated by an independent research group at $5.5 million annually plus another $1 million in night shift differential payments. A major multiproject program in the Police Department included new plainclothes anticrime units which, with 6 percent of the police manpower, soon accounted for 35 percent of all felony arrests with an average conviction rate of 84 percent. Central booking saved over 200 man-years of police time annually. Other projects included extensive substitution of civilians for police officers in office assignments, a major computerization effort, crime and traffic alert programs to reduce officer time in court, and integrated precinct commands including detectives.

The Citizens' Budget Commission (CBC), a nonpartisan civic research organization supported by public contributions, reviewed the productivity program and, departing from its more usual highly critical stance, gave the effort qualified praise. The following comments from the summary statements on the programs in the respective agencies:

1. On the Police Department: ". . . The Productivity effort in the Police Department represents a major attempt to make limited city funds go farther in providing security and service to the City's residents, and one which CBC believes has already achieved substantial success."[3]

2. On the Fire Department: ". . . The City has successfully sought to improve the service and increase productivity. New equipment is being acquired by the adoption of a ten-year replacement cycle. Modern technology is being applied and the development of new patterns of response and manning have been introduced. In CBC's judgement, arrived at after careful onsite study, we believe these changes to have been much in the public interest."[4]

3. On the Human Resources Administration: "The Productivity Program in HRA has been designed to achieve the twin goals of ensuring that only eligible recipients are on welfare, and that the management systems are established to provide accurate information on and control of the caseload. Within the broad framework of the Productivity Program, there are a number of programs which, once fully operational, will result in significant management improvements in HRA operations."[5]

4. On the Sanitation Department: "For some years, with strong and mag-

netic leadership, this department has been focussing on true productivity measures, i.e., the most effective delivery of services at the lowest cost, and deserves high marks for what has been achieved. . ."[6]

There are, of course, summary judgments, and, in detailed reports, CBC criticizes various aspects of the program, most commonly for omissions or lagging progress.

The program was also presented to numerous visitors from other cities and some states as well as potential investors in city bonds. It drew, throughout, strongly favorable reactions.

Program Characteristics

There are three important characteristics of the program. One was the strong initiating role of the staffs in the Executive Office of the Mayor. The mayor's project management staff (PMS) initiated and did the basic analysis for the park cleaning, vehicle maintenance, and fund control projects; PMS was eventually made part of the Bureau of the Budget. The Bureau of the Budget initiated and managed the Capital Construction Information System. Both agencies were heavily involved in the computerization projects. Over time, agency management improved markedly and built its own analytic capacity—partially by drawing personnel from Budget and City Hall. As this happened, an increasing proportion of improvements were made with little involvement by Budget or PMS. The New York City's RAND Institute's relation with city agencies was also, in the main, initiated and pressed by Budget.

The second characteristic is the typical but not universal tendency for developments to be a long time in the making. Only a few took less than two years to move from initiation to substantial accomplishment. In projects such as park cleaning and vehicle maintenance, it took an additional two years of what might be called fumbling with the problem before the right approach was developed.

The third and last characteristic is the strong role of outsiders to the established agency bureaucracy. Comparatively few long-time careerists played a significant role in either initiating or developing innovations. Among the exceptions were Chief John O'Hagan of the Fire Department, Commissioner Murphy's top uniformed command in the Police Department, the Police Department's electronic data processing team, and the Office of Productivity in Sanitation.

The Lindsay productivity program resulted in few direct reductions in the budget, although it certainly aided in the adjustment to the budget reductions required in the 1970–1972 period. The Mayor's primary concern was effectiveness, not efficiency. In Sanitation, for example, the productivity improvement in refuse collection made it possible to both meet collection schedules and to release manpower for street sweeping; the chief result was cleaner streets although by the end of 1973 the force had been reduced by about half the 1500 men added in 1970 just before the productivity effort began.

Initiation

The productivity program was the brainchild of Andrew Kerr and John Thomas, deputy director and assistant director, respectively, of the Bureau of the Budget. Kerr and Thomas had headed the project management staff in the Office of the Mayor which was transferred to the Bureau of the Budget in late 1971.

By 1972, the project management staff and its successor unit in the Bureau of the Budget had been involved in management improvement efforts in a wide variety of city programs and agencies. With a sizable staff experienced in the city government, Kerr and Thomas were confident that they could manage a citywide program of productivity and operations improvement. They developed a proposal to do this and put it before Deputy Mayor Edward Hamilton.

Hamilton was already calling publicly for productivity improvements and insisting on productivity concessions in union contracts. The Kerr-Thomas proposal was a logical extension of existing efforts, and Hamilton accepted it with enthusiasm.

Hamilton approved the program and obtained Lindsay's concurrence because it was a good thing to do, because it had become feasible with the passage of the high tide of union militancy and with rising citizen opinion critical of city employee performance, and because it would give Lindsay some recognition for substantial managerial achievements that had gone almost unnoticed in the city.

The program was supported by a considerable public relations effort. In addition to the initial announcement and the quarterly progress reports to the public, a productivity conference was held with mayors and other officials from large American cities. The Johnson Foundation financed a meeting on local productivity at Wingspread, Wisconsin at which Lindsay and Hamilton were the most prominent protagonists.

The program was a product of the Kerr and Thomas idea and Hamilton's entrepreneurship, but it fitted John Lindsay's needs and image. A mayor coming out of the regular majority organization might have been more cautious about introducing a highly publicized effort that was certain to be opposed by some municipal employees and by some of the employee unions. Lindsay, however, was a maverick politician, elected initially as a Republican far too liberal for his party and, later, a convert to the Democratic party. He was convinced of the inadequacy of municipal performance from the outset of his administration and almost totally committed to changes and innovations that offered the prospect of performance improvement.

The productivity program in New York represented an effort to bring under a single rubric a vast range of productivity and performance improvement efforts already underway in many agencies, to introduce similar efforts in agencies without such programs, and to systematize and manage the overall program on a citywide basis.

Hamilton describes the program as, in effect, the capstone of a six-year effort by the Lindsay administration:

In 1965 New York City was in no condition to mount a systematic productivity effort. The government was fragmented into more than 70 separate agencies reporting directly to the mayor. Most municipal salaries were so low that imposition of private work standards would have been justified cause for rebellion among city workers. An almost complete absence of analytic talent in city agencies made it impossible to install the complex management information systems necessary to monitor operations. Too often, there was no way to tell what, for example, a health inspector did with his day, nor were there quantified criteria setting forth what he ought to do—i.e., how long on the average should be required to complete a particular type of inspection. The city budget was not determined in terms of program categories, but in terms of sterile object class line items. The whole science of program-performance budgeting was in its earliest formative stages in the federal government and had not yet been applied in state or local contexts. In short, New York City, like other jurisdictions across the country, did not have the raw material to launch a comprehensive productivity effort.

We have acquired that raw material through a long and sometimes frustrating process of administrative innovation and reform. Mayor Lindsay has completely reorganized the government into 10 major administrations which group like programs, provide a point of coordination between them, and establish manageable lines of authority and accountability to the mayor. The roster of analytic specialists in all city agencies has expanded to the point where Fortune magazine and other business-oriented observers have called it the most impressive array of analytic talent at work in any government in the country. Management informations systems now produce more data on New York City operations than in any other state or local administration. The budget is enacted and administered by program categories and serves as a cost/benefit measure as much as a catalog of city expenditures. These advances, though too dull and drab to excite public attention, are the basic infrastructure which makes a systematic productivity program possible.[7]

Not all of these factors are equally important and at least one of them, the alleged inadequacy of city salaries, would be questioned by some. The most important was the build-up of analytic capacity in the city agencies. The super agencies contributed to the build-up by providing the critical mass necessary to support program analysis and evaluation staffs and the breadth of responsibilities necessary to attract competent staff. (At the same time, the superagencies have been criticized—not without reason—for adding a new impeding layer of administration.) Another critical factor was the trial-and-error learning process by which the mayor and his staff developed the capacity to find, identify, recruit, and, sometimes, develop competent and innovative managers for the various city agencies. Increasingly toward the end of the Lindsay administration, the Mayor turned to the young staff assistants and analysts for talent to fill line positions in the operating agencies.

The Development of Expertise

The New York City program, more than any other, was built on the skills, talents, and perspectives of a host of new recruits. New program planning and analysis staffs were created and staffed with recruits drawn from major business, law, and graduate schools. Experienced systems analysts were recruited from the Department of Defense and various research organizations. Industrial engineers and computer experts were attracted from private industry. The New York City Rand Institute was created as a joint venture with the Rand Corporation. Continuing and effective consulting arrangements were developed with MDC Systems and McKinsey and Company. The Vera Institute of Justice, which had pioneered in the reform of the bail system beginning in 1961, was enlisted in a wide variety of efforts related to the problems of the criminal justice system, including the launching of a major methadone maintenance program for drug addicts. The Urban and Policy Sciences Program of the State University of New York at Stony Brook used National Science Foundation funding to do yeoman work on sanitation problems.

The emphasis on program and operations analysis in New York was necessary because of the scale of the city government. The administrator of a large New York city agency or program simply could not perceive, in any real sense, the vast operations for which he was responsible. Fact finding, statistical analysis, and evaluation were necessary simply to know what was actually going on. Program changes had to be formally structured and carefully monitored to take into account the exceptions and the special problems in this complex world.

But analysts do not make the decisions or enforce them. This is the job of the administrators and commissioners. Lindsay's first term was beset with frustrations, many of them due to the lack of management that was both competent and innovative. The major pay-offs from the wealth of analytic talent did not come, in many agencies, until administrators and commissioners more strongly focused on improvement and innovation replaced the initial Lindsay appointees. For example, despite the mayor's great interest in the sanitation problem and the devotion of considerable analytic talent to it, the situation actually deteriorated during the first Lindsay term; the impressive gains in productivity and performance came later after the appointment of Jerome Kretchmer and Herbert Elish early in the second term. Similarly, the Health Services Administration remained largely moribund until the appoint-

ment of Gordon Chase as administrator. There was no significant and effective
use of analytic talent in police until Patrick Murphy became Commissioner.

Internal Accommodation

There was no special effort in the Lindsay administration to assure the cooperation of career senior civil servants except that their salaries were regularly
adjusted to keep them apace with the cost of living and with the gains won by
their subordinates in collective bargaining. Murphy in Police followed a very
tough policy of transfer and sometimes demotions for officers whose performance fell below his standards; at the end of two-and-a-half years, not a single
officer of the 182 above the rank of captain occupied the same position as when
Murphy had become commissioner. Elish in Sanitation did not follow so drastic
a course, but he did remove district superintendents he regarded as incompetent
and shifted headquarters staff to the extent he found necessary while at the
same time working hard and effectively to build pride and morale in the sanitation force. Chase, in health, managed a large part of his program outside the
regular organization with staff drawn mostly from outside the agency. In social
services and income maintenance, Arthur Spiegel built a huge analytic and
computer staff with new recruits from business, but Charles Morris, who was
responsible for the operation of the welfare centers, followed a strategy of
finding and using the best of the career staff. In other agencies, the pattern
varied.

There was little doubt that tensions and resistance developed as a result
among the senior career staff in the city. But it is difficult and probably
impossible to assess its magnitude and importance. The opposition to outsiders
in the Police Department certainly was the major factor in the termination of
the relationship with the New York City Rand Institute in 1969 by then Commissioner Howard Leary. Fire Commissioner John O'Hagan believes the introduction of "rapid water" was delayed for five or six months by problems that
were created on ostensibly technical grounds by officers who, in O'Hagan's
view, were simply opposed to change. The tension between the "new people"
and the "old people" was a definite problem in the income maintenance and
social services program.

In most departments, the senior careerists were skeptical of new recruits,
of consultants, and of proposed program changes. They succeeded in bringing
some of the more cautious commissioners around to their point of view and,
thereby, slowed the process of change. There is little indication, however, that
the careerists made any attempt to sabotage or delay the introduction of any
program supported by the agency head. In most departments, careerists continued to hold responsibilities they had held before the Lindsay administration
and many of them were important in the implementation (although not the
initiation) of innovative efforts.

The Unions

Until 1970, only the teachers and social workers had collective bargaining agreement provisions that dealt directly with workload and working conditions affecting productivity. The social workers' caseload limit of sixty had been introduced on the recommendation of a mediation panel at the end of the Wagner administration and was, in effect, bought back by the city in the collective bargaining agreement of 1969. The United Federation of Teachers had and still has a host of workload provisions in its contract with the Board of Education including class-size minimums and specified preparation and administration periods. The police and fire unions had shift and rotation schedules covered by provisions in state law—a 1911 act predating strong unionism in the case of the police, a more recent and more rigid provision successfully lobbied by the union in the case of the Fire Department.

Yet, union opposition was an important deterrent to productivity increasing changes. The police fourth platoon is an example. For seven successive years, Lindsay and Wagner before him had attempted to change the state statute to authorize a fourth platoon for the high-crime evening hours rather than maintain equal staffing in all three shifts. A court decision on the transit police who were subject to the same law and the deviations already in effect for traffic officers and others suggest that the problem was not, in fact, a legal matter. Given the adamant union opposition, however, an attempt by the city to make the change would probably have resulted in a strike. The legislature finally approved the change in 1969, partially because of a *New York Times* article on policemen "cooping" or sleeping in patrol cars on the inactive graveyard shift. The change, once enacted into law, was implemented largely through volunteers.

A much different story is that on one-person patrol cars. New York is one of only four cities of over 500,000 people to use two-person cars exclusively. The Police Department conducted an experiment in one-person patrol cars in Queens using approximately the same patrol force and, hence, double the normal complement of patrol cars. The experiment showed no increase in injuries to officers or accidents. The mayor elected to apply one-person cars in about one-fourth of the city's precincts, all low-crime and low-hazard areas. The union responded by threatening a strike and demanding the elimination of the experimental effort in Queens. The city caved in. Later, the two-person car was incorporated into the collective bargaining contract with the city.

In the summer of 1968, the fire officers demanded additional personnel in view of a quadrupling of the number of alarms over the course of a decade. They argued at the same time for the retention of the traditional response to box alarms of three engines and two ladder trucks. The city finally agreed to an immediate increase in staffing and resolution of the workload issue by the Office of Collective Bargaining, which resulted a year later in a second expansion in the fire force.

During this same period, the correction officers also protested and received additional staffing to reduce the number of "sticks," those instances where officers have to serve two consecutive shifts because their replacements did not appear for the next shift. The first increase provided no relief because absenteeism increased to nearly absorb the additional manpower, and a second increase was authorized.

Save for the case of the social workers, the city did not in the 1966–1970 period introduce workload and productivity issues into collective bargaining on the grounds that these issues involved managerial perogatives and were not bargainable. In fact, the agreement with the unions setting up the Office of Collective Bargaining had a "Catch 22" provision reserving these rights to management but giving the unions the right to bargain or carry as a grievance to the OCB any consequent changes in working conditions. As a result, unilateral action by the city, for example, to eliminate the short summer day introduced before air conditioning was common, was overturned by the courts. Or, alternatively, the unions would, as the Patrolmen's Benevolent Association did in the case of the one-person car, use muscle or threats to force the city to back down.

Productivity bargaining was initiated by the city in December 1970 with the city stating that it would sign no future collective bargaining contracts unless they dealt satisfactorily with productivity issues. The Uniformed Sanitationmen's Association formally agreed to change in the "chart," which would increase the force available on Mondays and Tuesdays when the refuse collection workload was heaviest—but accepted without formal bargaining or agreement an increase of 25 percent in the collection productivity of sanitation workers. Fire officers and fire fighters accepted a provision permitting reductions in engine company staffing as "rapid" water was introduced. The fire unions had at one time tentatively agreed to concurrent tours to concentrate more of the force during peak workload periods, but the city mishandled the issue and the union reconsidered.

Professor Raymond D. Horton of the Columbia University Business School argues that New York City's productivity bargaining effort under Lindsay was a failure.[8] Horton finds that the city's entry into productivity bargaining was, in effect, dictated by its past failures in labor relations. The high labor costs imposed on the city by past labor contracts made it necessary for the city to seek methods for performing its functions with fewer employees. At the same time, "the earlier dislocations of managerial power in the political and bargaining processes" made it impossible for the city to increase productivity unilaterally, without the consent of the unions. But productivity bargaining, in turn, reflected the same adverse distribution of power between management and the unions. The city secured the chart day change from the Uniformed Sanitationmen's Association. But from the Police, it gained only the benefit of half-hour daily training sessions at the cost of an eighteen-day reduction in the number of days worked by a patrolman in the course of a year. From the fire unions, it secured the right to introduce adaptive response that, in fact, reduced the workload on the average fire fighter. At the same time, the city paid very substantial increases in salary that resulted in an increase rather than a decrease in unit costs.

Horton's comments are, in some measure, correct. The city's productivity gains were achieved primarily outside the bargaining process, and the alleged productivity gains in the police and fire contracts are questionable. He misinterprets the police situation; it is generally agreed that the change in police work schedules to provide training time was a mistake, but it arose not from the bargaining situation but because the administration wanted that change. It is also not certain that the pay increases were larger than they otherwise would have been in the absence of productivity considerations. Furthermore, given the rising price level, the maintenance of real wages depended on significant dollar wage increases.

The major fact of the 1971-1973 period was that productivity was increased in many city agencies without union opposition, sometimes under an explicit agreement, more often without such an agreement. The difficulties came largely in the volatile police and fire unions, where any concessions were difficult to sell to the rank and file.

A standard general productivity clause was developed and inserted in collective bargaining agreements for employees in all the city agencies under the direct control of the mayor. There is little evidence that the clause had any impact on productivity.

Management and Implementation

Mayor Lindsay established in his first year in office a Police Planning Council (PPC) made up of himself and the principal officials in the Executive Office of the Mayor. By the end of 1967, the PPC had decided that the city's basic program problem was not policy planning but program implementation. It decided, accordingly, to form under the PPC a project management staff (PMS) to schedule and monitor the execution of programs, projects, and program changes of high importance to the mayor. PMS took on a wide variety of projects and handled them, with few exceptions, effectively. The staff expanded, eventually numbering 143, assuming responsibilities not merely for additional projects but also to provide management consulting and analysis assistance to the agencies. When Lindsay and Hamilton elected to undertake the productivity program, PMS—which had been made a unit within the Bureau of the Budget— was able to manage the program and monitor its progress. Without such a unit, it would have been extraordinarily difficult to mount and run a program of such great size on a quarterly reporting and review cycle.

Productivity under Mayor Beame

Abraham D. Beame succeeded John V. Lindsay as mayor on January 1, 1974.
Beame had been the City's budget director during Wagner's first two terms,
was elected comptroller in 1961, ran against Lindsay for Mayor in 1965, and,
after four years out of city government, was again elected Comptroller in 1969.
No Mayor in recent times had come to office with so formidable an experience
in the city's government and finances.

As comptroller and during his 1973 campaign for mayor, Beame had been
critical of some of the changes introduced by Lindsay, notably the super
agencies and the extensive use of contract consultants and researchers. These
were merely symptoms of the wide gulf in philosophy and perspective between
the two mayors.

The Lindsay administration was strongly change-oriented, highly critical
of departmental performance, convinced that new blood was needed to improve
it and committed to formal analytic problem solving and evaluation techniques.
The Beame administration was conservative and traditional, distrustful of
outsiders whether they were the "gypsy" analysts on the city payroll or the
systems experts of the Rand Corporation, intuitive in problem solving, less
critical of agency performance, and more skeptical of the possibilities of improvement. Beame was also more sensitive to political "realities" and determined
to avoid potentially destructive confrontations.

Productivity improvement in the Beame administration followed three
distinct and separate paths. The first was the continuation and modification of
the Lindsay-Hamilton program based on quarterly reporting against productivity
and performance targets. The second was Beame's effort to develop a cooperative union-management approach to productivity. The last concerns the productivity impact of the massive budget reductions resulting from the acute fiscal
crisis beginning in the autumn of 1974.

The Lindsay Productivity Program under Beame

The productivity program survived and, indeed, was expanded to include more
programs and objectives than in the Lindsay administration. The survival of the
program may, however, be more a tribute to the effectiveness of Hamilton's
public relations effort than to any conviction on the part of the new mayor that
it was a worthwhile endeavor. There is little indication that Beame took the
program seriously, and it certainly did not retain the importance given it in the
Lindsay administration. Beame's diffidence was not surprising given the program's close association with Lindsay and the hoopla with which it was introduced and marketed by Lindsay and Hamilton.

Within twelve to eighteen months of Beame's inauguration, the city had lost a substantial part of the capacity to continue an aggressive, large-scale productivity program on the Lindsay model. The analytic staffs built up over eight Lindsay years had been dissipated, in large part, by the end of Beame's first year, although there was no city hall effort to purge them. Many were provisional employees without civil service protection. Some were fired either because their administrators or commissioners didn't want them or because of budgetary stringency. Some with civil service status were encouraged to leave. More left because they found themselves unproductive in the new style and approach to city administration. The New York Rand Institute was continued during the 1974-1975 fiscal year at reduced funding and finally dissolved in June 1975—again under pressure of the fiscal crisis. The planned dismantling, initially of three super agencies and later extended to all of them, added further force toward the shrinkage of the capacity for analysis.

Productivity program reports had been issued on a quarterly basis through 1973, but the Beame administration did not issue its first report until February 1975. *The New York Times* reported that the program had undergone major changes under the Beame administration and that some officials, especially Lindsay administration hold-overs, felt that the result had been a sharp reduction in the effectiveness of the program.

There were several different aspects to the change in the program. One was the administration's intent to rely more heavily on joint development with union representatives of productivity improvements through the Productivity Council (discussed below).

A second aspect was a seeming willingness to reduce the productivity pressure on the agencies and to recognize some of the alleged adverse impacts of the productivity program. This seems best illustrated by the Highway Commissioner, who discontinued the inspection and follow-through program on potholes because he believed his men were "demoralized" by the productivity standards. The Commissioner conceded that the data would show declines in the number of potholes repaired and miles of concrete sidewalks redone but said that the quality of the work had gone up greatly. With "quality" determined by subjective evaluation, this argument carries little weight with most advocates of productivity improvement programs.

Another case was the Beame administration's agreement at the request of the union to drop the provision negotiated in the Lindsay administration to put more sanitation workers on duty on Mondays and Tuesdays. The administration was reported as believing the productivity loss was negligible and that the morale of the workers was greatly improved.[9]

Some officials saw the new approach as conciliatory toward both employees and agency heads with the expectation that in the new climate of good feeling, it would be easier to achieve productivity improvements.[10]

City Councilman Robert F. Wagner, Jr. carried out a phone survey in the summer of 1975 of agency officials charged with supervising the productivity program. He reported the following responses to the question: "Does your agency use the productivity report?":

This productivity stuff is okay if you want to impress the politicos. (Corrections)
It's not the system we use for our management effort. . . . To a large extent, it's a political document where agency heads make sure they're not embarrassed. . . . Most of the time, the commissioners just sign off on it and that's it, and ask themselves, 'How are we going to get around this?' (Addiction Services)
This year, it hasn't been, to be honest. We've been involved in layoffs, so we've made our productivity program an inadequate measure. (Personnel)
The level of detail is not yet that great for management decisions. (The official in Human Resources stressed "the public relations value of this document.")
The report itself, I would say no. . . . The report, per se, is just a matter, like, for the public to view. (Hospitals)
It is not consistently examined. (Health)
We go to the Bureau and discuss their figures with them. . . . The Commissioner has them but I don't know what he does with them.[11] (Fire)

It seems evident that productivity targeting and reporting in the Beame administration became a largely pro forma exercise and was no longer a serious management tool.

The third aspect of the change concerned the impact of the loss of analytic talent. The adverse effects were conceded by some agency officials. On the other hand, James A. Cavanagh, Beame's deputy mayor in 1974 and 1975 and a careerist who was Deputy Budget Director in the Lindsay administration, discounted the importance of the analysts: "Most of these guys come in from the Defense Department and places like that. They never became a part of the fabric of government. A lot of them may have eliminated inefficiencies in their departments, but do you keep a big staff in there even after they've already done what they could? It's wasteful."[12]

One hold-over Lindsay administration appointee in the Bureau of the Budget was critical of the "mediocre" quality of Beame's appointments but sympathetic with the mayor's handling of the productivity program. He saw Beame's opportunities as greatly constrained by the fiscal crisis and, moreover, believed that recognition should be given to the need for changes as the program evolved over time.[13]

The administration made few specific claims of gains in productivity. Robert Bott, the Deputy Director of the Office of Management and Budget, responsible for productivity programs, spoke in March 1975 of a new management audit approach to productivity that had avoided city spending of $50 million and was expected to prevent the spending of another $80 million in the next year. He reported in August that his office had completed seventeen unspecified projects in 1974 that saved the city $28 million and produced $45 million in additional revenues.[14] He also reported new inspector routing schemes that increased consumer affairs inspections by 53 percent and elevator inspections by 50 percent.

There was also one new actor. The Mayor's Management Advisory Board, a new organization quite detached from the city government, took over some responsibilities for management analysis, personnel reform, and productivity. The Board also implemented pilot projects in Management by Objective in the Fire Department and the Department of Highways.

The administration seemingly toyed in 1975 with the idea of eliminating the productivity report in favor of a new semiannual report on program indicators covering work force and workload but without explicit productivity targets or performance data. The new report was issued, but by the spring of 1976 there was also a new productivity report, greatly improved by classification of its 263 measures as productivity (93), program effectiveness (50), or program accomplishment (120) indicators.

The data in the report did not permit easy comparison with prior performance back to the beginning of the productivity program. Many of the ninety-three productivity indicators were new without either 1973-1974 or 1974-1975 base data. In others, the unit of measure was revised, e.g. the substitution of "square yards" for "maintenance miles" in pavement resurfacing.

A review of some of the measures where tracking is possible produces a mixed pattern of results:

Refuse collection: Average tons per truck shift up from 9.95 in fiscal 1973-1974 to 10.07 in 1974-1975, a gain of 1.2 percent. First half of fiscal 1975-1976 was 1 percent above first half of 1974-1975.

Water meters: Visits per man-day steady at fifty-two for both 1973-1974 and 1974-1975. First half of 1975-1976 down 10 percent below first half 1974-1975. Decline attributed to change in policy to give priority to meters of large water users.

Catch basins cleaned: An increase from 9.6 per crew shift in 1973-1974 to 12 in 1974-1975, a 25 percent gain. First half of 1975-1976 is about 11 percent over first half of 1974-1975.

Potholes filled: A decline from 28.7 per man-day in fiscal 1973-1974 to 26.5 in 1974-1975, an 8 percent drop. The first half of 1975-1976 was another 25 percent below the first half of 1974-1975.

These were selected from activities with minimum ambiguity, but there are virtually always questions of variation in quality. The wide difference in productivity performance was fairly representative of those operations to which fairly "hard" measures of productivity apply. The mixed performance can be regarded as evidence of a lack of strong central management of the productivity program. It reflects as well the limitations of productivity reporting systems not supported with the resources necessary for the work reorganization or program redesign often required to achieve gains.

The Beame administration's discomfort with the Lindsay format for productivity improvement seems obvious. Presumably, the survival of that approach was motivated primarily by the desire to avoid the criticism that would have been incurred by openly junking the effort.

The Beame approach as it emerged in stories in the press was apparently intended to be selective rather than comprehensive, less directive and more sensitive to agency and union objectives, less dependent on the OMB initiatives. Yet, the productivity program reports covered more measures than the Lindsay program. The difference was a matter of level of effort. By mid-1975, the city's sharply reduced analytical staff had been diverted to the more pressing issues of the fiscal crisis, and the time committed to the formal productivity program could scarcely have been sufficient to maintain it at the 1973 scale.

There were two basic factors. The first was the administration's skeptical view of the Lindsay productivity program and the staff who ran it. As Deputy Mayor Cavanagh put it: "The Lindsay people were very Johnny Light-Touch on productivity. You always got a picture of great activity and great efficiency. But you have to take what they say with a grain of salt."[15] The second factor was the fiscal crisis, which left little managerial time to develop alternatives to Lindsay's productivity program. Beame and Cavanagh, both former budget hands, well knew that there was no hope that productivity programs could generate reductions of the magnitude needed in the time required. It was a time for the meat axe, and productivity analysis could play no more than auxiliary or supporting role. It was a secondary priority during a period when secondary priorities were never reached.

The Productivity Council

The Productivity Council was, on the other hand, a Beame administration innovation established by new language in its collective bargaining contracts. The Council represented a joint union-management approach to productivity improvement. The following language describing the arrangement is taken from the contract with the Uniformed Sanitationmen's Association:

... the signatories to this agreement will participate in a City-Wide Productivity Program. In the development thereof a City-Wide Productivity Council will be established consisting of an equal number of representatives from management and the unions. The first Deputy Mayor will be management's chief representative and serve as chairman of the Council. This Council, in order to aid the

Department's Labor-Management Productivity Committee, will determine the scope of the program.

The Department's Joint Committee shall consist of two designees of the Department and two designees of the Uniformed Sanitationmen's Association. The Joint Committee shall aid in the determination of its scope of activity by making recommendations to the City-Wide Productivity Council.

In the event that the City-Wide Productivity Council is unable to resolve a dispute, such dispute may be referred to an arbitration process which shall be created by the City-Wide Productivity Council.[16]

This provision, in effect, legitimized productivity by securing recognition by the union and provided a means for resolving any productivity difference except, of course, those that were protected by specific provisions in the collective bargaining agreement.

The Productivity Council approach—in emphasizing the role of union power (as opposed to Lindsay's emphasis on analytic expertise) and in using a mechanism for working out differences (and avoiding confrontations)—can be regarded as an accurate reflection of the Mayor's style and beliefs.

The citywide Productivity Council included representation from three of the largest employee unions, the directors of the Budget, the director of Personnel, and the deputy mayor who serves as chair. The Council's mission was to work out ways of increasing the productivity of city employees. The primary initial problem was finding an approach in which the traditional adversary relationship between management and unions did not become an impediment. The Council decided to function through task forces to be established in four separate city agencies with the charge to develop productivity programs, including goals, objectives, implementation plans, and output measures. The agencies selected included the Department of Sanitation, the Department of Parks, the Office of Housing Code Enforcement, and the Health and Hospitals Corporation. In each agency, two task forces were established: one at the agencywide level including top union and agency officials, the second at the level of the unit or division selected as a test site and actually working in that unit.

In Sanitation, the district-level meetings began with an airing of past complaints, but a consensus emerged that a principal problem was an overcentralization of authority that left little or no autonomy in the districts. The task force consequently recommended a decentralization of management to the district level, adding that if effective management could not be found within the department, outside recruitment should be considered. The last is, for New York City unions, an heretical departure from a long-sustained defense of the filling of supervisory positions by internal promotion. The task force also recommended a salary-based incentive plan under which salary increments would be paid only to those workers increasing output. The alternative of producer cooperatives of sanitation workers was also suggested.

The Parks Department task force also recommended a decentralization of management as well as relief for the on-going problems of inadequate tools and equipment, preventive maintenance programs for vehicles and mechanical equipment to reduce down time, and the creation of a single civil service title, parks maintainer. The latter would eliminate the problem posed by the use of several different civil service titles, for each of which some part of the work of park maintenance fell out of title. Union acceptance of this notion was surprising.

In the Office of Code Enforcement, the major problem was ineffective computerization; nine out of ten cases handled on the computer had to be done manually. The computer required reprogramming, but no one in the agency seemed to have the authority to do it. There were few managerial positions in the agency, and virtually all supervisory jobs were filled by promotion upward from entry level jobs.

The Productivity Council, on the basis of these experiences, recommended a citywide program to "reestablish" management capacity while at the same time decentralizing decision-making authority. Key aspects included the restoration of an effective managerial pay plan, the introduction of a mandatory managerial training program, and the removal of supervisors from the same bargaining unit as the workers they supervise. No action was taken.

Robert Schrank, who served on loan from the Ford Foundation as staff director for the Productivity Council, summed up the council effort as follows: "The local task forces, the real heart of this project, began to produce some genuinely exciting results in the planning stage just when the fiscal crisis and resulting layoffs put a hold on their efforts. We expect the task forces to resume their work in the agencies when the city begins to resolve some of its current difficulties . . ."[17]

The Fiscal Crisis as a Productivity Program

By the spring of 1976, little remained of either the program or the supporting analytic capacity inherited from the Lindsay administration. Beame's own initiative, the Productivity Council, had foundered at least temporarily without any concrete achievements in productivity improvement. Over the administration's first twenty-seven months, it could claim few successes from formal productivity programs.

The results reflect, in part, both the low value placed by the administration on the inherited program and staff and the limitations of the favored joint union-management approach to the problem. More important, however, has been the effect of the fiscal crisis. Since the spring of 1975, when the city lost access to the money market, the administration has been concerned with little save the financial survival of the city government. City management had little time for productivity programs and almost no capacity to make the commitments necessary for productivity agreements with the unions.

Yet, under the mounting pressure of the crisis, the city reduced its work force by over 50,000 or about 15 percent of the total employment at the beginning of the Beame administration—with further substantial reductions in prospect. No analysis has been made of the impact of the cuts, but it seems certain that they have resulted in some significant increases in productivity as well as reductions in the quantity and quality of services.

The Fire Department, for example, responded to 208,913 alarms in the July-December 1975 period with a total staff, uniformed and civilian, of 12,508. During the comparable 1973 period, there were 14,613 men and 163,578 alarms. The United Firefighters' Association has repeatedly claimed that the cuts have resulted in dangerous reductions in fire protection. The Department used the Rand response model to help determine where cuts would have a minimal impact on response time. It monitored subsequent fire responses and found little indication that the reduced manning had significantly affected response time or the capacity to mobilize men and equipment for larger fires. If we ignore the apparently modest reduction in quality and effectiveness, the department is meeting the city's fire protection needs with 14.4 percent fewer men, a productivity increase of 16.8 percent. If we were to use the number of alarms per man as a productivity measure, the increase in productivity would be 50 percent.

In Sanitation over the same two-year period, the number of employees was cut 16.5 percent from 14,897 to 12,436. Refuse collections increased slightly from 1,740,000 tons to 1,760,900 thousand tons. Service was cut back by reducing the frequency of collection. The number of mechanical broom routes swept dropped by 40 percent, accounting for about one-tenth of the jobs terminated. Vehicle maintenance deteriorated with trucks out of service increasing from 15.7 percent in 1974–1975 to 31.4 percent in December 1975. Productivity in refuse collection increased by very modest amounts.

Oddly, it doesn't really all add up. If the 12,436 remaining workers had done the work of the original 14,897, the productivity gain would have been 20 percent. Neither identifiable reductions in work performed (street sweeping and vehicle repair) nor increases in direct productivity (refuse collection and barge loading) can account for the full 20 percent. Obviously, a large part of the cut must have been effected through a tightening of various indirect cost areas —administration and supporting services. Interestingly, the Scorecard project of the Fund for the City of New York found average street cleanliness at the end of the period to be about the same as it had been a year earlier—before the largest reductions in manpower.

Large reductions in staffing were made in virtually every other city service area with varying results. For example, a reduction of 3151 uniformed and civilian Police Department employees seems to have had little impact on the

number of arrests, but, presumably, the intensity qnd quality of patrol surveillance has suffered. In the public schools, the large increase in the pupil-
teacher ratio represents to some a cut in quality, to others an increase in productivity, and, to still others, some combination fo the two.

Ray Horton in a March 1975 American Society for Public Administration
meeting called productivity "frosting on the cake," saying the single most
important productivity gain would come from efforts to restrain or cut labor
costs directly. The evidence bears him out—emphasizing the powerful role of
necessity as the mother of both invention and accommodation. The recognition
of the reality of reduced resources has made the city government more malleable
and the process of adaptation has resulted in some significant increases in
productivity.

Almost everywhere, the solutions are limited to those possible within
existing organizational and program structures. More sophisticated redesign
of work process has been rarely possible. This reflects the pressure of time as
well as the difficulties both in performing that redesign with few management
analysts and industrial engineers and in securing union agreement.

The fiscal crisis is also changing the basic structure of collective bargaining
in New York City. The Emergency Financial Control Board, created by State
Legislature in September 1975, has the authority and responsibility for approval
of a three-year city plan and for assuring that the city's financial commitments
remain with the limits imposed by that plan. The Board has approved a plan, prepared by the city administration, that imposed a three-year freeze on all salary and
wage levels for city employees. The Board initially rejected the contract with
the Union Federation of Teachers and required the parties to renegotiate its
terms. Arvid Anderson, Chairman of the New York City Office of Collective
Bargaining, says that: "For all practical purposes, the Emergency Financial
Control Board has created a new bargaining structure in New York City and
New York State."[18]

The Office of Collective Bargaining has previously held that the city had
the managerial authority to lay off employees but was required to bargain about
the impact of the increased workload on the remaining employees; the city has
challenged that ruling, and the matter is now pending before the New York
State Supreme Court. In the meantime, the unions have brought several such
cases before the Office of Collective Bargaining. One, brought by the United
Firefighters, was resolved by a decision supporting the city but prohibiting
further reductions in the fire force on grounds of the risk to public safety;
that decision is being appealed by the city.

There is little doubt that the realities of the city's financial problems have
eroded union resistance to workload increases and that the legal support for
union rights in this respect is also vanishing with new legislation and a new
perspective on the part of both arbitrators and the courts. The teachers have
conceded back to the Board of Education some of the time allocated to teacher

preparation periods in past contracts. More often concessions are not made in contracts but simply accepted in the higher workloads resulting from layoffs.

Many productivity gains cannot be as simply achieved, requiring first some significant reorganization of the work or a change in unit manning. Here, the layoffs and burdens imposed on employees created a climate not conducive to cooperative city-union relations.

A new phase in the relationship with the unions began with the review of the cost-of-living adjustments included in the proposed contract with the Transit Workers Union in the spring of 1976. The Emergency Financial Control Board (EFCB) eventually limited the cost-of-living adjustments and, further, specified that such adjustments could be paid only from "actual accrued productivity savings, exclusive of reductions in service."

With contracts under negotiation with the various city employee unions, the Board elected to approve a policy prohibiting general increases in wages and fringe benefits and requiring savings in pension and fringe benefit costs. With respect to cost-of-living increases, the Board specified that such increases could be paid only if: ". . . funded by independently measured savings realized, without reduction in services, through gains in productivity, reductions of fringe benefits or through other savings or other revenues approved by the Board, all of which savings shall be in addition to those provided in the financial play." The policy, which has been accepted by the unions, provides, for the first time, real incentives for union cooperation in securing productivity gains. However, the cost-of-living increases do not depend exclusively on productivity gains or fringe benefit reductions; they can be paid from "other savings or other revenues." Given EFCB's insistence on conservative revenue estimates, "other revenues" may be a more likely source of funds than productivity savings at a hard to achieve annual rate of, say, 6 percent.

Only July 17, 1976, a *New York Times* story reported the first meeting of "a newly constituted labor-management committee on productivity." The committee was a result of the June 30, 1976 collective bargaining agreement and replaced the productivity council provided for in the expiring agreements. John Zuccotti, the city's deputy mayor, pointed with pride to a new supporting management information system and the management by objective approach: "Probably no government of any kind has brought as much sophistication to management as we have." A union representative was optimistic about the prospects for improved productivity because of the incentives provided by the new contracts.

A New Phase

The city's problems have made it subject to outside scrutiny and direction of a kind it has certainly not faced in at least forty years, if then. The Emergency

Financial Control Board, the Municipal Assistance Corporation, a new Special
Deputy State Comptroller, and the U.S. Secretary of the Treasury are the
enforcers of new perspective quite alien to New York City government. The
supervising agencies have reasserted public control over areas of operation and
decision long preempted by the unions and strong political constituencies. They
have demanded orderliness and a kind of conservative rationality that might
have been drawn from the good government groups of half a century ago.
Directly and indirectly, they have exposed more of the city's operations to
public scrutiny.

The mayor was forced to make changes. He was successfully pressured to
fire Deputy Mayor James A. Cavanagh, a knowledgeable and able budget careerist, because—like the Mayor himself—he was a long time participant in the city's
fiscal arena. Cavanagh was replaced by John Zuccotti, a Lindsay hold-over as
Chairman of the Planning Commission and a former official of the U.S. Department of Housing and Urban Development. Beame's widely criticized budget
director was also forced out and replaced by a professional with experience in
both business finance and federal budgeting. Earlier, a new deputy mayor for
finance was appointed from private industry.

One result was a return to the analytic school of management advanced
by Lindsay and largely abandoned by Beame at the beginning of his administration. The brain drain from OMB stopped, and by early 1976 recruitment was
underway to rebuild the Office's analytic capacity. The Mayor's Management
Advisory Board, set up in what seemed a defensive gesture by the Mayor, built
a staff capacity and, beginning with the two MBO experiments began to be
involved in the city's management issues. A parallel group, the Temporary Commission on City Finances, contributed a complementary fiscal perspective.
Zuccotti, from the time of his appointment as deputy mayor, focused on the
city's management systems and the need for formal management planning.

The Management by Objective experiments in the Department of Highways
and in the Fire Department had two principal aspects: a management plan and
reporting system and the provision of unusual flexibility in budget and personnel
management. At Zuccotti's insistence, Jack Ukeles, the Executive Director of
the Management Advisory Board and Bott of OMB developed the MBO management planning and reporting system for application to all agencies beginning in
July 1976.

The Management Plan and Report replaces the productivity program. There
are five components:

1.   missions, priorities and organization;
2.   a Performance and Resource Plan
3.   a Revenue Plan
4.   management improvement projects and key milestones by major mission
5.   critical executive management issues that are being faced and key decisions
     that need to be made by the agency head or the mayor

The agency plans for the first year were received in July 1976. Reporting against approved plans will be on a monthly basis. Public release will probably be limited to the mayor's plan, a compilation of the most important elements of agency plans plus some additional issues of special mayoral concern.

This is a very ambitious undertaking and difficult to do well. One major element will clearly be the already established reporting and targeting scheme covering the 263 items in the productivity program. But the new system requires the agencies to go beyond these indicators to deal comprehensively with the agency's programs and problems and to lay out specific management ·improvement projects and schedules.

How well the job will be done and how effectively it will be pursued in the future is necessarily uncertain. What is clear is that the effort will not survive as a serious contribution to policy making without both the continuing and detailed attention of the office of the mayor and a substantial continuing commitment of manpower in the agencies and in OMB.

An Overview

New York's productivity improvement effort defies any simple and straight-forward assessment. Even the city's own officials must confront a maze of questions, qualifications, unknowns, and uncertainties in assessing the impact of the program on this huge and complex government. Yet, a few salient points stand out in the city's productivity program experience.

First, the success of the Lindsay productivity program should not obscure the long and painful process by which it became successful. Some of the key elements were: The productivity program was the capstone of a frustratingly slow six-year effort to improve the performance of city government. It was based on a massive and unprecedented investment in analytical talent—industrial engineers, management analysts, systems analysts, and program planners— eventually numbering more than a thousand, in addition to contract consultants and researchers. The major productivity and performance pay-offs did not come until the new analytical capacity was coupled with aggressive, innovative agency managers. Indeed, it took most of Lindsay's two 4-year terms to bring the effort to significant success.

Second, productivity bargaining, with few exceptions, cannot be regarded as a success in the Lindsay administration and, in its first two years, the Beame administration did no better. The leadership of some unions, notably the Uniformed Sanitationmen's Association and AFSCME, have tolerated or infor-mally accepted productivity improvements—but attempts to negotiate formal, public productivity agreements have been largely unproductive.

Third, the city's capacity to continue a large centrally managed produc-tivity program was sharply reduced with the departure of most of the analysts in the first year of the Beame administration; beginning in 1976, some of that capacity was being restored.

Fourth, the loss of analytical staff exposed the principal shortcoming of reform in the Lindsay administration. The productivity program was created and managed by new recruits—a paste-on over the careerist civil service. The program was not successfully institutionalized nor were the city's senior civil servants coopted.

Fifth, the work of the Productivity Council emphasized again the critical weaknesses of the city's middle managers—a problem neglected in the Lindsay administration and on which the Beame administration has made the barest beginning through the Urban Academy set-up within City University to train city employees.

Sixth, the adaptation to the large budget reductions has fallen far short of the optimum, but it has, undoubtedly, resulted in substantial productivity gains in selected areas. The unions have made substantial concessions—implicit or explicit—in work rules and manning in the face of the new reality.

Last, the productivity increases to date are the result of the ad hoc adaptation to very large reductions in work force primarily in agencies with uncontrollable workload, e.g. sanitation and fire. There remains both the potential and, given the additional cuts in prospect, the need for further gains that will require a restructuring of work process or deployment; the city's current capacity to do this is limited.

Notes

1. Hamilton, Edward K., *Productivity: The New York City Approach,* Public Administration Review, November/December 1972.

2. Ibid.

3. *New York City's Productivity Program: The Police Department,* Citizens Budget Commission, Inc., November 1973.

4. *The New York City Fire Department: Recent Achievements and Present Problems,* Citizens Budget Commission, Inc., December 1973.

5. *New York City's Productivity Program: The Human Resource Administration, the Administration of Welfare,* Citizens Budget Commission, Inc., January 1974.

6. *New York City's Productivity Program: The Department of Sanitation,* Citizens Budget Commission, Inc., March 1974.

7. Hamilton, op. cit.

8. Raymond D. Horton, "Productivity Bargaining in the Public Sector: Caveat Emptor," in *MBO and Productivity Bargaining in the Public Sector,* Chester A. Newland et al., International Personnel Management Association, 1974.

9. Weisman, Steven R., "Productivity Program in the City Drastically Changed by Beame," *The New York Times,* February 23, 1975.

10. Ibid.

11. Wagner, Robert F. Jr., *Re: Productivity Program,* July 1975.

12. Weisman, op. cit.

13. Ibid.

14. Ranzal, Edward, "City Discloses 3 Programs under Study To Cut Costs," *The New York Times,* August 6, 1975.

15. Weisman, op. cit.

16. 1974 Labor Agreement between the City of New York and the Uniformed Sanitationmen's Association.

17. Schrank, Robert, "Management-Union Efforts Key to Productivity," in *Labor-Management Relations Service Newsletter,* February 1976, vol. 7, no. 2. Most of my summary of the work was drawn from the Schrank article. See also *Report to the New York City Productivity Council: Improving Productivity in Municipal Agencies—A Labor-Management Approach,* prepared by Productivity Council Staff, October 1975.

18. Anderson, Arvid, "New York City Fiscal Crunch Rattles Labor Relations," *Labor-Management Relations Service Newsletter,* January 1976, vol. 7, No. 1.

7 Palo Alto

Palo Alto is a small city with a stable population just under 60,000. The community has a high average level of both affluence and education. The city budget for 1975–1976 provides for expenditures of $15.7 million. The city also manages five utilities (refuse, electric, water, gas, and sewer) with aggregate 1975–1976 expenditures of $23.3 million including $4.3 million in surplus funds used to help finance the city's regular budget.

The city has been prudently managed. It has no indebtedness and routinely finances capital improvements from current revenues and reserves. For the first time in recent years inflation, a slowing economy, and energy conservation (because of the impact on utility revenues) have eliminated General Fund financing for the Capital and Street Improvement Funds.

This is scarcely an augury of serious future financial problems. Palo Alto continues to be able to finance an extensive range of services for its residents within a moderate tax structure. It faces no financial problems that demand a strong effort to secure early and significant gains in productivity.

Service Management System

Palo Alto's major citywide productivity effort is the Service Management System (SMS), a sophisticated program budgeting, evaluation, and management information system conceived in 1973 largely at the initiation of City Manager George Sipel. In addition, there is a handful of analysts in a few city departments working on efficiency and effectiveness projects of interest related to SMS objectives.

The proposal to Housing and Urban Development that brought in first-year funds for the SMS project described its goals as follows: ". . . to improve the City's decision-making capabilities by delineating techniques in which output and effectiveness of the delivery of municipal services and their impact upon the community can be measured, evaluated and enhanced."[1] In practice, this was seen as involving everything from improved needs assessment (as through

---

This chapter was co-authored by Daniel Rubin.

citizen surveys) and work with departments developing operational objectives and output measures, through to specific impact analyses and encouraging the City Council to make its decisions in a more rational-evaluative manner.

The Service Management System is an integrated, program budgeting and management reporting system. It employs a program structure with 5 major program categories, 39 programs, 125 subprograms, and nearly 400 subprogram elements. This basic program structure is outlined in Exhibit 7-1. Goals are established for each of the categories including subprogram elements. The goals are, with few exceptions, concrete and specific and are stated in quantitative terms wherever feasible.

Exhibit 7-1
Palo Alto Program Structure

I.   Personal and Property Safety
To create an environment in which people can live, move about safely and feel reasonably confident that they and their property are protected from criminal harm and the hazards of fire and natural and man-made disasters.
    A. Animal Services
       1. Animal Control
       2. Animal Care
       3. Spay and Neuter Clinic
    B. Police
       1. Support Services
       2. Field Services
       3. Research and Training
       4. Police Community Services
       5. Investigative Services
       6. Administration and General
    C. Fire
       1. Fire Suppression
       2. Fire Prevention
       3. Fire Training and Research
       4. Paramedics
       5. Administration and General
    D. Transportation (partial)
       1. Traffic Operations
II. Community Health and Environment
To promote healthy, attractive environmental living conditions enhanced by safe, clean, and reliable utility service with minimum hazards of water, air, noise, and surface (visual) pollution.
    A. Light and Power
       1. Engineering
       2. System Acquisition and Construction
       3. Customer Relations
       4. Operations and Maintenance
       5. Energy Conservation
    B. Water
       1. Engineering
       2. System Acquisition and Construction
       3. Operations and Maintenance
       4. Water Transmission Operations

Exhibit 7-1 Continued

II. Community Health and Environment (continued)
    C. Gas
        1. Engineering
        2. System Acquisition and Construction
        3. Operations and Maintenance
    D. Sewer
        1. Engineering
        2. System Acquisition and Construction
        3. Operations and Maintenance
    E. Waste Water Quality Control
        1. Treatment and Disposal
        2. Industrial Waste Treatment
    F. Refuse Management
        1. Solid Waste Disposal
        2. Collection and Customer Services
        3. Recycling
    G. Inspectional Services
        1. Building Code Enforcement
        2. Zoning Standards and Municipal Code Enforcement
    H. Planning
        1. Comprehensive Plan
        2. Development Monitoring
        3. Special Studies
        4. Inter-governmental Coordination
        5. Housing
        6. Environmental Control
        7. Administration and General
    I. Streets (partial)
        1. Street Cleaning
    J. Parks (partial)
        1. Parkway Maintenance
        2. Street Tree Planting and Maintenance
        3. Electric Line Clearing
        4. Utility Landscaping
III. Individual Development and Enjoyment
To promote individual self-development and to provide all citizens, to the extent practicable, with a variety of leisure opportunities which are accessible, safe, physically attractive, and enjoyable.
    A. Library
        1. Bibliographical Services
        2. Readers Services
    B. Recreation
        1. Parks and Playgrounds
        2. Physical and Sports
        3. Enrichment and Social
        4. Aquatics
        5. Special City Wide Events
        6. Administration and General
    C. Arts
        1. Performing Arts
        2. Visual Arts
        3. Administration and General
    D. Nature and Science
        1. Instruction
        2. Exhibits and Collections

Exhibit 7-1 Continued

III. Individual Development and Enjoyment
   3. Maintenance
   4. Administration and General
   E. Social Services
      1. Community Relations
      2. Senior Adult Community Resources Coordination
      3. Community Drug Abuse Project
      4. Child Care Services
      5. Registration
      6. Facilities Rental
   F. Parks (partial)
      1. Parks and Grounds Maintenance
      2. Golf Course Maintenance
      3. Administration and General
IV. Transportation
To provide multi-mode access to desired destinations in a safe, quick, comfortable, and
convenient manner for all segments of the community without causing major harmful side
effects.
   A. Streets (partial)
      1. Street Maintenance
      2. Sidewalk Maintenance
      3. Traffic Control
      4. Traffic Signal and Street Lighting
      5. Storm Drains
      6. Administration and General
   B. Transportation (partial)
      1. Transportation Planning
      2. Administration and General
   C. City Treasurer (partial)
      1. Parking
      2. Parking Enforcement
      3. Civic Center Garage
V. General Administration and Support Services
To formulate City policy to effectively meet community needs and assure implementation
through effective and efficient management and support services.
   A. City Manager
      1. City Council
      2. Staff and Organization Development
      3. Inter-governmental Relations
      4. City Manager's Time Priorities
   B. City Clerk
      1. Meetings and Minutes
      2. Elections
      3. Council Support
      4. Records and Filing
   C. City Controller
      1. Resource Utilization and Control
      2. Data Processing
      3. Systems Development
      4. Administration and General
   D. Budget and Resource Analysis
      1. Program Evaluation and Operations Analysis
      2. Budget Preparation and Administration
      3. Legislative Analysis and Research

Exhibit 7-1 Continued

V. General Administration and Support Services
    E. Reproduction and Mailing
        1. Reproduction
        2. Mailing
        3. Administration and General
    F. Purchases and Stores
        1. Purchasing
        2. Delivering
        3. Stores
        4. Administration and General
    G. Communications
        1. Operations
        2. Maintenance
    H. Building Maintenance
        1. Repair/Maintenance/Construction
        2. Janitorial Services
    I. Equipment Maintenance
        1. Equipment Repair, Maintenance, and Operations
        2. Equipment Replacement
    J. Real Estate
        1. General Real Estate Services
        2. Property Management
    K. City Treasurer (partial)
        1. Cashiering
        2. Customer Service–Office
        3. Customer Service–Field
        4. Meter Reading
        5. Administration and General
    L. Personnel
        1. Recruitment and Selection
        2. Employee Development
        3. Safety, Health, and Workmen's Compensation
        4. Classification and Pay
        5. Employee Relations
        6. Employee Services
    M. Public Works Administration
        1. Budget Analysis and Special Studies
        2. Management Development in the Public Works Organization
        3. Develop and Monitor Affirmative Action in Public Works
    N. Streets (partial)
        1. General Field Services
    O. Parks (partial)
        1. General Field Services
    P. Engineering
        1. Engineering Office
        2. Surveying
        3. Inspection

Source: *City of Palo Alto 1975–76 Program Statements*, pp. i–vi.

For each subprogram, SMS provides for a set of performance measures. Targets are set for the year for each item covered by a performance measure. The agencies report quarterly to the city manager on performance and a semi-annual report is prepared by the city manager to City Council. Exhibit 7-2 shows how one subprogram, investigative services in the Police Department, is presented in the semiannual report.

Exhibit 7-2

Goals, Objectives, and Performance Measures for Palo Alto Police Investigative Services Subprogram

Subprogram: Investigative Services

Goal: To provide an accurate, legally sound basis for discovery resolution and disposition of criminal cases; to utilize community resources as an alternative to the justice system for Juvenile offenders; and to provide other administrative support functions.

a. *Element: follow-up Investigations*

1. To maintain an overall clearance rate of Part I offenses of twenty (20) percent so as to correspond with the national average, and to increase the number of Part I offenses cleared to correspond with the probable numerical increase in those offenses.

2. To increase clearances of burglaries to twenty-five (25) percent by 1976, and to increase the number of burglary clearances so as to correspond with the probable increase in burglaries.

3. Through a federally-funded program, enter into the second year (Phase II) of alternative police investigatory procedures for rape. Phase II will concentrate on evaluating the first year's efforts and training for Palo Alto officers as well as other law enforcement personnel in Santa Clara County will begin. The end results will be aimed at increasing the number of reported rapes, while providing for a more modern and humane approach by the investigator in dealing with victims of rape.

b. *Element: Fraud*

1. Maintain police involvement in the prevention and investigation of consumer fraud through the use of referrals and our own fraud investigators. To increase the number of reported consumer frauds by 25% through public awareness of our availability for such a service.

c. *Element: Juvenile Operations*

1. To continue the partial funding of a professional social services worker so as to increase counseling capabilities and provide for on-going family crises counseling. Because on-going counseling is not currently provided, we are unable to judge how many individuals or families would benefit. Such a measurement will be developed after our first year's experience.

2. To reduce the repeat rate of multiple offenders of W & I code Section 601 by twenty-five (25) percent through the use of a social worker.

3. To continue efforts in diverting youths (as defined in Section 601 of the W & I Code) who are first-time offenders, from the justice system to local agencies by increasing the diversion rate to ninety (90) percent.

d. *Element: Special Investigations*

1. To provide effective narcotics enforcement, concentrating primarily on illegal production and sales by exploring the feasibility of providing person-power to the county drug enforcement task force or by not providing person-power but utilizing the county's enforcement capabilities.

Exhibit 7-2 Continued

Performance Measures	Actual 1972-73	Actual 1973-74	Target 1974-75	Target 1975-76
Part I clearance rate	9.3%	14.0%*	20%	20%
Part I numerical clearances	N/A	380 *	445	500
Burglary clearance rate	14%	19.8%*	20%	25%
Burglary numerical clearances	N/A	184	180	200
Number of reported rapes	N/A	18	11	36
Rape clearance rate	N/A	44.4%*	45%	40%
Rape numerical clearances	N/A	8%*	5	16
Percent of 601 arrests diverted	58%	73%	75%	90%
Recidivism rate of first-time 601 offenders	N/A	42.9%	40%	35%
Number of consumer fraud cases referred or investigated	N/A	10	20	30

Source: *City of Palo Alto 1975-76 Program Statements*, pp. 10-12.
*Calendar Year Figures

The semiannual report to the Council is submitted as a companion volume, *Program Statements*, to the annual budget. Beginning with the 1976-1977 budget, the budget and the program statements will be integrated into a single presentation.

The performance measures cover a number of different aspects of program operation including unit costs, cost recovery rates, workload, program results, citizen attendence or program usage, user evaluations of programs, response times, service frequencies, program variety, and others. Some of these measures directly reflect the characteristics of agency performance, but many deal with phenomena where agency control is limited or nonexistent. The targets vary accordingly from presumably achievable management objectives to estimates of external factors.

Performance measures and targets were determined initially on the basis of "best professional guess." It is contemplated that, with experience, irrelevant and weak measures will be weeded out and new better measures added.

The Service Management System in Palo Alto is, primarily, an information system rather than a structure for program analysis. Its value depends on the usefulness of a systematic information flow to program heads, department directors, the budget staff, the SMS staff, the city manager and the City Council in decisionmaking. It is hoped that these data will uncover otherwise buried problems in performance as well as changes in needs and demands.

The work of the Service Management System is supplemented and supported by a program evaluation effort. Most important from the longer range perspective is the commitment of the SMS staff to design an evaluation component for each significant new program undertaken by the municipal government.

Evaluation studies have been undertaken in several areas. These include: the Fire Department's paramedic program; a contract drug abuse program; the teen coffee house; child care services; the operation of a senior citizen center; and the Police Department's burglary prevention program.

The Citizen Survey

The SMS team's citizen survey, administered experimentally in 1974 to a sample of 600 Palo Alto residents, can be regarded as a supplement to the information gathered through departmental performance measures. The survey's purpose was described as follows:

In simple terms, the survey's purpose is to provide for a citizen's evaluation of Police and Recreation services in Palo Alto. In addition, certain factual usage and incident data will be collected. Furthermore, for the first time, there will be systematic data available on non-use of public services and the citizen's reasons why. All this information will be combined with existing departmental data to provide a more comprehensive citizen-oriented evaluation. Data on non-use may highlight correctable deficiencies and unmet needs.[2]

Besides basic demographic information (age, sex, race, income, housing type and location, length of residency), the sixty-five-item personal-interview survey included questions regarding:

General perceptions: overall satisfaction with city services, neighborhood and downtown safety, respect for police, summary evaluations of Police, and Recreation performance in several program areas.

Measures of service quality for city handling of complaints, information and service requests; for contacts with police; and for participation in park and recreation programs. Quality measures included courtesy, speed of response, correctness of information, and (for recreation facilities) convenience, safety, and cleanliness.

Crime victimization, including whether actually reported and reasons if not.

Extent of use for a list of recreation facilities and programs, with reasons for non-use (interest, convenience, health, cost, quality, etc.) where this was the case.

Palo Alto previously had made fairly extensive use of both special purpose planning surveys and more traditional means of community input: public meetings, contact with associations, comments channeled through Council members or city officials. The rationale for a survey stressed the sporadic and often unrepresentative nature of such special-occasion information. By contrast, "if standardized and conducted annually," a survey could "more routinely collect citizen input that represents the total population, in a usable clear format" that would allow year-to-year tracking of "broad effectiveness trends within the city."[3]

The actual use of the pilot-year survey, however, does not suggest early accomplishment of this goal. The sample survey was tabulated and analyzed, and some relatively minor effects can be attributed to it: new signs directing patrons from busy tennis courts to others nearby that might be less crowded; deferral of building two more courts at a particular site; a decision not to go ahead with plans for a central complaint bureau. But with the end of HUD funds, which paid for the 1974 survey, there has been no move to continue the venture on a regular basis. Consequently, quality measures introduced in the survey have not been carried over into the system of "Program Statement" performance measures.

Initiation

The idea of a citywide Service Management System, coordinated with budget preparation, originated in informal discussions between Palo Alto City Manager George Sipel and management consultant Richard Hughes. Sipel was not a newcomer to Palo Alto; he had been city manager since 1972 and assistant city manager before that.

The city previously had been involved in operation audits in several areas including police, inspections, and purchasing, and in the beginnings of PPBS development. In addition, a few departments had analytic staff. Sipel—a strong believer in the fruits of systematic analysis—felt that the time was ripe for a comprehensive effort at rationalizing many community decisions.

Part of the impetus to go ahead derived from Sipel's knowledge that federal funds would almost surely be available for the experiment. The HUD regional office had already approached the city to solicit an application for "701" planning funds. Application resulted in a grant of $40,000 for 1973–1974, to be matched by about $25,000 in locally contributed services. This made it possible to finance the additional positions and supporting consultant services without using local funds.

Sipel also was encouraged to proceed with plans for the SMS by the City Council's established interest in analysis and evaluation. In particular, the Council's Finance and Public Works Committee had expressed a desire to review all city departments systematically and in depth, apart from the pressure of budget hearings, at the pace of a few departments per year. The Council majority was, in fact, receptive, despite some specific opposition to the federal funds ("boondoggle," "strings attached") and the absence of visible direct community service in the project.

Developing the Program

Detailed planning for the SMS was conducted by Hughes (then with Booz, Allen, and Hamilton) under a $12,000 consulting contract. Hughes' role at this point involved advice on implementation as well as technical expertise in designing the system. Except for a $7,000 contract with Diridon Research Corporation of San Jose for administration of the citizen's survey later that year, all other development of SMS was done by city staff.

A two-person Service Management System staff was created within the Budget and Staff Services Department to take over the task of planning and coordinating the system. To serve as SMS Director, Sipel recruited George Barbour from the International City Manager's Association, where he had been overall project director of their productivity efforts, including a performance measurement project in St. Petersburg, Florida, and Nashville, Tennessee. Ed Everett, the sole operations analyst, came with community experience as a VISTA volunteer and analytic training at Princeton's Woodrow Wilson School.

The city had other assets relevant to SMS in the several small pockets of analytic talent. The Department of Budget and Staff Services had one budget analyst in addition to Director Clayton Brown, who himself had been a program analyst in Phoenix prior to coming to Palo Alto and had performed master's degree research on PPBS. This staff had been involved in reviewing various budget systems in other cities, as well as early stages of implementing PPBS stemming from a commitment in 1969.

Police Chief James Zurcher had actively supported the use of a civilian analyst added to the department's staff in 1969 by his predecessor in keeping with the recommendation of a Booz-Allen-Hamilton consultant (Hughes). When the Service Management System was created in 1973, this position—coordinator of research and training—was occupied by its third incumbent, James Hudak, with training in economics and public policy and experience in municipal government cost accounting. Hudak and his predecessors helped establish a Police Information System, adapted for Palo Alto use a model by which investigative time is allocated to burglaries on a point system, and successfully argued for changes in shift hours to improve patrol density during peak crime hours. These and other projects varied in success and reception, but Chief Zurcher's enthusiasm about rational decision making was enhanced rather than diminished during the period.

The Utilities Department has had two analysts since 1974, both permanently funded by the city as of the 1975–1976 budget. One analyst is employed in Public Works. Their experience has been a major asset to the survey components of SMS.

Palo Alto also has used outside assistance. The city participated for a time in the Public Technology, Incorporated (PTI) program and used the PTI fire station locator model to analyze fire-fighting needs before withdrawing this year dissatisfied with benefits. In addition, a strong relationship exists with Stanford University.

Barbour's strategy was to first develop a model approach to the Service Management System in two departments. This permitted a start to be made with the most interested and cooperative department heads. More important, Barbour and Everett could, with this limited initial application, provide substantial assistance to each of the two agencies. The agencies chosen were the Police Department and the Recreation Department. The first was especially important given the highly favorable orientation of the Police Chief and the short but significant history of the use of analyses in the department.

In the second year, the Service Management System manual was to be prepared and SMS extended to all the agencies of the city government. It was hoped that the experience with the two pilot agencies would make the extension to the remaining agencies relatively easy.

Two approaches were used to improve departments' analytic capabilities and their understanding of the Service Management System. An initial task has been for SMS staff to train departmental staff. The SMS team conducted a two-day training session for all police sergeants and lieutenants to familiarize them with the format of the system's new reporting by quantified objective and to give them some sense of what might be found by manipulating these data. Similar training for key staff was conducted in Planning, Public Utilities, and Public Works. A more extensive training apprenticeship was also developed, in which the first participant, from Public Utilities, spent three months as an assistant on analytic projects. All these variants play on the same theme of personal indoctrination by SMS analysts, and all increase the pool of department staff potentially receptive to the centrally located analysts and their ideas.

Another approach used by Sipel involves his personal approval of new analyst candidates, and annual contracting on all analyst positions between the city manager and Department Directors in which roughly 25 percent of each analyst's time is reserved for projects of interest to Sipel, either in the home department or elsewhere in the city, on which they report directly to Ed Everett. This, in effect, aims at a split loyalty for the analyst between his departmental supervisors and the manager's priorities.

Internal Accomodation and Implementation: Relations of SMS to Departments

Despite strong backing from City Manager Sipel and at least moderate enthusiasm from the City Council, the SMS faced major obstacles in winning cooperation from the city's departmental officials. SMS required of the departments an onerous data collection effort and, at the same time, raised the threat of new hurdles to be cleared in the budget process. The pressure was intensified by an exceedingly ambitious schedule for implementation.

Initial plans called for development of a citywide program structure the first year, complete with goals, performance criteria, and quantified objectives down to the level of departmental "subprogram units." All departments were to file 1974–1975 budgets based on these program formulations. In addition, the SMS staff would work intensively with two departments the pilot year, making models of them. It was anticipated that full implementation citywide could be achieved the second year, with far less SMS staff assistance needed in other departments after a year's experience and the examples of the two pilot departments had taught them what the process was all about.

The extreme optimism of this timetable was soon evident. By the publication of the *SMS Handbook* reporting pilot year achievements in July 1974, implementation had been rescheduled over a five-year period. And a year later, the five-year schedule had been scrapped.

Police

Police Chief Zurcher involved his department at his own initiative. He was enthusiastic about the analyst position he inherited on assuming the job, and he was convinced of the usefulness of better management information. Participating as an SMS pilot department represented a chance for assistance in reaching his own objectives. Confident of benefits, he was comfortable with a large contribution of police staff time: over 550 hours (mostly from Jim Hudak) as opposed to 130 hours from the other pilot department, Recreation.

However, interest in SMS within the department was strictly limited to the chief and a few of his top staff. Most officers responded to the system with apathy or with mild irritation and cynicism about this new "paperwork exercise." For example, even though objectives and measures were being discussed as the coming basis for budgets, an attempt to set up an internal police committee to advise on the objective-setting process met with negligible interest. Practical discussions on objectives and measurement did take place—for example between Hudak and patrol officers searching for a workable stand-in for "street crime"—but they tended to depend on initiation and continued pressure from above.

Even among those high police officers whose administrative responsibilities made SMS a potentially useful management tool, interest was far from uniform. The importance of personal predisposition toward analysis is neatly illustrated by the two captains heading the Inveisitgations and Uniform Services Divisions during that pilot year. After the chief and Hudak, these two were probably the most taken with SMS. However, the response from the investigations captain was clearly more intense, and Hudak compensated by spending more of his own time with Uniform Services as the two divisions developed measures and objectives. At first it appeared that the difference stemmed from the more frenetic problems of day-to-day administration in Uniform Services. But a year later, when the two captains had reversed duties as part of a rotation system, the two divisions' relative involvement in analysis shifted along with their leaders.

The Police Department made outstanding use of the chance to draft measures and, largely as a result, prepared "unquestionably . . . the best departmental budget submitted"[4] for 1974–1975.

However, use of the system since then has not been consistent. The first year, Chief Zurcher's personal interest was high and provided the impetus for a few top aides to do the hard work involved in initial development. By the end of the year, though, his interest had passed on to other matters. City Manager Sipel, noticing the difference, pressured him to improve the department's compliance with the reporting system just established. In essence, a stronger coordinator was needed—pulled in fewer directions than Zurcher, but higher in status than Hudak and his successor (who has little proclivity for quantitative analysis) as Research and Training Coordinator. The gradual decline in collection and use of information also reflected an upsurge of resistance to the task of collecting data, the usefulness of which was not clear beyond doubt.

Parks and Recreation

Parks and Recreation was chosen as the other pilot department to provide a contrast with Police. Although the Department lacked sophisticated analytical staff, George Barbour's work at ICMA had familiarized him with research from the Urban Institute and elsewhere, which lay the groundwork for output and effectiveness measurement in recreation. Also, he felt confident of his ability to provide strong support when it came to developing parameters and objectives. Finally, Recreation Director Keith Bruns, while not excited about the project, would make a conscientious effort at implementation.

From their first discussions with Bruns, in which he was asked if he wanted in, Sipel and Barbour offered the lure of some special purpose surveys to meet Recreation's immediate needs. This was an effective move. In fact, Bruns' recollection of those early contacts focuses on surveys. His apprehension about the Department's effectiveness being rated through a citywide sample survey was offset by general confidence in the services he provided. The offer of SMS help in running smaller surveys—to evaluate the use of the municipal golf course and expansion proposals for a neighborhood park—resonated with his sense of practical planning. Once he decided to go along with the project, he took it seriously and made it clear to his recreation supervisors that he expected them to do the same.

But Bruns was never struck with the value of SMS on its merits the way Zurcher was in Police. A lack of clarity about the nature and uses of the system probably contributed to his underestimation of the amount of energy it would require.

Given the lack of departmental expertise in analysis, Barbour's familiarity with a useful literature, and Bruns' unclear notion of what good objectives would look like, the two SMS staff spent more time with Parks and Recreation than with Police the first year. However, the involvement of middle-level Parks and Recreation staff was stronger and incrementally more important than was the case in Police. The interaction between Barbour and Recreation staff was successful enough that Bruns does not now sense any depth of resistance to using the reporting system devised. Even though it is energy consuming to collect the data, the only complaint he could pinpoint (with one major exception) involved not the overall utility of this quantity of data, but the appropriateness of a particular measure.

The one notable incident of Recreation staff resistance to SMS objectivication involved a newly established teen coffee house program. Fearing that initially low attendance would lead to budget cuts, the supervisor-counselors who ran that program refused for three quarters to file quarterly reports. Instead, they wrote to City Manager Sipel and the Council, claiming that quantified measures of success were inappropriate and inviting them instead to come for a visit to assure themselves subjectively of the program's essentiality and quality. Interestingly, after the program was better established and drawing more kids, resistance to reporting attendance was dropped.

SMS and the Budget: Citywide Objectives and Performance Measures

In addition to the close attention to Police and Recreation, the SMS staff gave limited assistance to all other departments during 1973–1974 in formulating program organization, measures, and objectives to be used in budget preparation. This more cursory exercise was not expected to produce results of consistently high quality. And as expected, some participating departments did not understand, or were unwilling to treat seriously, the charge. But at the end of the pilot year, the SMS staff made the following assessment: "The early involvement of the total City in the project, while cumbersome initially and putting a severe strain on the limited resources available, was clearly a good decision. Now, in the follow-on years of implementing SMS, the formats, style, and terminology are known city-wide and the early indoctrination is being reinforced through usage."[5]

The themes of familiarity and indoctrination sounded here are echoed in descriptions of analytic training for department staff and other SMS components. Careful groundwork was seen from the start as crucial to educating department officials, Council members, even the city manager to use the system effectively as an evaluation and management tool. For example, the initial sketching of program structure for the whole city was performed unilaterally by SMS staff. This was done "to expedite the process," and represented no more than a necessary dictation from above—ultimately, from the city manager's office—of a scheme that was going to cross-cut department lines and inevitably step on some toes. But it is worth mentioning that not everyone bought into this concept merely by following directives on a new reporting and budget preparation format. Even Recreation Director Bruns was uncomfortable with the lumping of "his" teen center counseling program with those of other departments.

The nexus between SMS and Palo Alto's budget process is so close that Barbour himself concedes the system can be viewed as "nothing more than an elaborate program budget process."[6] In the fall of 1973 all departments were instructed to prepare goals, objectives, and performance criteria as a "backdrop" for the 1974-1975 budget. Late that year, Sipel and Budget and Staff Services Director Brown held a series of meetings with top department staff to review the material prepared and discuss directions prior to preparation of draft budgets.

The process this first year had some characteristics of a formal exercise. Programs discussed in the prebudget sessions had not yet been costed out in most cases, and "decisions" made on a program budget basis were likely to be risky. In addition, the review of budgets by the Council's Finance and Public Works Committee followed quite traditional lines, with most discussion centered on work force and dollar requirements.

The SMS staff's plans for 1974-1975, as conceived following the first year's experience, involved greater synchronization between budget and objective preparation deadlines and an effort to provide better selected material to the Council (less financial detail, more reminders of objectives and outcomes) to nudge them in the direction of evaluation.

The Second Year: Public Works

This scenario was interrupted, however, by a major disruption in the relations between SMS and a key department. The Public Works Department was under fire for both sidewalk repair policy and chronic failure to meet schedules for funded capital improvements. The Department responded to the latter criticism by setting up a new position of Manager of Capital Projects, which was filled by police analyst Jim Hudak. SMS staff, under pressure from the City Council to show direct payoff from analysis, shifted their plans for work in Public Works to include not only improving the performance measures and objectives but also cost savings analysis. Sidewalk repair was to be the first component of this study. The analysis that ensued led to a budget cut of one position for Public Works. It was a small victory for productivity but a setback in establishing the credibility of SMS staff within departments.

The Director of Public Works was irate with the results. Other planned studied there were cancelled and further involvement with SMS was limited strictly to completion of the sidewalk study. As a result, Sipel placed the department off limits for the SMS staff with the proviso that the Public Works director would undertake with his own staff analyses of two pressing program needs—the programming of street repairs and the improvement of park maintenance.

The Department of Utilities also decided to do the analytic job internally. A new department director is learning the ropes, and the department has two highly regarded analysts to work on its problems.

The friction with DPW is no gain to the implementation of SMS, but one might argue that performing the analysis within the department is simply another way of skinning the same cat. However, both Barbour and Everett believe strongly that program analysis cannot be effective unless it is centralized. They are joined in this view by Clay Brown, the director of Budget and Staff Services. The argument rests both on the greater technical competence possible in a central unit and on the absence of the protective and defensive attitudes of the line departments. There is a directly contrary argument—made by Jim Hudak— that analysis cannot become an effective guide to program management until it is done in the departments.

Meanwhile, the SMS staff has put in place its basic system of performance measurement and reporting. It has limitations and imperfections, but it exists. It is buttressed by the commitments of at least a few departments to undertake program analysis.

The basic problem goes beyond the conflict with Public Works. It is that a majority of the department heads are not much interested in, or inclined to use, performance measurement and program analysis. City Manager Sipel, who "grooves on measurement and analysis," is reportedly disappointed that it has produced no comparable reaction in department heads who were largely selected by him. The limited acceptance by the heads of the operating agencies, if it continues, would seem certain to slow the rate of progress and reduce the usefulness of the system.

The Unions

Municipal employee unions have not been dramatically strong in Palo Alto, compared to, say, Eastern cities. For example, the Palo Alto Police Officers Association, representing 100 officers, is not a local unit in any national or international union. The Association has proved neither highly resistant to change nor interested in discussing, pro or con, the department's experiments with analysis and management information systems. Police officers have preferred to respond individually—with apathy, cynicism, or moderate cooperation—rather than en masse through the agency of union policy. Palo Alto's police ranks have been passing through a period of heavy turnover, and the force is now younger than most, better educated (median education three years of college), and better sexually integrated (14 percent of sworn officers are women). The significance of these changes for unionization are uncertain.

The city's fire fighters are more strongly unionized. The union is a local of International Association of Fire Fighters. Changes affecting the duties of work of fire fighters are cleared with the union, but this seems to have raised no obstacles to change thus far. More problems may be likely in the future.

Most of the remaining city employees are members of the Service Employees International Union (SEIU). The union went out in July 1975 on a one-month strike. Although the major stakes were wage and fringe related, an expansion of bargaining units to include many seasonal park employees was also at issue—a realm in which the city would lose much flexibility to alter programs and reassign personnel. Clearly, the potential for union stands antithetical to productivity measures is here in evidence.

SMS Director Barbour became intimately involved in labor relations, including the negotiations in the SEIU strike, through a new responsibility for analyzing every proposal to determine its costs and implications for productivity. The rapid escalation of leave provisions for city employees—educational leave and a guaranteed monthly three-day weekend as well as traditional sick and vacation provisions—had made this particularly useful. Comprehensive costing-out was an unprecedented procedure, and the unions lacked information and preparation to respond with detailed "counter analysis." In addition, the city's bargaining agents themselves were shocked at the magnitude of the costs implied by apparently simple proposals. Current negotiations with the fire fighters will be aided by Everett, using the cost analysis model developed by Barbour.

City Council

The early attitude of the Council toward the SMS proposal has been described: general approval tempered with a few reservations about the dangers of losing autonomy in federal programs and getting caught up in overhead activities providing little public service benefit. With the end of the one-year HUD pilot grant and the consequent increase in local costs, concern with the cost-effectiveness of analysis itself became more important.

When the Finance and Public Works Committee expressed its interest in gradual review of the directions of departments, SMS with its federal subsidy seemed to most members a good way to help this happen. Whether the Council's view of the review sessions matched the perceptions of the SMS staff, however, is unclear. "Now, for the first time," said Barbour of the first year's meetings with Recreation and Police, "the discussion was not the number of people to be employed or put in the street for patrol, but what impact these specific objectives were going to have on response time, on the crime rate, or the accessibility to recreational programs."[7] But Recreation Director Bruns recalls that many of the Council's questions related more to the choice of effectiveness measures than to the objectives of his department; the SMS as well as Recreation was under scrutiny. Similarly, the Committee's budget hearings that year, in which citywide use of objectives and effectiveness reporting was first introduced, followed usual lines of cost and staffing debate.

The Council's desire to put SMS to work for *it* was evident the second year of the program. The original SMS model called for setting priorities for intensive SMS staff work with the departments on the basis of a rating scheme that assigned points for the size of departmental budgets, the number of citizens served, the magnitude of current operating problems, and an assessment of the Council's interest (as perceived by top administrators). This list was revised substantially, however, in response to political pressures such as the Council's desire to examine sidewalk repair operations right away.

When it came time to prepare the 1974-1975 budgets, Council support of the SMS project had diminished to the point that there was initial resistance to including Project Director Barbour's salary. The Council was unwilling to rely on long-term benefits of program budgeting. Pressure was applied, in effect, for the system to earn its keep with immediate payoff projects such as the sidewalk analysis, Palo Alto-Stanford University fire consolidation, and involvement in labor bargaining. Whatever the relation of cause and effect, these new missions have' gone hand in hand with a reduction in the trust of departmental officials for the SMS staff, and a slackening of work on the improvement of objectives and performance measures for the SMS.

Achievement and Prospects

The achievement of the Service Management System proper, to date, are not negligible: use of objectives and output measures as a matter of course in all budgets; a requirement of budget modifications for all changes in level of service; and familiarizaton of city administrators and Council members with the intent, mechanics, and vocabulary of the system. In the two departments that received most careful attention, the improved information is at least partly responsible for a few identifiable changes: (1) operation of a high school swimming pool shown to have low usage was terminated; (2) construction of two planned tennis courts was deferred in a park development; and (3) a reduction was made in the budget for the Department of Public Works sidewalk repair program. Of course, the new data may make a contribution to the decision-making process without necessarily determining the results. For example, the city manager pointed out to the City Council that the approval of a proposed new park in the eastern part of the city ran counter to the citizen survey data showing that the unmet needs for parks were almost entirely in the western sector of Palo Alto. The Council nonetheless approved the eastern city park under strong neighborhood pressure—motivated in part by the fear that the land would otherwise be preempted for low-rent public housing.

George Barbour sees broader implications in the SMS data—for example, the evidence of changing demography on the demand for city services. The demand for child-serving activities is declining in library, recreation, and other programs. At the same time, there is an increasing demand for recreational and educational programs for adults. But these insights have yet to have a significant impact on program decisions. Similarly, Barbour sees, in the citizen survey, the negative attitudes toward police of citizens who have been stopped or ticketed. To him it suggests the possible need to improve on police behavior— but the Police Department does not see it as a serious problem.

Budget and Staff Services Director Clay Brown could not identify, after the first full year of the Service Management Systems, a single major program decision based primarily on SMS data. Nor was there any indication of dramatic improvement in the targeted program measures. The lack of impressive results is disappointing but scarcely surprising at this early stage of the process.

The job of using the Service Management System data is substantially more difficult than the work that went into its development. The data tend not to provide answers but to suggest questions that, in turn, demand some significant effort in further fact-finding analysis. This would, without doubt, strain the capacity of the small number of program analysts working for the city.

The limited acceptance of information systems and analyses by line officials is a major impediment. Both the hostility toward second guessing by the city's top staff units and the disinterest in analysis are very common problems. They are, at the same time, very real problems that, unless corrected, will limit the impact of SMS. It may be that SMS can make its greatest contribution by the pressure it can place upon the agencies through the budgetary process. This frankly adversary process can conceivably lead to a situation where the agencies see the need for a more analytic posture, if only to better defend themselves.

The SMS staff completed two evaluation studies in the fiscal year 1973-1974 and three more in the first half of 1974-1975. The studies have provided some important inputs to program decision making.

One completed evaluation reached favorable conclusions with respect to a drug abuse prevention and treatment program operated by a private group under contract with the city. Despite the supportive evaluation, the City Council elected not to renew the contract apparently because council members looked askance at the counterculture attitudes and political activism of the group that managed the program. The teen coffee house program was also favorably viewed with, however, a recommendation for some reduction in the program budget.

The study of child care services recommended a continuation of the program with the existing contractor, Palo Alto Community Child Care. Among the specific recommendations accepted by the City Council and the PACCC board were the development of better cost and effectiveness measures of component elements of the program and more adequate information on program impact on parent employment.

The most complete cost-effectiveness evaluation is that done for the Burglary Prevention Program. The program functions through crime prevention meetings with small groups of householders or businesses in burglary affected areas and through security checks of specific buildings. During the 1974-1975 fiscal year, there was one household burglary for every thirty-two residences in the city; in residences covered by the program, the rate was one burglary per fifty-one homes. One out of every twenty-two businesses covered by the program was burglarized compared to the one out of six businesses citywide. The average averted burglary saves an estimated $400 in property losses and $167 in investigation expenses. The savings from an estimated 57 burglaries averted were, then, $32,319, compared to a program cost of $46,560. The net costs of $14,241 represent about $250 for each averted burglary, an interesting lesson in the economics of a *successful* anticrime program. Yet, interestingly, the analysis recommends an expanded program using lower cost personnel and utilizing the Burglary Probability Factor to focus work more on areas with high burglary prospects. But, ultimately, the cost of the program must be partially justified by intangible benefits from "improved community relations, communications and public safety awareness."

The Palo Alto budget credited the SMS effort with savings in the last six months of the prior fiscal year of $47,000, attributable chiefly to the cuts in the sidewalk repair program. A new overtime scheduling program in the Fire Department saved $9600 in the last quarter of the same fiscal year, with expected full year savings of $43,000.

For 1975-1976, the budget established a target for savings of $118,000. This was based on the assumption that the city should realize annual savings in each year of 2.5 times the amount of its own funds in the financing of SMS. This was clearly responsive to the City Council view that the SMS unit must earn its keep by analyses that lead to budget reductions.

The press for concrete money-saving performance may be regarded as a symptom of the insecurity of SMS. Clearly, the city manager's strong support and interest were not sufficient to generate the needed City Council support beyond the initial trial period. The goal that an analytic staff develop annually savings equal to 2.5 times its own costs is by no means unreasonable, but the developing situation placed the SMS staff under special tensions that made the task more difficult.

First, the maintenance and improvement of the Service Management System required staff time with little or no resulting contribution to budget cutting. In addition, the agency cooperation needed for most effective development of SMS was likely to be jeopardized by the increasing focus of the SMS unit on budget reductions.

Second, the unit was hobbled by the inconsistencies in strategy between the Council and the manager. The Council demanded an aggressive program to effect productivity savings—while the manager responded to departmental complaints by placing some of the prime targets for such savings off limits to the SMS staff.

Third, the resignation of George Barbour in September 1975 to enter private consulting practice deprived SMS of its one experienced hand—although it was understood from the inception that Barbour would leave after the system was functioning and that no replacement would be recruited.

In the autumn of 1975, the future of the program seemed very much in doubt. Less than a year later, the effort seemed to have weathered the crisis and secured the support necessary for its continuance.

In December, City Manager Sipel delivered an annual performance report to the City Council and to the city. He was able to report (in addition to the savings in sidewalk repair and fire fighters' overtime) such successes as the reduction in power usage from a projected 734,000 megawatt hours to 728,000 mwh, a cut in average police emergency response time from a projected 3 minutes to an actual of 2.8 minutes, and the completion of 306 low- and moderate-income housing projects compared to the 244 estimated.

Palo Alto was under rising fiscal pressure. One reason was the continuing effect of inflation on city costs. Another special problem arose from the failure in the courts of Palo Alto's attempt to prevent development in its foothills area through use of zoning powers. The resulting acquisition costs of $7.5 million for the first group of affected properties virtually eliminated the city's accumulated reserves.

In this climate, City Manager Sipel understandably, began to take a tougher line with his department heads. He proposed to cut city employment by fifty jobs over a five-year period and to make the reductions where he found them appropriate unless the departments developed acceptable alternatives. In addition, the moratorium on SMS involvement in Public Works and Utilities had expired without either department having effected any productivity improvements.

Sipel next introduced a "productivity contract" with each of his department heads and any future salary increases will be pegged to their performance of that productivity contract. By June 1976, contracts had been developed for half of the team.

At the same time, Ed Everett and the SMS staff were proving increasingly useful to the city. They had, for example, become regular and valued participants in the city's labor negotiations. Most important, they had provided the extensive analysis that made it possible to carry to fruition the long-discussed merger of the fire forces of the city and Stanford University. The merger was a major coup for the SMS staff. Over a seven-year period, the joint personnel savings to the university and the city will aggregate about $3 million. The city estimates its own annual savings after the seven-year period at $550,000.

In addition to the consolidation, SMS staff work resulted in the following 1975–1976 savings:

1. $10,500 annually from the determination of minimum fire department (preconsolidation) staffing levels;
2. Half of the $3200 annual increase in revenue from a new method of billing participating communities for sewage treatment costs;
3. $16,200 a year from work performance standards for janitors;
4. $9,300 a year for 13 years from a financial analysis of an automatic library circulation system;
5. $30,300 a year from changes recommended in management of city hall pool cars.

Three studies have not yet been implemented. These include a marketing study of the industrial waste system with recommended savings of $17,600; new sick leave policies expected to save $82,500; and the proposed sale of surplus city property with an expected yield of $375,000.

Work is continuing on analyses of police scheduling, utilization of police vehicles, utility meter replacement, and a plan to consolidate the Stanford and Palo Alto communications center.

The staff is still small. At the time Barbour left, Everett was assigned two positions for analysts, one to be filled by rotation from other city departments, the other to be filled with an employee funded from federal funds under the Comprehensive Employment and Training Act (CETA). Subsequently, the CETA job was converted to a permanent city position, and an additional position was requested in the 1976–1977 budget.

Notes

1. Quoted in *Palo Alto Service Management System Handbook*, July 1974, p. 44.

2. Ibid., p. 40.

3. Ibid., p. 40.
4. *SMS Handbook,* "Executive Summary," p. x.
5. Ibid., p. 46.
6. Ibid., p. 25.
7. Ibid., p. 2.

8 Phoenix

Phoenix is different, a new metropolis unlike any other large city in America. With a 1975 population of 668,000 people, it is indisputably one of the nation's great cities, the seventeenth largest according to census reports for 1973. The city is spread over 270 square miles, only 10 percent less than the land area of New York City, which has twelve times the population.

Phoenix is the largest of the cities of the American desert. Desert, here, is not meant in the sense of relative aridness used by the famous Texas historian, Walter Prescott Webb, in describing as the Great American Desert the entire area from the Sierras and the Cascades to the Mississippi. In Phoenix's Valley of the Sun, the desert is real and unambiguous. Without the water from the Salt and the Colorado, Phoenix could not survive, and the valley's rich agriculture would vanish to be succeeded by the mesquite and cactus.

Most large American cities and some metropolitan areas are declining in population and in jobs. Phoenix and its region are still growing. In fact, the construction and development-oriented sectors of economic activity constitute a major source of employment and income in Phoenix. Phoenix has no problems of water supply and no watercourses to pollute. The automobile is the main threat—and a limited one—to the purity of its air. Dependence on public transportation is minimal and, given the dispersion of employment centers as well as housing, virtually certain to remain minimal. With low densities, Phoenix has few significant problems of traffic circulation. Its slums are limited and, compared to the East, relatively new as well as low in density. It does have a high crime rate— but only by virtue of the high level of burglaries.

Starting the Phoenix Productivity Program

Phoenix's present productivity improvement program had its genesis in the review of the budget by the City Council in the spring of 1969. The Council then faced the need for an increase in taxes to finance the budget. Reluctant to increase taxes (which, ultimately, they were unable to avoid), they turned to the possibility of increasing the productivity of city government. As a first step they

149

decided to engage a management consultant to study the city government and develop recommendations for the most effective approach to increasing productivity.

The Council turned to management consultants, because some of its members were familiar with two cases in which consultants had been effectively used to improve management in a large Phoenix bank and in a local utility. It became clear early in the Council's discussions with the city manager that the proposed management study could make no contribution to the solution of the immediate budgetary problem: the decision to proceed was made on the basis of anticipated favorable effects on future budgets.

A proposed scope of services was drafted by the Council together with the city manager and the director of finance. Proposals were solicited from eight or nine firms. The Council's conviction was basically that government could profit from the application of the management techniques and practices of private business; initially, they wanted the selection restricted to firms that had worked only in the private sector, but they were finally persuaded that this was not practical.

Booz, Allen & Hamilton was selected to do the study. The initial study, completed in November 1969, was an overall diagnostic appraisal of the city's organization and management systems. The Booz, Allen & Hamilton recommendations led to a complete reorganization of city government. The city's conventional departmental structure was broken up into some two-dozen smaller and more homogeneous departments. These departments might have been grouped into superagencies but instead, following the consultants' recommendations, positions were set up for four deputy city managers each with responsibility for a group of related departments. The Bureau of Research and Budget was taken out of the Department of Finance and set up as a staff agency to the city manager.

The Booz, Allen & Hamilton study also recommended the following changes in the city's budget system:

Establish overall municipal objectives as the basis for detailed budget planning.

Develop program statements for each department once overall municipal objectives are approved.

Apply Planning-Programming and Budgeting System (PPBS) approaches to a pilot department.

Hold prebudget Council-manager planning sessions prior to detailed preparation of departmental budget requests.

Emphasize cost reduction awareness and concern in the budget process.

Establish, adopt, and update annually an integrated, multiyear capital improvement program.

Restructure the operations and the staffing of the Budget and Research Department.

The first of these recommendations to be implemented was the restructuring of the Budget and Research Department, chiefly through the addition of an Operations Analysis Division.

The second phase of the Booz, Allen & Hamilton study was the development of a work planning and control system in conjunction with the new Operations Analysis Division, which would administer the program. A staff of thirteen was recruited for the division from among city employees, trained, and put to work. The Work Planning and Control program was thus launched in April 1970.

Action was also taken to implement the consultants' recommendation for a multiyear capital improvement program. After voter approval of a $177 million bond issue in 1970, the city, for the first time, programmed all capital improvements whether or not bond financed. The multiyear program was approved by Council but funds were not appropriated. Instead, appropriations were requested each year as a separate capital budget section of the budget. Budget and Research Director Charles Hill regards the annual review and updating as the key to successful capital programming.

The city moved more slowly into the PPB system recommended by the consultants. A ten-hour orientation was given to eleven Budget and Research Department staff members responsible for program analysis. This group, with consultant assistance, prepared for the City Council an evaluation of the prospects of PPBS in Phoenix. The report was submitted in the summer of 1971 and recommended implementation of PPBS in a pilot department. The Council agreed and selected solid waste management as the pilot area.

A full year's data collection effort was undertaken in the actual use and character of uncontained refuse collection. Alternatives were analyzed and recommendations made on questions such as frequency of collection, limitations on type and volume, and the desirability of self-supporting service charges. The analysis struck paydirt by demonstrating that needs could be met with less frequent collections, since the usage survey found that less than 1 percent of the households put out uncontained refuse twelve or more times per year.

The Council gave the go-ahead for full implementation of PPBS in 1972. Phoenix calls its system Program Analysis and Review (PAR). Responsibility for PAR was assigned to the Division of Program Analysis in the Department of Budget and Research. While the Work Planning and Control system was intended to improve efficiency and productivity, PAR would be concerned with program objectives, the service levels needed to attain them, and program effectiveness.

Talent

Phoenix has relied almost exclusively on the staff of the Budget and Research Department to carry out its productivity improvement program. There are no staffs in the agencies for program or operations analysis or for work measurement.

The work measurement staff was set up in Budget and Research pursuant to the consultant recommendations and was staffed by employees already on the city payroll. Applications were sought from all city agencies and thirteen were selected from among them. The new recruits were put through a two-week training program given by the consultants in industrial engineering and work measurement. After Booz, Allen & Hamilton completed its second-phase study, the city recruited one of the firm's resident consultants to serve as the city's Operations Analysis Administrator to supervise the program during the following year. Eventually, an industrial engineer experienced in municipal government was recruited as permanent administrator of the unit. He was Harry Kelman, who had participated in the successful effort to increase productivity in New York's Department of Sanitation during the second Lindsay administration.

The Program Analysis Review program is managed by the Program Analysis Division in Budget and Research, with a total professional staff of twelve. The typical staff member of this unit has been recruited from a graduate school in public administration or public policy and has a master's degree in that discipline. Few have significant training in quantitative analysis techniques.

Booz, Allen & Hamilton played a major role in the reorganization of city government and in the installation of both the Work Planning and Control and Program Analysis and Review systems. There was little doubt about the significance of the Booz, Allen & Hamilton contribution. Part of the success must be attributed to a work plan that required consultant participation in the process of initial implementation as well as the training of city employees to carry on the system. Continuity was also enhanced by the retention of Booz Allen for three successive phases of the work: diagnostic and reorganization studies; the Work Planning and Control system; and the Program Analysis and Review system. Obviously, the individuals involved had something to do with the success of the effort. The high regard with which Richard Hughes, then with Booz, Allen & Hamilton, is held in both Phoenix and other cities in which he has worked is perhaps symptomatic of the situation.

Other talent from outside was also used. Arizona State University in suburban Tempe provided a computer model simulation for the study of garbage collection. The Public Technology, Incorporated (PTI) fire station location model was used as were some of the findings developed by the New York City Rand Institute in its analysis of fire department response to alarms in New York City. PTI also assisted in a study of microfilm records retention.

The City of Phoenix financed the initial engagement with Booz, Allen &

Hamilton and the staff for the new Operations Analysis Division from city funds. The second-phase contract, which included the provision for training city staff in PPBS that led eventually to the PAR approach, was also financed from city funds. However, federal comprehensive planning grant funds were available for the development of PAR. The grant funds for the three years through 1975 totaled $85,500 and are estimated at $21,700 for the 1975-1976 fiscal year. Without the Federal funds, Phoenix would have still proceeded with PAR but the pace would have been slower.

Work Planning and Control System

The Work Planning and Control system has been in effect for over six years since its inauguration in April 1970. The objective of WPC is to establish work performance standards for every employee of the city government for which work measurement and work standards are regarded as appropriate. The major exclusions were the Fire Department and all of the Police Department except Property Management, the Information Bureau, and the Communications Bureau. Of the 7570 positions in the 1975-1976 budget, 4547 were scheduled for WPC coverage; as of October 1975, standards had been set for 3231 of these positions.

Work measurement and work performance programs have a fifty-year history in municipal government, and the term has covered a wide variety of different programs. Most commonly, measures and standards have been applied to organization units carrying out a single activity. A typing pool is a typical example. A refuse collection work force is another.

In Phoenix, however, the standards are applied to individual positions, the only approach that accounts for qualitative differences in the workload, work organization, and differences in the type of equipment used. To do this requires a very substantial investment of industrial engineering time to set the initial standards and to revise them as required. It is, hence, not surprising that, as the city manager noted in his 1971-1972 budget message: "No other city had used this program on the scale recommended to reduce costs."

For all jobs for which standards have been set, the departments report monthly on actual performance in relation to standards. The Operations Analysis Division prepares a program-by-program summary that goes to the city manager. There is, as a result, a process of continuing monitoring of performance and a distribution of data that brings performance and changes in performance to the attention of the chief officials of the city and the departments.

In the 1971-1972 budget message, the city manager attributed $734,900 in budgetary savings to the Work Planning and Control system during its first year in operation. Offsetting the savings were costs of $215,200 for operating the program. The city manager cited Booz, Allen & Hamilton as estimating first-year economic savings at $1,573,600, this amount representing the annual value of the improvements in manpower utilization and of time-saving improvements in work methods. The ultimate direct and indirect impact of the program was estimated by Booz, Allen & Hamilton at $5,247,000 in reduction of need to increase the city budget in the future.

The largest of the savings identified in the budget were:

$94,000 in street maintenance from converting four- and five-person street repair crews to three-man crews;

$124,000 in sanitation by reducing three-man collection crews to two men;

$130,000 in building inspection resulting from travel time savings from permitting inspectors to take their cars home at night thus avoiding checking in and out at the office.

It should be emphasized that all three of the above cases involve some reorganization or change in the work process and are not simply the result of standards requiring more work from employees under the same work conditions and workload.

At the end of the first year of WPC, 1299—22 percent—of the city's permanent full-time work force were covered. A year later, in the 1972-1973 budget message, the city manager reported, "Studies are underway and nearing completion involving 1,187 additional employees." The utilization rate, or performance against the standards, for the employees covered in the first year had increased from an initial average level of 85 percent to 90 percent a year later, a growth of sixty-five man-years of usable work time, "representing an avoidance of over $500,000 in recurring costs . . . in addition to the recurring savings of $735,000 accomplished last year. . . ."

The manager also reported on three specific WPC studies:

1. The one-person contained refuse study on the basis of which the first 19 one-person trucks were purchased making it possible to avoid for the first time in many years the addition of new sanitation personnel.

2. The parks maintenance study which distributed the work force among four geographic districts. This will reduce travel time by the equivalent of seventeen man-years, a cost avoidance of $137,000 annually when fully implemented.

3. The new city courts arraignment procedures study to increase courtroom utilization and reduce police officer time in court.

In the 1973-1974 budget message, a year later, WPC coverage was reported at 2520 employees and the average utilization rate at 90 percent. No specific savings were detailed, but the manager estimated the value of the increase in utilization over the initial 85 percent as $983,000 in the current year and $562,000 in the prior year for a total of $1,545,000.

The budget message for 1975-1976 makes no mention of the work planning and control system, although WPC had been extended by then to 71 percent of the jobs for which it was planned.

Program Analysis and Review

Patrick Manion, a senior member of the program analysis staff, has described Program Analysis and Review as incorporating "a management by objectives approach with an analysis of program alternatives to brief the City Council on the basic effectiveness and potential service level changes for individual departments and programs." The words have the ring of the PPB vocabulary, but the Phoenix version departs sharply from the original federal model.

The federal PPB attempted, with limited success, to force on the operating departments of government a rational planning and budgeting structure embracing a program structure, multiyear planning, and cost-effectiveness analysis. PAR imposes no comparable apparatus or demands on the agencies. Rather, it is a system of program analysis or evaluation carried out by a central staff of analysts. It has not achieved—nor has it attempted to achieve—as did PPBS, concurrent coverage of all agencies.

In three years, the Program Analysis Division has carried studies of programs in twelve—or about half—of the city departments and done followup analyses in two of these. All city agencies have been asked to develop detailed statements of goals and objectives.

A Program Analysis Review is the equivalent of a program memorandum in the Planning-Programming-Budgeting System. It is an effort "to wrap it all up," identifying the city objectives the program is intended to meet, the extent to which those objectives are being met, the effectiveness of the program, and any changes or alternative approaches that should be considered. Work Planning and Control data on work performance are one of the inputs to the PAR process, but PAR may result in a recommendation for a detailed work analysis in some particular area.

PARs often result in recommendations and actions that have limited direct relevance to the budget. The impact of PAR may be best indicated by examples of its results:

Court case dispositions have been expedited by the introduction of a "meet and confer" pretrial disposition conference.

Faster resolution of traffic cases was obtained by a mail-in bond procedure.

Police emergency response time was reduced by designating special "E cars" that respond only to emergencies. This is one of several recommendations on improving available patrol time that resulted from a thorough study of patrol time use and a projection of manpower requirements.

Constant full strength manning in the Fire Department will help improve fire-fighting capacity and elevate from Class 4 to Class 3 Phoenix's rating by the fire insurance underwriters. In addition, operations plans were developed for the emergency medical service, and a construction plans review process to maximize fire safety was also inaugurated.

Seal coating was given a higher priority in street maintenance. The current level of streetsweeping was judged to be adequate.

In traffic engineering, recommendations were implemented for upgrading street marking and lighting. Subdivision street lighting policy was revised to require lights to be installed at initial development.

In planning, emphasis was increased on the total zoning process and systematic zoning inspection was intensified. Time requirements for the development application hearing process were reduced.

A classification system for maintenance service levels was introduced as an aid to projecting manpower requirements and steps were taken to strengthen both development planning and fiscal control.

From these examples, the chief impacts of PAR seems to have been the improvement of the quality of performance and the effectiveness of city services and the establishment of appropriate service levels. Quantitative productivity gains and cost reductions do not loom large in the results.

The Refuse Collection Case

In the 1971–1972 budget, one of the more significant savings achieved by the Work Planning and Control system was the reduction from three to two workers in the crews used in the biweekly collection of uncontained bulk refuse.

In the autumn of 1971, the Departmentof Sanitation asked Budget and Research to analyze the performance of the Shu-Pak truck against the rear-loader compactor trucks then used for regular collections. The Shu-Pak truck is described as a "side-loading, frame mounted hopper, continuous packing, dual-drive vehicle primarily designed for a one-man operation; the one man driving on the right and exiting the stand-up cab to load the collection hopper directly behind the cab." The Shu-Pak system was not new. An attachment to the evaluation study listed twelve local governments already using Shu-Paks, including Inglewood, California, which had used them since 1960.

The Operations Analysis staff established time standard data for one person operating a 29 cubic yard Shu-Pak truck. The staff concluded that using Shu-Paks, the city could collect refuse with as little as 46 percent of the collection work force required for the rear loaders manned by a driver and two servicemen. There would be some offsetting costs for additional trucks snce one man in a Shu-Pak would collect only about three-fourths of what three men in a rear loader collected. The report recommended the gradual replacement of the collection fleet with Shu-Pak, with nineteen to be ordered immediately and twenty-five more in the 1972–1973 fiscal year. Savings from the use of the first forty-four trucks were estimated at $467,800 in the first full year and increase with progressive replacement to nearly $900,000 in the 1976–1977 fiscal year. The estimates reflected a proposed 5 percent premium for Shu-Pak drivers. The recommendations were accepted.

Interestingly, William Donaldson, then the City Manager of suburban Scottsdale, had, during the prior several years, achieved a national reputation for an innovation based largely on "Godzilla," a garbage truck with a side mounted hoist to lift, empty, and return standardized plastic refuse containers. Godzilla required only a driver. In the course of this analysis, Phoenix considered Scottsdale's Godzilla and rejected it. The primary concern was the maintenance cost and vulnerability to damage of the "arm" used to pick up the containers.

But mechanization was on its way to Phoenix. In 1974, the Department of Sanitation and the operations analysts of the Budget and Research Department tested "Rapid Rail," a mechanized collection device with two short grappling arms that move out a few feet from the truck at hip level and close around a container. The grappling device holding the container then rides up the side of the truck along two vertical rails (hence the name), turns the container upside down with a jerk to empty it in the hopper, and executes the return trip to restore the empty container to its original position on the side of the road or alley. The operation is entirely mechanized, controlled by the driver from the cab.

Rapid Rail is mechanically simple, compared to Godzilla, and very fast, taking only about twenty seconds to empty a large container. But there is a rub. It will not take the usual assortment of garbage cans but must be adjusted (as does Scottsdale's Godzilla) to a uniform standard container. The container, a 90-gallon wheeled plastic barrel with a hinged cover, costs $70 and has a ten-year life. Alternatively, a 300-gallon container costing $125 can be used for three to four families.

The cost analysis showed that the city could install Rapid Rail, pay for the containers, and still come out ahead. The savings depended on the extensive use of the larger container. A truck equipped with Rapid Rail collecting from a 90-gallon container for each family could do no better than a manually loaded Shu-Pak. With three-to-four family 300-gallon containers in the alleys (from which 55 percent of Phoenix's refuse collections are made), the potential savings were very large. Rapid Rail could function at 75 percent of the costs of manually loaded Shu-Paks and at 53 percent of the costs of three-man-crew rear loaders.

The containers are guaranteed for ten years normal use by the manufacturer but not, of course, against vandalism. Perhaps only a New Yorker would ask what happens if a fire is set within a container. The answer: It collapses like a plastic dish in a warm oven, a total loss.

Citizen reaction was clearly crucial. A questionnaire was distributed to 431 households in the test area, and 345 replies were received. A surprising 97 percent requested the retention of the Rapid Rail system, and 96.5 percent said the system had improved the appearance of the alleys.

The city elected to proceed with conversion to Rapid Rail over a five-year period. When the system is fully in force in 1978–1979, it is estimated that the city will collect refuse from 17 percent more households with 35 percent fewer trucks, 63 percent less manpower and a 32 percent reduction in costs compared to actual 1974–1975 costs. The annual savings will be over $2 million. Twice-a-week refuse collection will be provided to a projected population of nearly 900,000 people with only 107 trucks and a work force of 149. (See Exhibit 8-1.)

Phoenix, like most cities, provides, in addition to regular collection of containerized refuse, less frequent collection of bulk or uncontainerized refuse. Bulk refuse includes everything from old sofas and refrigerators to tree cuttings. Phoenix has developed a mechanized approach to bulk as well as containerized collection. This is done with three-man teams equipped with a termite tractor with a large front-end loading claw scoop and two goose neck tractors each pulling two large open gondolas. The termite loads the refuse into the gondolas far faster than it could be handled manually and keeps two goose neck tractors and their gondolas busy, filling one while the other takes a load to dump. The termite system used initially for 25 percent of the crews has been extended to 70 percent coverage. At the same time, service was cut from twice to once monthly as a result of the Program Analysis Review. As a result of the two changes, staffing was reduced by one-fifth while city population was increasing by 5 percent.

The Centralized Office Copying System

The development and perfection of the copying machine has spurred a revolution in office practices over the past two decades. The Xerox machine has become as much an office fixture as the water cooler. The making of copies of anything and everything has become common, because it has become both cheap and easy.

However, Phoenix discovered that the total costs were far from negligible, and they were rising rapidly. In the fiscal year 1973–1974, the city government's thirty-one decentralized office copiers produced a total of 8.6 million copies with machine and supply costs of $264,000 and estimated total costs of $342,000 including labor—nearly three times 1969–1970 costs. Moreover, costs were continuing to rise at 25 percent or more per annum.

Exhibit 8-1
Stages in Development of Phoenix Refuse Collection System

	Projected Operating Statistics and Cost Comparisons of Fully Implemented Systems[a]		
	Rear Loader	*Shu-Pak*	*Rapid Rail*
System:			
Equipment	5 yd. rear loader	33 yd. side loader	33 yd. side loader w/Rapid Rail
Crew	2 packers plus driver	1 worker	1 worker
Productivity:			
Households/truck			
shift	700	535	1000
Tons/truck shift	9-12	7-10	12-15
Tons/man-day	3-4	7-10	12-15
Resources Required:			
Number of trucks[b]	153	200	107
Number of men[c]	553	251	149
Annual Costs[d]:			
Dollars/household	$36.98	$34.11	$26.32
Dollars/ton	$31.64	$29.15	$22.52
Total Cost/year	$9,335,000	$8,600,000	$6,644,000

Source: Budget and Research Department, City of Phoenix, Arizona.

[a]Estimates assume that all contained refuse is collected by the specified system. In fact, Phoenix still uses some rear loaders, although it began the shift to Shu-Pak in 1971 and has not yet equipped all Shu-Paks with Rapid Rail. By 1978-1979, all collections will be by Shu-Pak trucks or comparable side loaders equipped with Rapid Rail. Both refuse volume and costs change over time. Therefore, in order to provide a true comparison of the different collection systems they are all based on (1) current (1975) costs, and (2) projected refuse volume in 1979 when the Rapid Rail system will be fully implemented.

[b]Includes the number of vehicles required for route collections plus 27 percent for maintenance and standby equipment.

[c]In addition to scheduled collection crews, includes approximately 40 percent for pool and relief personnel for six days per week collections.

[d]Includes all operating costs in current (1975) dollars plus annual amortization of trucks, Rapid Rail, and containers.

A Budget and Research analysis found that nearly 50 percent of the copying was done in runs where fifty-one or more copies of the original were made. A decision was made to set up a Rapid Copy Center in the City Print Shop and require city agencies in and near city hall to use the center when more than fifty copies were required. Special envelopes and a messenger service were introduced to make sure that work was expedited. The center used an Addressograph-Multigraph Total Copy System. The high-speed bond copiers were removed from the city offices, and slick paper, low-speed electrostatic copiers were substituted.

By March 1975, after four months of the new system, nearly half of the copies were being made in the Rapid Copy Center at an average cost of 1.7 cents compared to the previous 3.2 cents per copy for the high-speed office copiers. The average cost for the center and the office copiers together was 2.3 cents per copy. The total savings on this basis were running close to $9,000 per month and over $100,000 per year.

Comments from using agencies were mixed. Complaints centered on the copy center's difficulties with large orders and with low quality of the convenience copies that replaced the Xerox machines.

The success of the Rapid Copy Center as a money-saving effort was, however, qualified by the apparent stimulus the center's existence and services provided to the demand for copying. Total production by both the center and the office copiers increased to 32 percent above the base level in three months, partly due to a diversion of normal print shop business to the faster copy service. Thus, there was a net gain in volume of about 17 percent, which reduced the savings by some $2,000 per month.

Building Inspections

When the Work Planning and Control system was inaugurated in 1970, Building Safety Director Michael J. Sienerth was waiting for it. Sienerth, himself, had come to the Department of Building Safety from a background in work study and industrial engineering. He welcomed the city's decision to build an industrial engineering capacity in the Department of Budget and Research and was eager to use any help the new staff could give him. Moreover, he had definite ideas for increasing productivity in building inspection.

The situation suggests an immediate question. Why was Sienerth waiting? Why did he need Budget's Operations Analysis staff? Apparently Sienerth needed help because he had no supporting staff to speak of in his own office to do the job.

The first big step was the creation of the general inspection program in 1970. Prior to that time the department had followed the common practice of four different specialized inspections at each construction project. Hence, there were not only building inspectors but also electrical inspectors, plumbing inspectors, and mechanical inspectors. Most of the activity was generated by the tract builders of single-family houses. Sienerth reasoned that one person could be trained to perform all the inspections competently for the relatively uncomplicated single-family house and provide better service than a succession of different inspectors. Moreover, this could be done with only about half the number of trips to the construction site required with specialized inspections.

On this basis, the general inspection program was set up. Inspectors assigned to this function were given training in all four specialties. Regular continuing periodic meetings were set up where the general inspectors could raise technical questions with the specialists. The General Inspection Section was given responsibility for all tract developments of single-family homes, custom homes, minor accessory buildings, fences, mobile homes, swimming pools, town houses, and "quads" with up to four units. The program now accounts for 53 percent of all inspections but only 25 percent of the total number of inspectors. The annual savings from the general inspection program are now estimated at $750,000 annually.

In the same year, a change in vehicle usage policy produced a marked increase in inspector productivity. Inspectors had reported to departmental headquarters at the beginning of the day to pick up assignments and a city car. They would return at the end of the day to turn in the car and report to their superiors. Under the revised policy, the inspector retains the car overnight, reporting to the first inspection site at the beginning of the working day and completing work at the last assigned site at the end of the day. Cars are equipped with two-way radios so that assignments can be received and work reported without returning to headquarters. This seemingly modest change resulted in an increase of 13 percent in the average number of inspections performed per man-day.

At the same time, Budget's Operations Analysis Staff was doing work measurement studies that resulted in a system of measuring, forecasting, and balancing work that achieved an additional gain of 11 percent in the average number of inspections per man-day.

Thus, three successive productivity improvements resulted in major gains within a relatively brief period of time. (See Exhibit 8-2.)

In April 1972, the building permit system was changed. Hitherto, the city had required four separate permits (building, electrical, plumbing, and mechanical) for each building project. The requirement generated a great deal of confusion, much paper, and many unnecessary trips to the municipal building. The April 1972 change scrapped this system in favor of a single building permit issued to the general contractor. It produced obvious advantages for the contractor and reduced by 50 percent the department's costs for paper, copying, and filing.

Accommodating to Change

Members of city councils must vote the taxes and bear the brunt of criticism about the rising cost of government. Naturally, they have an interest in economy and expenditure control. Nevertheless, they usually see governmental economy and expenditure control as depending on political forces rather than on management styles and actions. One reason for this is that Council members tend to be drawn from the law, real estate, and insurance agencies and from the leadership of labor, veterans, and civic organizations. Consequently, they usually

Exhibit 8–2
Building Inspections in Phoenix

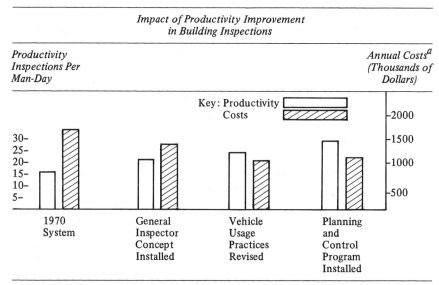

Impact of Productivity Improvement
in Building Inspections

Source: Budget and Research Department, City of Phoenix, Arizona.
[a]Costs calculated for 1975 volume of inspections.

have limited if any experience in the management of large organizations and, more often than not, little faith in management consultants or any of the other approaches associated with large-scale management. Therefore, even when it would seem logical to use the services of an outside management consultant, it is very unusual to see it done on the initiative of a council.

Moreover, legislative bodies rarely propose major changes in managerial and administrative practice. Thus, Phoenix is a double exception to what might be considered a norm: first, because the City Council, not the then city manager, wanted a formal effort to improve productivity and reduce costs; and second, because the City Council initiated the idea of a management consultant study of city government. This situation is indicative of the fact that the Phoenix City Council, certainly circa 1969, was rather different in perspective and outlook than most other city councils. (See Exhibit 8–3.)

Clearly, legislative initiation made the Phoenix effort different from the outset. No one had to sweet-talk a skeptical council into appropriating funds for a management consultant study or for an operations analysis staff. Nor did ideas for investments in management improvement meet the more usual bureaucratic quiet death when the boss says to a subordinate (or to himself): "Forget it. I could never sell it to the Council."

Exhibit 8-3
The 1968-69 PHOENIX CITY COUNCIL

Phoenix municipal elections are held in odd-numbered years. The mayor and six Council members are elected at-large on a nonpartisan ballot for two-year terms commencing in January of even-numbered years.

Mayor Milton H. Graham, businessman, owner of laundry supply firm. Graham was a World War II fighter pilot. He was first elected Mayor in 1963 and was reelected in 1965. He was defeated in his bid for a fourth term in the 1969 municipal election.

Vice-Mayor Frank G. Benites, labor leader, president of the Phoenix Building and Construction Trades Council and a member of the Arizona AFL-CIO executive board. He was first elected to the Council in 1965. Benites was active in the City's antipoverty program, is a member of the Arizona Academy, and is on the board of Samuel Gompers Memorial Rehabilitation Center.

Councilman Charles G. Case, businessman, owner of a Phoenix tire business. He served on the Municipal Aeronautics Board for five years and was a member of the Boy Scouts Advisory Board and Boys Club Board. He received his degree in business administration from the University of Arizona.

Councilman John F. Long, businessman, became the nation's number 2 homebuilder in 1962. Long was named to the City Council in 1966 to serve out the unexpired term of a vacated seat and was elected in his own right in 1967.

Councilman Milton G. Sanders, businessman, general agent for a life insurance company and formerly vice-president of Central Arizona Light and Power Company. He majored in liberal arts at the University of Arizona.

Councilwoman Dorothy Theilkas, civic worker. She had long been involved in city civic organizations, including the Phoenix Public Library, municipal bond program promotion, and legislative, school, and juvenile delinquency activities. She directed the Charter Government Committee campaign in 1963. Her most recent civic activity has been editing and publishing educational materials on the city's government for use in each elementary school grade.

Councilman Morrison F. Warren, black educator, elementary school principal for 15 years. He was first elected to the Council in 1965. He served for three years with Patton's Third Army in Europe, and graduated from Arizona State University.

Note: All members of the 1968-69 Phoenix City Council were sponsored by the Charter Government Committee, a municipal reform group, which was responsible for strengthening the city's Council-Manager form of government through amendments to the City's Charter in 1948. The Committee had been successful in electing candidates to all mayor and Council member seats at each municipal election up to and including the 1967 municipal election.

The Council initiated the program with the specific purpose of generating productivity improvements that would lead to budgetary savings. Therefore, the city manager and the consultants were faced with need to come up with those savings. That they did so after only a year of WPC was, undoubtedly, critical in maintaining Council support for the effort.

Public opinion seems not to have played a major role. However, since 1970, there has been extensive citizen participation in the budget process through informal public information sessions and hearings well before the date on which the Council is legally required to adopt the budget. In addition, the Council created a City Financial Advisory Committee and, in December 1974, a Citizen

Bond Advisory Committee. The latter successfully promoted the $206 million new bond authorization approved by the voters in April 1975. The local Chamber of Commerce makes regular annual reports on its recommendations for city budget priorities.

Difficulties with officials of the operating agencies were inevitable, since they were confronted with a far more intensive review than before, which used new and unfamiliar methods and aimed at cutting or holding down their budgets. It would be astonishing if they did not regard the approach as threatening. Budget and Research Director Charles E. Hill noted some of the problems:

None of these changes in the budget process was accomplished without difficulty. The application of industrial engineering work measurement and time standard techniques to department operations was particularly difficult. Empathy of department problems, constant persuasion and salesmanship made inroads in the innate human reluctance to undergo new approaches and change. In some cases, the Budget and Research Department freely admitted false starts and inept approaches to gain operating department acquiescence to begin studies anew to successfully complete and place in operation the work planning and control program. Only after operating departments realized the work measurement techniques were to be used to their benefit to justify their operating needs to management as well as a basis for rejecting their requests have they come to accept the program.

In retrospect, Hill believes that confrontations might have been averted by the assignment of staff analysts to the operating departments "to develop a technological dialogue" with Budget and Research Staff.

At that, both the city manager and the Budget and Research Director undoubtedly had an easier time of it, because they were marching at the insistence of the Council rather than on an initiative of their own.

More serious problems could be anticipated with the city work force. In some strongly unionized cities, an effort to do work measurement studies and set work performance standards would, in itself, be regarded as an adequate cause for strikes or job action of some sort. Phoenix had few problems of this kind although some might well have developed had not the Police and Fire Departments been excluded from the work measurement program.

Collective bargaining by municipalities is not authorized by Arizona law. Most Phoenix city employees are not unionized. But there are unions, and they are not of negligible importance. The police force is organized as a local association without international union membership. The fire fighters are organized by the International Association of Fire Fighters. The sanitation workers are organized as the Service Workers' Association. A recent development has been the organization of less commonly unionized employees in the Administrative, Supervisory, Professional, and Technical Employees' Association.

Limited bargaining under a "meet and confer" procedure was introduced
in 1976. Even before this, however, the unions were not ignored. Compensation
and other issues have been important enough to justify extended meetings including, in recent years, day-long retreats for discussions by the Council and city
management with union leaders. With all this, the unions are a limited factor
in the Phoenix government and display little of the muscle of their brethren on
the east and west coasts and in the midwest.

The city took steps from the beginning to allay employee concern with the
productivity improvement program. In explaining the program, the emphasis
was placed on the creation of improved and simplified work procedures rather
than on having employees work harder. More important, the city guaranteed that
there would be no layoffs; any reductions in staffing would be effected through
attrition or through reassignment of employees to other jobs.

The sanitation service workers have been more affected than any other employee group by changes introduced since the inception of the program in 1970.
The shift from the three-man rear loader to the one-man Shu-Pak truck increased
the amount of lifting required of each worker per day from three to four tons to
between seven and ten tons. A 5 percent pay premium was provided in recognition of the additional work and responsibilities. Rapid Rail shifted the lifting to
a machine but also meant that the work force would be only half as large as it
would have been with three-man rear-loaded packers.

Worker concern came to a head after an accident in which a child was killed
by a Shu-Pak truck. The child was to the left of the cab and allegedly invisible to
the driver using the right side controls. The driver was charged; he argued that
the accident occurred because the truck was unsafe. The sanitation workers went
out on strike and went to court to seek the banning of the truck on grounds that
it was unsafe; they demanded that a second worker be assigned to each truck. The
city presented accident record data indicating that the one-man truck was safer
than the three-man truck. The judge found the union argument without merit.
The servicemen returned to work after three weeks. Minor modifications have
been made in the truck, notably a glass panel in the lower part of the left-hand
cab door to increase visibility for a driver operating from the right-hand side.
The installation of Rapid Rail continues according to plan.

Problems have also occurred with the fire fighters. The analysis recommend-
ing full manning of fire companies at all times also noted that this would permit
fire fighters to be trained and used on a part-time basis for regularly scheduled
commercial fire code inspections. The Department's Fire Prevention Division was
already responsible for inspecting schools, hospitals, and public assembly buildings. The fire fighters argued that the additional work entitled them to an increase in pay; a 5 percent increase was ultimately provided by the Council. The

pressure for pay increases continued, however, and would continue so long as fire fighters did not have salary parity with police.

The city agreed in 1975 to a new assessment of changes in fire-fighter workload and productivity to be carried out by the Budget and Research Department. The work covered a historical review of fire fighters' work activities, an intercity salary and work comparison, and a work measurement study. Although the work was done in response to the union's request, the union head flatly told the city administration that the fire fighters would go on strike if any work measurement analyst so much as entered a fire house. As a result, the city did the study from data in departmental records.

The study concluded that fire fighters' activity had increased in scope and quality of services but that about the same amount of time was being spent on each job-related activity as in 1967. In the intercity comparisons, Phoenix was a low-cost, high-program department. On the basis of this information, the Council approved parity pay for the fire fighters effective July 1, 1976.

The partly unionized water meter readers complained that their work standards were too high. The issue, according to Patrick Manion, served "as an impetus to higher salaries, a long standing grievance." The issue was at least partially resolved by the recognition that the major problem was an unequal distribution of workload. Workload was subsequently balanced within each of the four geographic divisions.

Management and Implementation

The city has had few serious difficulties in the implementation of specific productivity improvement projects once a decision has been made to proceed with them. One exception may be the park maintenance project, which after three years is still not fully implemented.

Only one project involved a great many complexities in the implementation process. This was the change in refuse collection, which required a scheduling of truck acquisitions, work-force training, collection route modifications, and arrangements for personnel transfers. The operations analysis staff developed the schedules and generally assisted the Department of Sanitation in the process.

The Building Safety Department similarly depended on Budget and Research for the staff support and expertise in managerial systems necessary to carry out the changes in the inspection and permit system. The installation of the Rapid Copy Center seems to have been even more closely and directly managed by Budget and Research to make sure that the service was provided according to plan.

The work measurement program includes a system of monthly reporting of employee utilization so that performance can be monitored by the operations analysis staff. The major problems with the system have been the difficulty in certain activities of establishing meaningful and useful standards and the general problem of keeping the standards current.

There is a more general problem of enforcing or, more accurately, using the standards. The existence of a standard does not necessarily mean that it will be met. Sometimes, and in some jobs, there will be good reasons for not meeting standards.

One case covers those jobs where there are day-to-day variations in the demand for services; staffing may be designed to meet average load or peak load, depending on the service, but some underutilization is inevitable. Temporary, part-time, or new employees may function at lower productivity levels than experienced employees. External factors may have an impact on productivity. The point is, the problems associated with the failure to meet work standards are hetereogeneous, enmeshed in varied specific situations, and often complex. Hence, utilization figures may merely indicate possible problem areas. To determine whether a case of underutilization is correctible and, if so, to develop a means of correcting it demands staff time of a magnitude that cannot be fully met by thirteen people, given their other responsibilities.

Overview

Few cities in the country have done as much to improve productivity and have been as successful in doing so as Phoenix. Virtually no other city has done the job "by the book," sending operations analysts out to examine nearly every city job (outside of police and fire). Few monitor performance in anything like the detail or scope of Phoenix's monthly work planning and control reports.

The Department of Budget and Research estimates that increasing utilization of city employees through Work Planning and Control has resulted in aggregate savings today of $3 million and that methods improvement from special studies is responsible for aggregate savings of $4 million, largely from the sanitation service. Methods improvement savings should increase very rapidly from projects already in process; Rapid Rail alone will contribute about $2.5 million annually. Charles Hill calculates the balance sheet to date as comprising total benefits of $7 million against costs of $1.6 million for a "profit" of $5.4 million and a benefit-cost ratio of 4.5 to 1.

The largest productivity gains in Phoenix have come not from the Work Planning and Control system but from the reorganization of certain work processes. The mechanization of refuse collection, the general inspector idea, the change in inspector motor vehicle use, the restructuring of park maintenance and street repair operations are the cases that have produced the gains to justify the program. The common characteristic of all these is that they were not routine. They all required the investment of significant analytic time to identify and evaluate alternatives and to design program changes.

We tend to measure the effectiveness of a productivity program by the improvement it has produced. In many cities, the improved level of performance still leaves much to be desired. This is not so in Phoenix; its improved building inspection and refuse collection services are, for example, probably as efficient as any comparable operation elsewhere.

This is partly due to the fact that Phoenix is a curiously uncomplicated city. It is a low-density city, largely single-family homes with some apartments and a handful of highrise buildings. It spreads over the flat valley floor around the few topographical outcroppings, such as Camelback. A uniformly hot dry climate is interrupted only by a gullywashing rain storm or two in the course of the year.

Social and political factors are also less complex than in older cities. Labor relations are still relatively benign and simple enough so that most changes can be put into effect without an endless hassle of negotiations. Few service delivery patterns are so enmeshed that the population regards them as immutable.

Both physical and sociopolitical characteristics contribute to Phoenix's ability to improve the performance of its government. Refuse collection is a good example. The city could make changes with drastic effect on worker productivity and work force without bargaining or negotiation; the sanitation workers' strike was almost happenstance with no effect on the mechanization program. Contrast this with the tough bargaining on productivity in cities like Detroit and Flint. Phoenix could, unlike Milwaukee, for example, mechanize without having to wean citizens away from long-established backyard refuse pickup. It did not, as would New York or San Francisco, have to take action to assure truck access to the curb. It could use, as could no large northeastern city, a container that is totally destroyed if a fire is lit within it. There was no need to consider performance in snow or on significant grades. There were no serious complications from wide variations in requirements for refuse collection among city neighborhoods.

The city government of Phoenix has taken good advantage of a milieu favorable to change and improvement. As Phoenix accumulates some of the social and political problems of our older cities, the habits of analysis, standard setting, and performance improvement will make it far better prepared than most of our older cities to deal with those problems.

9   Tacoma

The City of Tacoma, Washington, midway between Seattle and Olympia on the southeastern shore of Puget Sound, includes about 59 square miles and a population of 156,000 people. It is the population center, economic hub, and county seat of Pierce County, 1975 population over 413,500. Both city and county populations are rising, Tacoma's at an average yearly rate of 3.0 percent and Pierce County's at 4.5 percent.

Tacoma's history has taken it through many changes of image. The city's frontier history bound it up with the wild life of seaport, lumber town, rail center. Later the expansion of war industries and military bases during World War II continued the abundance of "single men looking for action." A notably open city during the immediate post-War period, Tacoma was "sanitized" in a reform movement peaking in 1953, when the city shifted to a Council-Manager charter, brought in a manager and police chief who closed the downtown brothels and gambling halls, and began a reform administration that was to last for the next sixteen years.

The government organization established in 1953 separated the city into two divisions: General Government under the Council-appointed city manager, and Public Utilities (Light, Water, the "Belt Line" municipal industrial rail system and, since 1973, the Data Processing Division) directed by a separate director and Utility Board. In addition, there are a number of independent boards and commissions, some of which have been involved in city productivity measures.

Tacoma's 1975-1976 budget is $117.6 million, of which Public Utilities accounts for the lion's share. The General Fund budget is less than $30 million. Municipal employment (permanent and project) totals about 2700, of whom some 1800 are in General Government. The city has no significant fiscal problems.

There is nothing in Tacoma *called* a productivity program. But there are a multitude of activities, astounding in scope and variety, which are aimed at efficient and effective government services. Some approach this goal through intro-

---

This chapter was co-authored by Daniel Rubin, who did virtually all of the field work and prepared the initial draft, most of which survives in the current version.

169

duction of new technology. Others are centered on management and decision processes, seeking to improve their quality and efficiency through better cooperation, participation and motivation. This whole panoply of activities is organized for the most part in a decentralized system of departmental projects and interdepartmental liaison.

Mr. D., the Man Who Gave Us "Godzilla" . . .

The great majority of Tacoma's productivity-related programs and projects can be attributed to William Donaldson and the climate he engendered in city government after his appointment as city manager in 1971.

Donaldson's appointment was no ordinary changing of the guard at City Hall. A crisis of elected leadership of heroic proportions had created the need for an outsider with great negotiating skill and strong professional credentials to restore order and reputation to the city.

Tacoma's city manager from 1956 to 1969 was David Rowlands, who ran the city in highly centralized, directive fashion. During his term of office, Tacoma gained a national reputation as a well-managed city and, in the later years, became known for innovative social programs, especially urban renewal and model cities. Rowlands subsisted on narrow council majorities, often 5-4. Finally, in 1969, after the election of a conservative Council, Rowlands resigned.

The majority Council bloc, adamantly opposed to the manager charter and to federal social programs, proceeded to embroil itself in scandal and thoroughly alienate the city's minority and liberal voters. A seventy-six-year-old civic-minded retired military officer was appointed city manager as a "caretaker" until the system could be dismantled. The police chief and the head of urban renewal were fired. A cable television franchise was granted to a friend of the new council members. When much higher raises were given to police and fire fighters than to other city employees, labor support for the administration began to erode. Finally a successful recall campaign was mounted in 1970, resulting in the ouster by a 2-1 vote of five of the nine council members. The vacant seats were filled appointively with political unknowns.

As the smoke cleared, the new Council looked through professional organizations for a top-notch manager. Donaldson came highly recommended with a just-emerging national reputation for technical innovation earned during his five years as manager of Scottsdale, Arizona. The Council and Mayor Gordon Johnston were impressed also with his smoothness and responsiveness to their needs. Donaldson was unanimously chosen by the Council.

Donaldson might be said to have ridden to fame on a garbage truck. During his administration as city manager, Scottsdale developed a highly efficient mechanized refuse collection system using compactor trucks with a side-mounted hoist and city-purchased standard large plastic household refuse containers. It was an impressive performance especially for a small city that had to put together the needed equipment configuration in its own shops, develop specifications for the containers, and find a firm able to produce them inexpensively. In a widely distributed Urban Institute Report, *Technology for the Cities,* the truck, nick-named Godzilla, shared honors only with the New York City Rand Institute's polymer additive "slippery water" for fire fighting. Donaldson, as a result, be-came widely known not merely among the professionals in city government but also in such unlikely places as the Rand Corporation and the National Science Foundation.

The reputation was deserved. Donaldson, who says he has no professional accreditation save a certificate as an apprentice embalmer, has a special genius and taste for technological applications. He couples this with a probing curiosity about how things work and how things are done. It has led him to riding fire en-gines (in New York as well as Scottsdale), mechanical street sweepers, refuse col-lection trucks, and police patrol cars.

Donaldson's talent in the technology area was coupled with a high recogni-tion by and rapport with the grantors of funds for technology projects. There could, consequently, be litle doubt that as city manager of Tacoma, Donaldson would initiate efforts to improve the technology—particularly hardware—in city operations.

In addition to his strong orientation toward technology, Donaldson had a second important characteristic. This was his unconventional posture on person-nel and organization. Donaldson's managerial style is commonly referred to as "informal." He talked, when he first came to Tacoma, of wanting to take down the internal partitions that set off the hundreds of separate offices and, in his opinion, impeded interchange and communication. He was concerned with the difficulty of getting to know Tacoma's 2600 employees in the same way he had known a quarter their number in Scottsdale.

Some of this sounds like the discomfort of the jump from a small pond to a bigger one. But it was more than that. The partitions did come down in the city manager's office, and the empty spaces filled with the desks of members of the manager's staff. The city manager sat in this cluttered office accessible not only to his own staff but to anyone else who walked in. Interchange was not merely facilitated; it was unavoidable. For a wholly private exchange with the city manager, the corridor outside offered greater opportunities than his office.

The Donaldson style is an assault on the substance as well as the symbols of hierarchic organization. He saw the principal role of the city manager not as making "right" decisions but in getting other people to make right decisions. In this context, an order from the city manager to a department director is a confes-sion of failure, indeed of grievous failure, because it means that the department head has persisted in a course that is not merely wrong-headed but also serious and immediate in its repercussions.

Donaldson also accepted the legitimacy of widespread participation in gov-ernment decision making. Council members have an obvious interest and so do interested citizens. But employees also have an interest in the way their agencies are managed and staffed, and the unions mirror some of these interests as representatives of the employees. Every city department has a valid concern with the quality of administration in the Department of Personnel or in the budget allocations proposed by the Department of Finance. This attitude suggested an extensive use of group decision making that did, in fact, result. Donaldson's basic attitude was that anyone who wants to come should either be invited to the party or have a representative there. If there were problems or differences, the people involved should sit down and try to work it out.

Donaldson made it clear very early that he intended to make no changes in top departmental positions. He brought no one with him from Scottsdale and made no significant effort to recruit new staff. This was especially surprising given Donaldson's penchant for technology—a posture more usually linked to the recruitment of staff with new skills and attitudes. But, Donaldson's policy was, as he put it, "to grow people" rather than to recruit them.

He made known his interest in innovation and his belief that substantial improvements were feasible. He committed himself to an effort to provide resources and support for departmental projects. Above all, he pushed questions, work, and responsibility out to his own staff, to the departments and, frequently, to teams and task forces.

Response from top city staff was mixed. For years, they had dealt with a diametrically opposite management style. In the brief conservative regime, they had had to run their own affairs with little help from the manager's office. But enough staff were enthusiastic to make a start. Some projects were underway within the first year, and the momentum began to build up.

Technology from Totem to Center

Donaldson's ability to obtain money and technical assistance was important to the launching of Tacoma's technology improvement efforts. It produced extra resources for the experimenting department heads, relieving, at least in part, the need for the new effort to compete for funds within regular operating budgets. Donaldson used his own reputation and his ability to gain interested audiences for proposals and presentations. Considerable ingenuity was used in devising avenues for funding. Tacoma's approach to the Maritime Administration was MARAD's first encounter with a city—for funds to survey requirements and develop specifications for a surface-effect harbor service craft. Equally imaginative was the Public Works proposal to the Environmental Protection Administration for the development of better street sweepers that would leave less residue to pollute storm sewers.

The majority of technology projects now in evidence owe their existence at least indirectly to the technology transfer program, called "Totem One" for most of its duration, which started soon after Donaldson took office in April 1971.

Extension of technology to more city services was one of Donaldson's strongest interests, and it received much personal attention from him. However, most of the work of setting up the transfer program was done by the Technology Coordinator, Harvey Singleton, who joined the city in June 1971 to write a proposal to National Science Foundation and stayed as a full-time consultant to administer the efforts eventually funded through it.

Singleton, with Donaldson's support and agreement, assumed the role of a broker for technology transfer. Over a period of months he became acquainted with the directors of operating departments and discussed their ideas about what technology could do for them. Later, when strong working relationships were established with Boeing and other outside experts, he worked to keep communication informal and friendly, expectations realistic. But departments were always encouraged to run their own projects and deal directly with outside technologists.

When Donaldson arrived in Tacoma there was already some technical innovation going on, notably in the Public Works Department. Most current projects, however, have been nurtured by the Totem One program, which made a concerted effort to combine the experience of city officials with the specialized expertise of technologists. The departments that have made the strongest use of technology—Fire, Police, Public Works, Transit and the independent Municipal Court—all do their own project coordination at this point.

The range of projects undertaken in the city is evident from Exhibit 9-1 covering the Fire and Transit Departments. They include new devices, adaptations of existing machines, scheduling models both custom made and imported, and even an economic study on apportionment of fire charges to users. The substance of these projects will receive considerable analysis later; for now our interest is the organizational devices by which Tacoma has nurtured this extraordinary mélange.

The NSF grant to Tacoma, amounting to $70,000 the first year (1972-1973) and $180,000 over three years, covered Singleton's services and funds for contract exploratory consulting work. During the first year of this transfer program, Donaldson began discussing the concept of an "Urban Laboratory" in which Tacoma would receive funding for detailed development and implementation of a group of technical projects. The organization and intercity transfer role of such a project, however, was not resolved at this point.

In early 1974 NSF provided $60,000 for six months of planning toward a city technology transfer center. The proposal for this grant contemplated a center involved in three relationships: with sources of technical expertise, with city departments, and with other users (cities in the Northwest especially). In April of that year the Technology Transfer Center opened under the direction of Regina Glenn, former director of Manpower Planning. The Center's early funding consisted of $32,000 in city money, $24,000 of the NSF planning grant, and other project money. Tacoma's 1975-1976 draft budget included $50,000 in

Exhibit 9-1
Departmental Technical Projects in Tacoma

Project	Involved	Dates Status	Description	Cost/Funding and Effects/Savings
Fire Department Systems Analysis and station siting	Boeing NYC-RAND station siting model	1972: Analysis; siting model used 1973: One station closed, one changed to roving duty	General cursory analysis of Fire Suppression activities. Siting model used to explore effects (response time) of closing station, reducing manning of traditional units.	*Funds:* Totem One Boeing time *Effects:* led to further funded development work, and to closing of Station 5, reduction of 11 of 15 fire companies from 4 to 3 firefighters as of Jan. '73. *Saving* from manning reduction went to reduce firefighters' hours from 50 to 48.
Automation of logistic support for firefighters	Donaldson Boeing	1971: Idea discussed 1971–72: Reconceptualized into projects (see below)	Concept: reduce the number of firefighters unable to attack blaze due to support duties (manning hydrants, pumpers).	Analysis led to specific projects *Funds:* Totem One
Portable automatic hydrant	Donaldson Boeing	1972: Proposed to NSF (rejected) Idea dropped in this form	Idea: radio controlled hydrants which can be snapped into water main through connector in ground	*Funds:* Asked NSF for $90,000 *Effect* (if developed): frees a firefighter from hydrant duty. *Savings* would include reduction of permanent hydrants, thus of hydrant knockovers at $1500 each.

Item	Organizations	Dates / Status	Description	Funds / Effects
Automatic hydrant valve	Donaldson Boeing Battelle AEC (now ERDA) Heath-Techna Co. Technology Center (Glenn)	1972: Proposed to NSF (no) / 1974–75: 2 prototypes finished by Battelle/AEC and by Heath-Techna.	Idea: radio controlled valve which can be attached quickly to hydrant port. Two prototypes exist which can regulate water flow automatically once turned on manually.	*Funds:* ERDA–$25,000 NSF–$45,000 for testing prototype ('75) Time contributed by Boeing and Heath-Techna. *Effects:* Heath-Techna is considering marketing its version. If implemented, this valve frees a firefighter.
Portable extension mains (5" diameter hose)	Donaldson Denver & Littleton, Col. fire departments	1971: Idea; 1975: In use by 5 of 14 companies, will be extended to all	Using wider hose from hydrant to pumper means fewer lines to lay (time) and less frictional pressure loss (effectiveness).	*Funds:* City–about $100,000 for hoses
Adapters and quick-connect couplings	Storz Co. (manufacturer) Boeing City Water Division	1971: Idea 1974–75: Adapters installed on 4,000 hydrant ports. Now, 7 of 14 companies use Storz couplings	Permanently mounted adapters on hydrants allow 5" hose to be snapped on quickly using special fittings.	*Funds:* City from Rev. Sharing–$193,000 *Effect:* Speed in using 5" hose.
Light 2" hose		Tested and not slated for further implementation	Lighter hose for use between pumper and firefighter/nozzle. Tested in one company. Construction was poor.	*Desired effect:* lighter hose can be laid faster, e.g., up the stairs of a building. *Test effect:* not used. *Funding:* nominal; City.
Umbilical prototype	Boeing	Idea dropped in this form; broken into smaller project ideas	Idea: a unified hose, air line, and communications/equipment control cable.	*Applied* for NSF funds (denied). *Desired effect:* improve safety, improve effectiveness through better water control and control of automated equipment.

Exhibit 9-1 Continued

Project	Involved	Dates	Status	Description	Cost/Funding and Effects/Savings
Breathing system: mask and tank	Boeing NASA Scott Aviation Co. Dallas FD	1974: 1975:	Prototype tested in Dallas Tacoma lost interest	Idea: a better breathing mask and light air tank, adapting NASA space technology. Tacoma-Boeing proposal to test NASA model rejected.	Boeing contributed time. *Outcome:* City realized development and *marketing* of systems will take too long; replacement equipment will be bought sooner, on market. *Scott Avn:* "May manufacture" the system starting 1976.
Explosive ventilation	Rocket Research Co.	1973:	Idea RRC tests conducted	Idea: develop a shaped and/or unshaped charge to take the place of axes in entering roofs and ventilating fires.	*Funds:* NSF–$2,230 RRC–all time *Effect:* improves speed and safety. No commitment to purchase but cost looks low.
"Probeye" infrared			Tested. Deferred for later consideration of purchase.	Infrared viewer helps to locate fire hotspots and smoke-obscured fire victims.	Developed already and marketed. Tacoma has tested and may buy in the future.
Harbor Service Vessel	MARAD (Maritime Admin.) Boeing Tacoma Boat Building	1970: 1972: 1974: 1975:	Need established. Idea Requirement study done Proposal for 2 hull designs (surface effect, planning).	Idea: Tacoma's 1929 fire boat needs replacing. A study of requirements nationwide for harbor service functions confirms the possibility of building a widely useful high-performance vessel for less than cost of a traditional replacement fire boat.	*Funds:* MARAD–$53,000 rec'd for requirements study; $150,000 request for design pending. *Benefit:* Lower investment cost, higher total performance, higher proportion of boat and crew's time productive. Also meets new needs.

Project	Organizations	Year	Status	Description	Funds / Results
Equipment evaluation	Boeing National Bur. of Standards (NBS)	1972: 1975:	Proposed to NSF (no). Completed under NBS	Design and conduct performance tests for 5" hose, nozzles, valves to control pressure surges in hose, and water additives.	*Funds:* NSF –asked $108,000 (denied) NBS: *Results:* tests informed Dept. purchasing. In general, testing methodology helps fire depts. influence what is manufactured by specifying performance criteria.
Skills Degradation Study	Boeing Seattle Fire Dept.	1972:	Idea	A specialized firefighting skill was taught and then variously evaluated after a few months.	*Funding:* NBS– *Results:* Fast degradation of skills substantiated, giving more basis for present training expenses for about 10 hours/week per firefighter.
Firefighting systems requirements analysis	Boeing Seattle FD NBS Wash. Fire Service Training Program	1972: 1975:	Methodology developed. Boeing is testing in 11 cities	Task analysis of fire methods to establish skill and performance baselines.	*Funds:* NBS– *Effect:* (if extended to many skills): would allow inter-city and time-series comparisons of fire skills, aid in specification of equipment needs by use parameters (e.g., time for standard procedures).
Fire suppressant fogs test	Union (IAFF)			Suppressant fogs can be applied under various pressures.	*Union* performed. *Results:* confirmed present practice.
Large fire simulator	Boeing		Idea Built	A visual aid simulator which allows training of fire officers in fighting large fires which occur rarely and require tactical skill.	*Cost:* $7,000 *Effect:* Better training, and hopefully reduction in probably errors (estimated responsible for 50% of fire loss) in big fires. Also preserves skills of retiring officers.

Exhibit 9-1 Continued

Project	Involved	Dates Status	Description	Cost/Funding and Effects/Savings
Computer real-time simulator	Boeing, National Fire Protection & Control Act	1975: Proposed	A more sophisticated programmable simulator along the lines above, this one able to respond in real time with consequences of an officer's tactical decisions.	*Desired effect:* see above.
Fire Service Demand Charge	Boeing Booms Singleton	1974: In progress. 2nd draft report on concept and methodology complete.	Idea: to develop a charge assignable to each building which corresponds to value of fire services likely to be required, as a basis for fire funding and an incentive for fire safety. A heavily	*Funds:* NSF–$30,000 Unpaid Boeing time over amount paid. Phase 1 cost: $53,000 Very time consuming and far from implementation as assessed
Transit Department Transit Analysis	Boeing	1972: Complete	An organization study of the Dept. with sections on feasibility and probable course of many specific projects. Includes much analysis.	*Funding:* City–$20,000 *Effect:* established a baseline and an agenda which has been the source of almost all subsequent technical projects in Transit.
Bus alarm system	Boeing	1973: Implemented	To reduce vandalism, a low cost device to sound bus horns on entry was developed and installed in all buses.	*Funds:* Totem One (cost was very low) *Effects:* a large reduction in night vandalism *Savings* estimated at $10–12,000/year.

Project	Agency / Source	Status	Description	Cost / Results
"Service Improvement Program"	Boeing Urban Mass Transit Admin. (UMTA)	1973: Partly implemented, but mostly in progress	A catchall list, containing pool dispatching, dynamic routing, fare and ridership information, central business district (CBD) planning, and maintenance facility improvement.	*Funds:* UMTA—$30,000 *Effects:* See below for specific projects.
Pool dispatching	Boeing	1973–75: Not implemented. Model designed and run, schedules ready.	Analysis showed that, due to waiting times of various buses before their next scheduled run, there are always at least 2 buses idle. Redesign of schedules to "pool" waiting at the new CBD depot allows cutting these 2 buses.	*Cost:* *Savings* estimated at $30,000/year based on 2 buses cut. *Results:* model needed refinement to make it operational. This was done. Now implementation awaits completion of the CBD mall depot.
Dynamic routing	Boeing	1972: Model development start. 1975: Operational test disclosed problems. Future: uncertain	During night hours when bus use is light, a minimum of one bus/line is needed. This can be reduced as much as ½ by routing buses flexibly with a computer algorithm in response to phoned in "appointments" with patrons. A computer model was developed but requires complex data on city streets and has performance problems at present.	*Funds:* UMTA—$20,000 Another $100,000 is needed (est.) to complete development. *To implement,* an investment of $30,000 in computer and terminal equipment and operating costs of $12,000 are required. *Savings* were first estimated at $120,000 gross per year for cut buses. Model performance is not as good as hoped, so the latest estimate is lower.

(continued)

Exhibit 9-1 Continued

Project	Involved	Dates Status	Description	Cost/Funding and Effects/Savings
Origin-destination data collection	Boeing	1972: Recommended in Transit Analysis 1975: greatly simplified	Need: better information on trips and fares. Recommended: automated system in which passengers punch cards in and out for continuous data to be stored or transmitted for analysis. Done: one-time 5-day card survey of riders.	*Costs:* too high for automation. *Effect:* manual survey with keypunching and computer analysis was used to plan routes and schedules at new CBD mall depot (where the dispatch "pool" will be).
Maintenance facility improvement	Boeing	1972: 1975: Recommended Pending funds and arrival of orders.	The Transit Analysis recommended replacing outdated equipment for efficiency and service improvements.	*Funds:* UMTA pending *Results desired:* greater efficiency in use of maintenance employees.
Automatic operating data collection	Boeing	1972: Recommended. Since dropped.	Transit Analysis suggested automatic radio-interrogated sensors on buses to report in oil and gas use, temperature, etc., for periodic computer analysis.	*Cost:* high. *Effect:* would make preventive maintenance more accurate and improve bus retirement system (now by age not condition and maintenance costs).

city funding—not enough without supplementation to carry the Center's four staff: Glenn, two generalist assistants with training in law and applied industrial technology, and a secretary.

Totem One emphasized the first-phase priority of establishing good interaction between city officials and outside specialists, spinning off departmental projects as this became feasible. The Center seeks to perform an additional centralized clearinghouse function involving many activities hitherto conducted in more scattered and informal fashion. Glenn expects to enlarge cooperative relations with other technology transfer projects nationwide and with local universities. She also hopes to find an industrial science advisor to undertake such projects as an inventory of local technology capacities and the recruitment for a small Industrial Science Advisory Board. She is taking on the coordination of interdepartmental projects such as geobase data file development and a planned energy symposium, and intergovernmental projects, for example a City-County-Port of Tacoma adaptation of a Federal Air Pollution Control Agency model to help plan action on the severe pollution problem threatening further development of the city's industrial area. Finally, Glenn maintains close contact with major funding sources and legislators and serves as a broker and negotiator on proposals.

The network of contacts established since 1971 remains in place directly between local technologists and department officials. Departments continue to maintain their own national contacts through professional associations and in many cases through their own research and development staff. The importance of the Technology Center will depend on its success in meeting specific departmental needs for money, information, and speedy action. Certainly, it is unlikely that the most self-sufficient departments, Fire, Police, and Public Works, will give up any of their present autonomy except in exchange for new resources. The team building experience of the past years likely has increased departmental staff's ability to deal better with *either* style of work, self-contained or centralized.

Boeing! Boeing!

Tacoma's relationship with Boeing company was crucial to development of the technical projects. In addition to the large amount of systems and technical work directly performed by Boeing specialists, it was their impact that markedly increased many department directors' receptivity to technology in general.

The relationship began in 1971 at Donaldson's initiative. Sales personnel from Boeing Computer Services had approached the city with a proposal for refuse rerouting, but Donaldson chose to make his own approach, going directly to top executives of Boeing Aerospace. He voiced his conviction that a more client-oriented relation between high-technology firms and cities was needed, in which demeaning stereotypes (the technologist as arrogant egghead, the civil servant as grafting know-nothing) could give way to trust and respect. Donaldson suggested the assignment of Boeing personnel to the city for the education that a protracted work experience with city problems and officials could provide.

A series of executive-level exchange meetings ensued, including a tour of Tacoma's landfill and lunch at the city jail, and by the end of these discussions top corporate officers had been sold on a cooperative experiment. Boeing Aerospace was at the time interested in participating in the planning of new towns and had a special unit working in this field. From this group was detached a team of systems analysts and engineers, headed by C. Ray Turner, who set up camp in donated city offices.

Boeing contributed seven man-years or $350,000 of professional staff time with back-up in 1972 and 1973. To Boeing, this substantial commitment was justified as part of its strong effort to diversify to escape the severe effects of recession in the aerospace industry. Hopefully, the know-how developed in Tacoma might have commercial application in new product development, in the company's new towns effort, or in technological services to other cities.

The effectiveness of the arrangement was greatly aided by both Singleton's skillful coordination and by the personalities of early Boeing team members. The Boeing staff were casual, relatively low key, and willing to learn operating details by means including participation as a transit driver or fire trainee. Several department officers feel that their good relations with these first Boeing contacts were crucial in building a favorable perspective that could stand later jolts from disappointing project outcomes or more abrasive technologists (including some more recent Boeing representatives).

The germs of most technology projects now underway were already evident after the first rounds of "wish list" meetings held between top department officials and first, Singleton, as the informal broker and, later, the early members of the Boeing team, especially Ray Turner, Joseph Muldoon, and Frederick Fath. Development next often took the course of general system or organization studies. Such work was performed by Boeing staff in Transit (1972, on contract), in the Fire Suppression Division (1972, on contributed time), and in the Public Works Refuse Utility Division (1973, on contract). In the Police Department, organizational analysis was performed by one of its own LEAA-funded specialists at about the same time.

By the time such initial studies were done, a close and informal department-consultant relationship had been established. Accordingly, the style of detailed project development—proposal writing, modeling of problems, specifications for information systems and hardware—was frequent conversation rather than occasional written reports. The directors of Transit and Fire, and other departments as they developed projects, were consequently more involved in development than would be typical of an in-and-out consulting job.

The sustained relationship between Boeing and the departments transcended the usual limitations of project-based contract research. The Boeing team developed an unusual understanding of the particular local circumstances and problems to which the relevant technology had to be adapted. The city staff became increasingly knowledgeable of the potential of new technology and technique; a visiting economist said of Chief Reiser: "I've interviewed fire chiefs in fifty cities and this is the first time I've heard the word 'tradeoff!' " Lastly, both groups began to understand and respect the capacities of the other.

Projects tended to evolve from a particular limited problem to a more comprehensive perspective of the operation. For example, the concept of automating logistic support to fire fighters so as to release more members of the company for actual fire attack has gone through several redefinitions. Early discussion separated "support" into the supply of water from city mains to pumper to nozzle, the supply of breathing air to fire fighters, and the maintenance of communication and control among people and machines. (See Exhibit 9-2.)

The Boeing contribution of professional staff was allocated within the company for specific projects, rather than blanket coverage of the whole team. In addition, some $83,000 in funded contract work was conducted over the two years. (See Exhibit 9-5). But these figures do not indicate the flexible way in which Singleton and the Boeing project team handled finances. There were three sources from which Singleton could fund Boeing projects: the $15,000 per year set aside from the NSF Totem One grant specifically for Boeing; a more general fund of Totem One money for "other high technology contracting"; and whatever city money departments could be convinced to spend for other work. Whenever Boeing internal money ran dry for the project team, Singleton would tap one of these sources for a Totem One assignment or a contract, or Donaldson would give Boeing executives a further "pep talk" to get company money flowing.

The order of projects reflected to a degree the week-to-week strategies of funding, in which a paramount concern was to keep experienced team members, already well established in the city, from being transferred off the project. But the work performed was in all cases responsive to departments' desires, and scheduled in a realistic professional manner. The minor workload problems that did occur—for example, formal reports being delayed several months after project completion due to a transfer to other work within the city—tended to reflect the difficulty of agreeing in advance what the scope of an "exploratory" analysis would be.

The Tacoma-Boeing relationship is at a point of transition. The main Boeing team now works out of Boeing Computer Services, not Aerospace, with no connection with the new towns project. The spin-off from Tacoma projects (especially transit and court scheduling) to other cities provides incentive for some corporate risk capital for project development but not at the high level of three years ago. Apart from funding shifts, the transfer team is in flux. Singleton has left Tacoma, and at some point other career pulls will move the last two "original" Boeing technologists, Joseph Muldoon and Dr. Frederick Fath, on to other

Exhibit 9–2
Tacoma Fire-fighter Logistic Support: Development History of Automation.

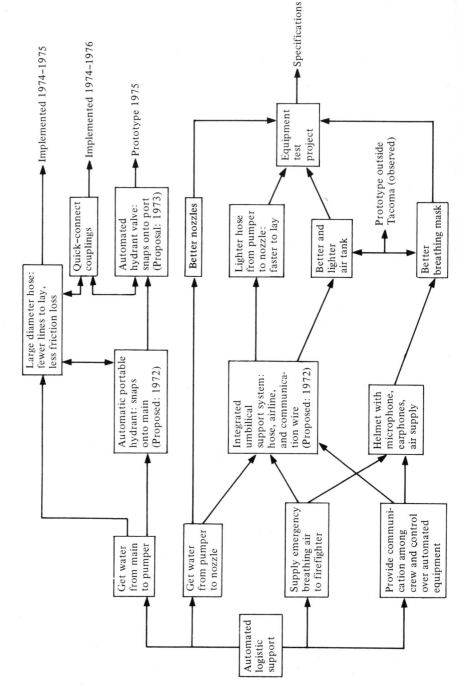

assignments. As this turnover occurs and the city's coordinating functions undergo at least partial centralization in the Technology Center, it is unclear what the nature of future contracts will be. What will certainly remain is a tremendous amount of learning by city officials about what to expect in good consulting relationships and how to use them.

Tacoma's overall view of the Boeing relationship is decidedly favorable. It probably should be. In over four years, the city obtained over half a million dollars in consulting services from Boeing, nearly 70 percent of which were contributed by the company. Federal funds accounted for nearly all the remainder; the city's contribution from its own funds totalled $33,700 for two small contracts. (See Exhibit 9-3.) Donaldson never had to sell the City Council and the public on the notion that technological advice was not only worth having but also worth paying for.

A rather different perspective of the project has been set out in a monograph by Joseph T. Muldoon ofthe Boeing team.[1] Muldoon emphasizes that, to the Boeing Company, the services donated to Tacoma represented an investment in the development of products and services that could be marketed elsewhere. In fact, the project developed few marketable service packages, the learning experience generated little business in other cities, and, even in Tacoma, Boeing lost every bid competition it entered because of its "lack of experience." The company's overall perception of its diversification opportunities also changed over the course of its involvement in Tacoma. Eventually funding and staff were cut back, and the company insisted that the project become self-financing.

With only limited continuing support from Totem One funds, the project became increasingly dependent on federal grants. This required the team to divert its efforts to areas where federal financing was likely, to spend an inordinate amount of time in the preparation of proposals for relatively small grants, and to endure delays between application and grant award so long as to make intelligent program management impossible.

In Muldoon's view, the success of the program in problem definition and solution development was not translated into equally successful implementation, largely because of inadequate funding. He argues, too, that much of the effort never moved beyond the definitional stage of the first year because the city never established the goals, provided real direction, or moved to integrate technological innovation into the mainstream of departmental management. Technology had to be sold to the department managers by Boeing staff, and some projects were never accomplished, because they "were counter to the inertia within the organization."

This situation seems, clearly, to reflect two factors. The first was Donaldson's deliberately nondirective management style. The second factor was the dependence on opportunistic funding.

As time passed other sources of outside expertise besides Boeing came into the picture. The Boeing team themselves acted as brokers for some models de-

Exhibit 9-3
Boeing Work on Tacoma Productivity Projects

Year	Donated Time[a]	Summary of Work Done		
		Percent of Year's Total Donated	Contracts	Yearly Total
1972	$200,000	78	$56,000	$256,000
1973	150,000	79	40,700	190,700
Subtotal 1972–73	350,000	78	96,700	446,700
1974	0[a]	0	49,000	49,000
1975 (partial)	0[a]	0	20,000	20,000
Totals 1972–75	$350,000	68%	$165,700	$515,700

Year	List of Boeing Contracts Included		
	Project	Amount	Source of Funds
1972	Totem One (various assignments)	$15,000	Federal (NSF)
	Transit Analysis	20,000	City (Transit)
	Municipal Court Calendaring and Judicial Information System	10,000	Federal (DOT) via State Highway Traffic Safety Council
	Economic Development Information System (EDIS)	11,000	City (Model Cities)
1973	Totem One (various assignments)	15,000	Federal (NSF)
	"Visibility Center" (for Program Management System)	12,000	Federal (EDA)
	Solid Waste Collection System Analysis Program	13,700	City (Public Works)
1974	Transit Improvement, Phase 1	30,000	Federal (UMTA)
	Technology Transfer Center	6,000	Federal (NSF)
	Fire Service Demand Charge	13,000	Federal (NSF)
1975 (partial)	Transit Improvement, Phase 2	20,000	Federal (UMTA)

[a]Boeing contributed time since 1973 has been zero officially, but internal corporate product development money has been used, and, in addition, reported hours worked on projects often were understated.

veloped elsewhere: the New York City Rand Institute fire station siting model, a police scheduling program designed for the Law Enforcement Assistance Administration and the City of St. Louis by Dr. Nelson Heller. Local academics became involved in several projects, starting with the work of Drs. Bell and Rosenzweig on organization development. Dr. Bernard Booms, an economist at Pennsylvania State University, arranged on his own for foundation support for an eighteen-month residence in Tacoma working on practical city problems and stayed another year as a consulting economist in the Department of Community Development.

Booms, Dr. William Baarsma of the University of Puget Sound, and others have been involved in bringing graduate students to the City. Students have performed responsible analysis in keeping with the requests of department directors: for example, a cost-benefit exploration of options for reorganizing city stores, and a now implemented comprehensive design for the new Department of Community Development.

The use of industrial technology has been extended far beyond the Boeing relationship, as well. Tacoma Boatbuilding Company was involved in development of specifications and prototype design for a multiuse harbor service craft. The Battelle Seattle Research Center has cooperated in planning and evaluating capacities. A scientist from Battelle's Richland, Washington complex developed one of the two automatic hydrant valve prototypes. Tacoma has long been involved in information exchange with the California Innovations Group (formerly the "Four Cities Project") and with a NSF-sponsored technology consortium. There is a proposal under consideration for a regional Pacific Northwest Innovations Group similar to the one in California, with which Tacoma would strongly associate.

The Tacoma program is changing as the availability of contributed expertise declines. It must pay for an increasing proportion of the services it needs, and, probably, a larger share of those costs must come from its own budget rather than from federal grants. Regina Glenn believes that one of the keys to future progress is an allocation for research in every agency budget. Manager Erling Mork is generally supportive, but the idea must be sold to the department directors. Better methods of identifying and using local expertise and new mechanisms for technology exchange are also in the picture.

Up the Organization

From the start of Donaldson's tenure as city manager, participative management and use of teams have been seen as ways to ease the way for technical change and to directly improve the quality and efficiency of decision making. The initial NSF application assembled by Singleton included $10,000 for consultants to conduct formal organization development work.

In January 1972, Donaldson appointed a special Federal Project Management Team of department directors to oversee the allocation of General Revenue Sharing money within the city and to coordinate other federal projects. The same group began to meet in June 1972 on technology transfer programs in sessions at which department staff and technologists described what they were up to. These meetings gave way by fall to department directors' luncheon meetings.

A key aspect of the group's development was the extension of its responsibilities from the initial assignment of distribution to revenue-sharing funds to a later more central role in the city budget process. By mid-1973, the team had full time staff support from the federally funded Program Management System in the Planning Department and had been redesignated the Management Team in recognition of its broad managerial responsibilities. The team meets now as necessary, usually weekly or more often and is attended by department directors or their principal assistants. Many specific responsibilities are delegated to subcommittees chaired by a team member. These subcommittees often include middle-management staff from the appropriate departments.

A considerable part of the frustration of the directors of the line agencies in any government arises from the controls and limitations imposed by the staff or overhead agencies such as budget and personnel. It is, hence, scarcely surprising that the team was interested in moving into the budget area and, later, under the Alderbrook program, into personnel. At the same time, it is also clear that Donaldson was no supporter of the traditional budget practices of the conservative director of finance. However, Donaldson, under his own self-denying ordnance, eschewed direct intervention to either introduce new procedures or replace the director. But, voilà! The Management Team appeared to play cat to Donaldson's monkey and pull the chestnuts out of the fire. Moreover, the staff support needed to make the team's new budget role effective was available under the Program Management System.

Meanwhile, at least forty other teams of varying importance and composition came and went, dealing with special problems (like writing proposals and designing new organization units) and continuing responsibilities (such as labor negotiation, legislative liaison, and budget review). Exhibit 9–4 presents a list of teams, with brief descriptions of origin and functions.

The same Donaldson-inspired release of departmental staff for special duties, which allowed teams to proliferate, also gave rise to a management internship in which middle managers marked for promotion spend three-month stints as a special assistant to the city manager. The diversity of this experience, especially given Donaldson's volatile style of delegating jobs to anyone handy, gave interns a breadth of knowledge about the city far beyond what they would normally acquire. Many maintain informal contact with other "graduates," creating a network for effective communication. In addition, this pool of broadly versed staff may include much of the city's future top leadership; two of them have already become department directors, and others have moved up to senior positions.

The city's formal program of organization development—or Organization Improvement, as Donaldson chose to call it—grew from contacts between Singleton and a former professor of his, Dr. Cecil Bell of the University of Washington Graduate School of Business Administration. After including $10,000 for contract services in this area in the NSF proposal, Singleton went about interesting Bell and a colleague, Dr. James Rosenzweig, in performing the work. Following a

Exhibit 9-4
Interdepartmental Teams in Tacoma

Name	Dates	Status of Members	Description/Purpose
Ongoing Interdepartmental Teams			
Program Management Team	1973	High	Coordinated allocation of Revenue Sharing money among 81 applicants within city; more generally, came to oversee federal programs. Members were department directors. Evolved, with growth of membership and of responsibilities, into Management Team.
Management Team	Evolved from Program Management Team	High	Wide-ranging coordination and decision making for General Government division of City. Frequently sets up other teams, generally subgroups of its members with other individuals added. All department directors are members.
Budget Review Team	1974	High	Annual review of department budgets, with staff support from Program Management System (Planning Department). Format of the review, and participation of citizens, has changed from year to year. Members chosen from Management Team.
Municipal Training Committee[a]		High	Established by ordinance. Coordinates all training, education, and job development activities in both General Government and Public Utilities. Has 3 members from each.
Training Team (General Gov't.)		High	Performs the same coordination as Municipal Training Committee, but within General Government.
Training Representatives		Middle/Low	Inform employees of opportunities for training, development.
Data Processing Advisory Board[a]		High	Coordinates data processing in both divisions of government. Most allocation decisions are made within the respective committees for General Government and Public Utilities.
Data Processing Coordinating Committee	1975	Middle	Coordinates data processing in General Government, including the allocation of system development time of Data Processing Department staff. Attendance 10-20.

(continued)

Exhibit 9-4 Continued

Name	Dates	Status of Members	Description/Purpose
Public Utilities Data Processing Coordinating Committee[a]	1972		Same coordination with Public Utilities.
Legislative Committee	1974		Liaison with State legislators on matters of interest to Tacoma.
Negotiating Team[a]	1972	High	Conducts labor contract negotiations for the City. Has 2 members each from General Government and Public Utilities.
Public Information Team		Middle/Low	Puts out staff quarterly publication; helps departments on employee activities.
Council Presentation Team	1974	Middle/Low	Schedules departmental presentations before the City Council; provides technical assistance in videotaping presentations.
Geographic-Base File Team	1974	High/Middle	Looks into uses of geobase data files among city departments. Officially ongoing but largely inoperative, as most activity is now within Planning Department. Recently acquired funds may reactivate broad interest.
Affirmative Action Team		Broad	Informally accepts complaints of discriminatory action by City. No decision-making authority.
Major Special-Task Interdepartmental Teams			
Research Team	1973-75	Broad	Conducted local portion of "Job Talk" employee attitude survey; analyzed interview data; designed and wrote 2 booklets presenting findings to employees; recommended action to Management Team.
Technical Team	1973	High	Coordinated planning throughout the City and designed the Program Management System (under HUD comprehensive planning grant to Planning Department).
Guidance Team		High	Studied possibilities for future of Model City and Human Development Departments when reorganization seemed necessary. Further related work continued by Community Development Team.
Community Development Team	1973	High	Designed the Community Development Department incorporating elements from Model Cities and Urban Renewal programs.

Exhibit 9–4 Continued

Name	Dates	Status of Members	Description/Purpose
EDA Team	1974	High	Developed a block grant application to U.S. Economic Development Administration (Department of Commerce). Members were high administrators from 5 departments, plus representatives from Port of Tacoma and two business groups.
Word Processing Team			Developed City policy and plans for use of automatic word processing machines.
Policy Advisory Team	1973	High	Reviewed and consolidated individual budget review recommendations and wrote guidelines for 1974 process.
County-City Combined Law Enforcement Support Agency Team			Set up permanent agency to coordinate area law enforcement.
Minor Special-Task Interdepartmental Teams			
Agenda Team			Assisted a U.S. General Services Administration representative in a study aimed at reducing the quantity of local paperwork.
Brochure Team			Prepared a brochure on historic monuments in Tacoma-Pierce County. 3 members.
Grooming and Dress Team	1973		Developed guidelines for city employees.
U.N. Settlements Team	1974		Wrote proposal for Participatory Management Process demonstration at U.N. Conference on Human Settlements, Vancouver, B.C., 1976.
Payroll/Personnel Design Team	1974		Designed a new organizational structure.
Public Works Maintenance Center Team			Prepared information for the most recent bond issue involving the funding of this project.
Print Shop Study Team			
Nonunionized Employees Benefits Team	1975	High	Recommended city policy on fringe benefits for employees not represented by unions. A Management Team subcommittee.
Miscellaneous Interdepartmental Teams			
Public Utilities Coordinating Council			
Personnel Committee			
Fleet Safety Team			Devise special action to combat a high accident rate.

(continued)

Exhibit 9-4 Continued

Name	Dates	Status of Members	Description/Purpose
Investment Committee	1965		Attend to investment of nonessential cash reserves.
Accident Review Board	1958		Recommend policies to prevent accidents.
Council of Emergency Services			
Contract Compliance Team			Coordinate administrative support for compliance reviews.
Bond Program Team			Prepare a LID bond issue.
Radio Users Committee	1974		Coordinate city communications
Northeast Tacoma Service Committee			Was intended to develop ways to improve services to northeast Tacoma. Defunct.
Suggestion Award Board			Created by City Council to judge cash suggestion incentive award system.
Planning Club			Was to work on comprehensive planning issues. Never got off the ground.
Urban Lab Team			To keep all departments informed on the progress of NSF-funded technology transfer projects.

[a]These teams contain members from Public Utilities as well as General Government.

series of meetings with city officials to gain approval and clarify objectives, Bell and Rosenzweig laid out a program of action including:

> Quarterly two-day team-building and problem-solving retreats for top administrators from General Government.

> Workshops and other activities with management and professional personnel from an unspecified "Department A" (line) and "Department B" (staff).

> Skills development seminars for department directors and assistants, to include administrative and communications exercises and lecture-discussion.

These activities were begun during 1973-1974, the first two years of the Organization Improvement Program. The off-site workshops, called "Alderbrook I" and so forth after the conference center where they first were held, have numbered so far nine and are continuing indefinitely. A new city Training and Development director, Dwight Faust, will be sharing actual leadership of these sessions with Bell or Rosenzweig by turn.

The Alderbrook workshops involved the membership of the Management Team meeting in a new setting under different auspices. Bell, Rosenzweig, and Donaldson knew that successful, strongly attended early workshops were a necessity. The influential Training Committee had satisfied itself as to what the consultants were up to but not the rest of the city's managers. As the time of the first retreat neared, pressure mounted for an agenda; and Donaldson finally announced that budget cuts would be discussed. With the incentive of up to two full days of talk about money, attendance was very good.

At one of the early Alderbrook workshops, Public Works was chosen as "Department A" and Personnel as "Department B". The departmental activities that followed met some problems, but one successful workshop was held in Public Works and three in Personnel. The Alderbrook sessions were limited to department directors; a seminar program to give assistant directors the same exposure to problem-solving technique was unhappily scheduled for Friday afternoon and poorly publicized and quickly died for lack of interest. Schuster was eager for Public Works to be "Department A," and the first session there, a two-day workshop, went extremely well. But before a second could be held, Schuster died while recovering from an operation. A followup was never held.

The Personnel Department was selected as staff "Department B" by department managers displeased with their service relations with Personnel. The department's nonclerical staff participated in a two-day workshop, a day-long "user conference" with representatives of other departments, and in a second later workshop. Although the process was resisted at first, the result to date has been successful implementation of a system in which every department has a permanent liaison at Personnel. Early feedback suggests that this arrangement has improved the situation.

In addition to these organization development activities suggested by Bell and Rosenzweig, several projects have developed at the initiation of others.

Fire Chief Reiser invited Drs. Bell and Rosenzweig in as department-paid trainers, hoping to draw his field commanders into the administration of the department. The first session with the department's top eighteen men went superbly. But before a second was arranged, the group decided to meet on their own— against Reiser's preference. The staff meeting that ensued was described as extremely exciting: slow, expensive (the time expended was calculated to total about $1500), but very successful at clearing up old problems. The staff meetings show every sign of continuing indefinitely without outside assistance. Erling Mork, who stepped up from assistant city manager when Donaldson went to Cincinnati in June 1975, requested Bell to conduct a series of organization development sessions with the central staff of his office. The first of these meetings was held in late August 1975.

There is one additional program of management change and team use which must be cited separately. Since 1970, before Donaldson's arrival, the Police Department has been involved in reorganization and reallocation of personnel with goals that include better communication among top officers, less patrol turnover, closer supervisory and working relationships in patrol, and improved morale to heighten efficiency. This was a team effort by Chief Lyle Smith and his top officers, with Police Foundation aid plus technical assistance from analytic and management specialists he had hired in 1971 using LEAA funds and with backing from Donaldson since he came.

Specific changes have included a top management team within the department reinforced by a number of efforts to improve communication among senior officers, and a team patrol system established in March 1973 when a new scheduling plan ended the previous isolation of officers from their supervisors and others working in their district. Participation has been broad; recently three allocation teams, of low-, middle-, and high-ranking police officers, have each reviewed a set of major proposals for changes in assignment aimed to permitting flexible response to crime patterns and to opportunities for preventive or investigatory work.

In sum, Tacoma's recent management changes and organization improvement efforts have been directed at department heads and, to a lesser degree, their top-echelon staff. The Job Talk project solicited information on attitudes, but response was general. There was no widespread attempt to systematically collect information about absenteeism, rates of transfer and turnover, and other data that might be related to improved motivation of line workers. Where these data were most available, in Police, there were such enormous morale pressures from other changes over the same period (e.g., a 45 percent increase in calls) that no connection with organizational changes is discernible.

Tacoma has some three dozen analysts and technologists, working in a dozen locations, whose work is closely tied to productivity-related projects. Exhibit 9-5 sketches the roles and background of these individuals and of administrators particularly active in project development. Whether the present pattern will change due to the activities of the Technology Transfer Center, previously described, remains to be seen.

Even in budgeting there is an extraordinary degree of decentralization, due in large measure to the strong allocation role taken by the management team and the other teams it delegates. The City Finance Department has never taken a strong role in evaluating program outputs; the tradition there has been accounting of dollars and people within a line budget. Over the past three years, however, there was simultaneously an extension of both citizen and bureaucratic participation in budget making and a gradual shift toward program budgeting with an emphasis on needs determination, objective setting, and evaluation. This effort involved Budget Review teams of administrators and a succession of devices for community input.

In preparing the 1974 budget, the management team had its budget review and made recommendations; in addition, department staff and seventeen citizens chosen by the City Council took turns (two citizens and two directors at a time) sitting in on the review of departments' budget, still in line form.

Exhibit 9-5
Location of Technical and Analytic Expertise within Tacoma

Department	Analytical/Technical Coordination Staff	Relevant percent of time	Source of staff	Date[a]	Funding Source
City Manager's Office	Technology Coordinator: An MBA with mechanical engineering degree and experience; general liaison for city technology programs in departments.	100	Recruit	1971–75	NSF
	Asst. to Tech. Coord.: Undergraduate training in business administration.	100	Recruit	1974–75	PEP/CETA
	City Manager: (a) From 1971–Spring 1975 incumbent was technically well informed and very interested in project development.	(a) 20	Recruit	1971–75	City
	(b) The present C.M., formerly Asst. C.M., has a background in urban planning.	(b) 10	Transfer	1975	City
	Asst. C.M.: An experienced engineer with additional training in business, urban studies. Assignments have included project coordination as well as wide-ranging budget and other responsibility.	20	Recruit	1971	City
Technology Transfer Center	The Center acts as technology liaison agency, locating expertise, seeking grants, administering some inter-department programs, and disseminating information.			1974	1974: NSF/City
	Director: MBA with strong organization development background; former director of Manpower Planning for City.	100	Transfer	1974	1975: City
	Technology Technician: degree in industrial technology (mixed traditional engineering and industrial trades)	100	Recruit	1974	
	Technology Engineer: attorney, former teacher	100	Recruit	1974	
	Secretary: work includes much liaison and dissemination	50		1974	

(continued)

Exhibit 9-5 Continued

Department	Analytical/Technical Coordination Staff	Relevant percent of time	Source of staff	Date[a]	Funding Source
Planning	Program Management System: described elsewhere, this unit is heavily involved in revision of budget and other allocation processes to permit management by quantified objectives and evaluation. In addition, of course, other Planning staff perform planning analysis of established varieties.			1973	HUD
Data Processing	Staff involved in system specification and development with departments of both General Government and Public Utilities.				City
Police	Research and Development Unit: Consists of a Captain, 2 Sergeants, a civilian analyst from a computer systems/finance background, and a secretary. One of the Sergeants has been trained by the Department as a programmer.	100	Transfer/ Recruit	1971	City/LEAA
	Technical Management Specialist: hired with LEAA funds; has worked on reorganization of Department among other things		Recruit	1971	LEAA
	Crime Analyst: Another civilian hired from LEAA funds, to develop pattern of crime analyses for use in selective patrol and investigation.	100	Recruit		LEAA
Fire	Technology Coordinator: A field Lieutenant on full-time administrative assignment doing detailed followup on technology projects in progress and initial assessments of new projects.	100	Transfer	1975	City

	%		Date[a]	Source
In addition, the Fire Chief spends an unusual amount of time directly involved in project development, due to a strong personal interest in technology.	20	Role shift	1971	City
Others in Department, variously	20	From pre-1971		City
Public Works				
Systems analyst				City
In addition, several top administrators and engineers are highly involved in development of new technologies for solid waste collection, compaction, and recycling. Also, some engineers are used at times as a high-technology resource by the Technology Center.				City
Transit				
Transportation Analyst: Using CETA funds, an analyst formerly employed by a private transportation consulting firm was hired to share coordination of technology projects with the Transportation Director and participate in Department planning, load counts, etc.	100	Recruit	1975	CETA
Municipal Court				
Has no analytical staff, but the Court Administrator, from a business background, is conversant with modern data processing and personally coordinates contract analysts in keeping with a phased automation plan.	10		Job: 1969 Role: 1972	PSCOG DOL
Community Development				
Economist: a temporary position filled in 1974–75 by Dr. Bernard Booms, who created (a) a foundation-supported "city internship" for himself (1973–74) and then (b) stayed under city funding to do economic analysis.	100	Recruit	1973–74	Foundations
		Transfer	1974–75	City
Human Development				
Research and Development Specialist:				
Law and Justice Planning				
Evaluator/Researcher:				

[a]Date office or position created, or beginning of relevant role for previously established official.

Prior to budget preparation for 1975-1976, a panel of citizens was chosen through lists of ten names provided by representatives of local organizations and agencies. These 187 individuals were administered a detailed attitude survey, from which summaries of problems and priorities were given to each department director. Both line and program budgets were prepared, and they were reviewed by a Budget Review Committee consisting of the assistant city manager, three department directors (two line, one staff) chosen by the Management Team, and the Finance director.

In 1975, citizens were surveyed as the previous year, but this time, in response to criticisms that the panel survey method was not representative, the sample consisted of the 1800 respondents to a random mailing of 5500 surveys. Departments were instructed by the City Council to respond in the preparation of their program budgets to questions raised by this survey. Line budgets were prepared but for department and accounting use, not Council review. Budget modifications are required for alterations of service level, and departments for the first time have included management objectives, many of them quantified, in their budgets.

Interestingly, citizen representatives were not enchanted with the opportunity to participate in long sessions on the details of the budget. Instead, citizen inputs are now provided for in a prebudget Council resolution prescribing budget policy.

Staff support for the transition to program budgeting was provided by the Program Management System (PMS), a unit in the Planning Department funded under a four-year Housing and Urban Development comprehensive planning assistance grant. This group worked closely with the former Program Management Team in developing priorities among the eighty-one applicants for local revenue-sharing money. As the broader Management Team evolved and assumed increasing control over the budget process, PMS did the staff work for citizen representatives and department directors reviewing the 1973 budget, conducted the citizen surveys of 1974 and 1975, and, over the last year, helped departments frame management objectives.

The future placement and uses of the core staff developed around the PMS is uncertain. There was fairly broad consensus that, when HUD funding ran out, the city would pick up the tab for some five to seven people hired under project money. But there was debate about the appropriate mixture of budget preparation, accounting review, and evaluation that the emerging unit should perform. The PMS staff themselves wished to avoid the departmental resistance that might ensue from combined budgetary and analytic responsibilities.

Job Talk—and the Rank and File

Tacoma was one of four jurisdictions in the United States selected to participate in a comprehensive employee attitude survey administered by National Training and Development Service (NTDS) under Department of Commerce EDA funding.

Called locally "Job Talk," the project was conducted between October 1973, when NTDS approached the city, and July 1975, when the Research Team of city employees formed for the Job Talk project was formally disbanded after final meetings with the Management Team to review findings and frame responses.

The Job Talk Research Team consisted of twenty-two employees from both General Government and Public Utilities, ranging from (then) Assistant City Manager Erling Mork and the City Treasurer to secretaries. Sixty percent of the city's 2600 employees accepted questionnaires and 1140 returned completed questionnaires. The Team interviewed 311 city employees, edited two reports on the interviews and the larger printed questionnaire, and reported to the Management Team with recommendations.

The Job Talk project directly involved more workers than any other innovation. It was initiated by NTDS rather than by the city; the Management Team made the decision to participate. Since the work involved locally would be considerable, Assistant City Manager Mork and Manpower Planning Director Glenn discussed the project with each department director detailing the timing and extent of participation of each employee contributing to the Research Team. Pains were taken to assure confidentiality to the point where Chief Reiser met Research Team objections in getting a printout covering Fire personnel. Later, the researchers, in reporting to the Management Team, had an unprecedented audience including the entire nonelective leadership of the city.

Tacoma's efforts to involve rank-and-file employees and to solicit their views has also been accompanied—at least in some instances—by a willingness to modify new procedures to accommodate the employee problems. In Municipal Court the original procedure for computing the ticketing rates of officers in order to assign future court time had to be simplified at the loss of some of the model's theoretical effectiveness, in response to clerks' complaints about the work. And in Transit, some variations from efficient rerouting have been made for purely humane reasons over the years, for example, to let a particular driver stay on a run that had become a center of his social life due to years-long relationships with passengers.

Cecil Bell believes that the changes in management style have penetrated deep in the city by improving the ability of top managers to hear and respond to dissatisfaction. He stresses the long range significance of Job Talk and the fact that the Management Team's responses, although general, included acknowledgement that vertical communication has sometimes been poor.

Some specific changes can be cited as well, whether directly related to Job Talk or not: for example, Transportation Director Walsh's new concern for internal memos so that changes do not hit the newspapers before all employees know of them, and the new staff meetings in the Fire Department. The Police Department's team patrol system was enthusiastically described in 1973 as effecting a "remarkable . . . positive change in attitude" among personnel involved and reversing a pattern of transfers out of the patrol division—but there is today less inclination to see significant long-term impacts on police attitudes.

The effect of all this on rank-and-file workers is uncertain. Workers have generally gone along with the innovation program. Although rank-and-file workers were skeptical of many new projects, there has been little resistance of note. Cynicism about mountains of reports, academics out to make a contract buck, and attention to office analysis and "gimmicks" rather than "letting us go out and do our jobs" did not go beyond the level of talk. The major exceptions to this, in Fire and Police, involved unions and will be discussed later.

Putting the Ideas into Execution

Tacoma seems not to have had serious problems in putting innovations, once developed and agreed to, into actual practice. There was, however, a high attrition rate of ideas in the course of evaluation and development and, for the survivors, a relatively long gestation period before execution.

This reflects Singleton's care to avoid pressure and haste in developing projects, the use of group decision processes, and the effects of the continuing interaction between the Boeing team and city program directors. All these characteristics tended to force the proponents of innovation to deal, early in the process, with possible problems and with different perspectives of the prospects. One of the curiosities of Tacoma was Donaldson's combination of relatively radical ideas with a very conservative and cautious method of deciding whether to actually carry them out.

Discussions between department directors and technologists about what to avoid were careful and explicit. In the traffic court problem, Boeing's Fath was instructed to leave police options about when to testify as wide as possible, to create a system simple enough to be applied manually by clerks until computerization was possible, and (to improve court atmosphere) to minimize the number of police officers in the small courtroom at one time. The patrol-scheduling analysis performed in Police followed the same approach to the point of overspecification. Between the objectives of creating group training days and overlapping shifts more effectively and the added requirements imposed by work hours legislation and traditional preferences within the force, no significant improvement was to be had.

The slow progress of the transit innovations—pool dispatching and dynamic routing—was a reflection of a diligent analytic effort that has uncovered a number of significant problems to implementation.

As previously remarked, the Fire and Public Works Departments have become deeply involved in equipment evaluation and the development of future-oriented performance specifications. In effect, these are attempts to share the risk of innovation with manufacturers.

Pilot projects were also used. When the Public Works Department decided to change from three-to two-person refuse crews, implementation started with a handful of crews before being extended citywide. Similarly, in Fire, use of 5-inch hose and special couplings were phased in company by company. The one company experiment with 2-inch hose for pumper-to-nozzle use was *not* extended due to poor results.

Projects involving several departments encountered some special problems. Generally, one department had to take a lead role and commit itself to carry through before anything happened. This was particularly true in the development of geobase data files, where a multidepartment team met indecisively for months before the Planning Department and county assessor's office got together on their own to begin work. But the network exists now for rapid extension of the project, which appears likely due to new funding and special interest from the Technology Transfer Center.

The Bottom Line

There can be no argument that there has been a drastic change in the government of the City of Tacoma. Its functions now under a new and vastly different modus operandi. Its staff is devoting an incomparably greater amount of time to problems of change, innovation, and improvement. The city is engaged in many projects that four years ago it would have regarded as beyond its competence and its legitimate concerns. Yet, calculating the bottom line—the accounting of what the effort has accomplished for Tacoma—is not easy. The diversity and complexity of the effort, the combination of the tangible with the intangible, and the heavy emphasis on process and attitude rather than final output preclude the simple and rigid discipline of cost and benefit.

Donaldson made "technology transfer" the name of the game. The detached observer might well wonder whether the game was really "technology transfer" and whether Donaldson, himself, believed it was "technology transfer." Whatever the case, technology is an important aspect of the program and the area for which Donaldson sought and obtained funds and technical assistance.

Prominent among the successful projects were the following:

Five inch hose and quick connect couplings in the Fire Department that, along with analysis using a siting model, allowed reduction of at least eleven fire fighters from attack companies as well as better utilization of the work force.

A municipal court traffic case scheduling project that substantially reduced the police time required for testimony.[2]

A shredder and compactor that will extend the life of the City's landfill.

Some other projects are complete but produce effects that are difficult to evaluate: A cooperative City-Pierce County police dispatch system is operating and producing detailed analytic information on type, location, and time of calls, as well as processing calls faster. But these benefits are hard to monetize for comparison with development cost. Also, some testing and evaluation projects—for example, those regarding fire suppressant fogs and a change in police scheduling—resulted in confirmation of present practice. But how much is the added certainty worth?

Projects in a third group are apparently near the end of development and seem destined for successful implementation in the near future. Two examples from this group include: resource recovery in solid waste, starting with fuel uses of separated trash and moving soon to ferrous metal recovery; and pool dispatching of busses that has proceeded to the preparation of schedules. Significant problems became apparent, and a refinement of the approach will be necessary, however.

These "nearly done" projects require a word of caution, though. Long delays can flow from overlooked operating details (e.g., the large turn radius of a bus, limiting routes) or from a wait for production and delivery of completed prototypes (e.g., for fire fighters' breathing systems.)

Also "completed" in a sense are those projects that have been abandoned for one reason or another with no prospect of early resurrection: for example, a cash management system to minimize the sum of non-interest-bearing reserves maintained by the Finance Department met with little interest. Also, automated collection of bus maintenance and ridership data was dropped when costs were computed; regardless of whether the project would be a good theoretical investment, the turnaround time was too long and absolute cash required too high. The mask and tank adapted for fire fighters from NASA aerospace research looks effective, but the City cannot wait the estimated four years until it would be commercially available. Finally, two versions of a "simple" transit bus vandal alarm were tested, but the costs proved prohibitive, and the project was, accordingly, dropped.

Within these four groups of projects on which closure has been reached or appears imminent, the score is good. The number of clear failures is small, and those projects abandoned have generally been terminated at a point of low city investment.

Evaluation of two additional classes of projects clearly must wait. A large number are in mid-development stages; they have undergone substantial work and significant progress is being made toward implementation:

1. Dynamic routing of buses during night hours when demand is small has been modeled, revised, and operationally tested using simulated call-ins of riders desiring service. Based on the test held in August 1975, it is clear that further work is needed before the investment in equipment (computer terminals, disc files of address locations and "navigable" streets) and personnel (an added night dispatcher) can be justified as a good bet.

2. Automatic hydrant valve: under development since 1972, two prototypes exist on this project, but they are useless to the city until commercially manufactured.

3. Geographic-base data file development, with the potential of automatic mapping and correlations of many data by geographic location, has begun in the Planning Department, where certain Assessor's records are being translated into an appropriate form for input to a computer file. However, the remaining work for conversion of major city records to this form amounts to between ten and twenty person-years.

Finally, many projects are in early stages of development. Not all are new, but for a variety of reasons including complexity and funding difficulties as well as recent concept, all are far from operational use. For instance, a multiuse high-performance harbor service vessel can be designed and built, it is thought, for less than half the cost of replacing the city's old fire boat with its modern single-purpose equivalent. But the project is now just entering its detailed structural design phase, amidst protracted negotiations over further federal funding. It appears that there are two years and many local dollars to go before a new city-owned boat reaches water. In another case, Fire Chief Reiser and others in the City became interested, in 1974, in the concept of allocating fire costs, actual or anticipated, directly to buildings in the form of individually assessed charges. Helped by a visiting economist and a $30,000 NSF grant, a proposed approach has been developed. The proposal obviously faces many political obstacles as well as conceptual problems.

It has been generalized sometimes that software and operations models are faster to implement than new hardware. The record from Tacoma, however, indicates that overestimates of benefit are also more likely for models and software. The police-scheduling assessment, dynamic routing project, and even the successful court-scheduling system all ended up with savings less than early predictions. This was not necessarily due to shortcomings in the analysis. The Police Department decided against the maximum possible reduction in police overtime on the basis of the argument advanced by some officers that some police would respond by increased moonlighting.

The overall results of the technology projects to date are clearly less than world shaking. Moreover, some of them, such as traffic court scheduling, are new only to Tacoma, similar projects having been undertaken in a number of other jurisdictions. Yet, the truly innovative projects—the harbor service craft, the automatic hydrant valve, the 5-inch hose and quick connect-release couplings—are remarkable undertakings for a city of Tacoma's size. For the departments of a municipal government to achieve a sense of their own competence and problem-solving ability sufficient to challenge the expertise of the manufacturers must be almost unique in city government.

While the overall effort was headlined "technology," Donaldson's broader objective seems to have been the creation of a milieu more conducive to innovation and change. This objective was served both by the technology transfer program and by the organization development and improvement efforts. By any measure, Tacoma's progress in this area was substantial.

Claims of an impressive change in atmosphere in the city are supported by the consistent testimony of many people, including outside observers and city officials initially suspicious of teams, technology, and workshops. Department directors who knew few of their counterparts well five years ago now interact regularly at workshops and are much more conversant with the operations of other departments. Allocation decisions formerly made by the city manager as arbitrator are now resolved successfully by teams. There is more delegation of authority by department directors and greater willingness to work with expert outsiders.

Note, however, that the progress was heavily concentrated in a few departments. Reportedly, Donaldson's ideas received the most enthusiastic early response from the heads of Fire, Public Works, Transit and Court Administration. Gilbert Schuster, then director of Public Works, had a long record of operations improvement and has been described as a "perfect manager." The Fire Chief and the Transit director were attuned to new approaches and ready to take risks to achieve them. Courtland Fawver, the court administrator, was comfortable with the idea and practice of computerized approaches to court administration. To all these administrators, the Donaldson regime offered immense advantages by improving the climate for change and reducing its risks, by providing new resources, by easing the bureaucratic obstacles, and by the enthusiastic support of the city manager's office.

Donaldson referred to change as a bandwagon that would leave behind anyone who chose to stay off. Those who did not jump on the initial bandwagon began, in fact, to see the early starters as a special in-group and a potential clique. Whatever their willingness to consider innovations in their own department, the outsiders were not willing to be excluded from such a group. They were, as a result, exposed to the plans and experience in innovation in the pathfinding departments. But the listing of the city's numerous technological projects suggests that the impact was marginal; the skeptics and standpatters were inched along, some more than others, but they did not become innovators.

Donaldson was more successful in making the government system more malleable and in reducing some of its internal stresses and constraints. In doing this, the unleashing of the Management Team on budget and personnel was a brilliant and apparently successful effort. It removed the manager from the thankless job of playing Doctor No, forced his department directors to confront the constraints of the budget first hand, put the budget decision making in a forum that was almost certain to deal tenderly with the projects in which the manager was interested and, lastly, took over for the manager in adapting one of the more conservatively managed and administered functions to his needs. The Management Team experience cannot but have educated its members to the problems at the city manager's level and to the needs and problems of other departments. It also substituted a sense of participation for that "bossed around" feeling. Perhaps most important, the new environment lowered the hurdles to be surmounted by the innovative administrator.

Without a host of new high-level recruits, the Tacoma program depended on the ability to develop talent within the government, in Donaldson's happy phrase, "to grow people." The more venturesome administrators have had a first-class education in the opportunities for innovation as well as the trials and tribulations of the innovatory process. In addition, however, the immense increase in demands on the time of department directors for both new projects and participatory management inevitably gave their subordinates increased responsibilities as well as increased exposure to citywide management problems. The middle-management internship in the city managers office gave the most promising of these subordinates direct experience with Donaldson; two of the interns have since become department directors, and others have advanced to second in command.

One example will illustrate. When Boeing first began work with the Transit Department, the present department head, C.R. Walsh, was a divisional director. Although working closely with the Boeing team and the now-retired director on a major organizational and technical analysis of the department, he was pessimistic about many of the projects discussed. Over the next three years, Walsh was involved in many products of management innovation. He served as a rotating intern in the office of City Manager Donaldson, where he came in broad contact with city activities and had to learn quickly how to operate the small municipal airport following an illness of its administrator. As Transportation director, he was drafted by his colleagues on the Management Team as one of the three department directors to sit on the Budget Review Team for the 1975 annual budget. Now Walsh retains a healthy skepticism about productivity gains from technical change but continues to be intimately involved in the development of several projects despite setbacks that he could easily use as an excuse to terminate the experiments, were he so inclined.

The impact of the Donaldson approach almost certainly produced changes in every department of the city government in one area or another. The most unambiguous success was in the Fire Department. The Fire Department has, with little question, become an innovative organization with the best record in the city on technology transfer. What is more, Chief Reiser, in the process, introduced extensive officer participation into the decision process. A different set of attitudes and the education from new experience have given the department a new capacity for continuing improvement and innovation.

Transit faces a different situation with far more difficult technical problems. It had a good top-management group at the outset, which advanced greatly on the learning curve as a result of its continuing experience with Boeing. Public Works and Police have had special unrelated management problems, but they, too, appear to be well along into new approaches. There are, of course, other new capacities in other line departments, in the infant Technology Center, and in the Program Management Staff.

There is no meaningful way to place a value on the changes. It is important to recognize, however, that the changes are real, and they represent an increase in the capacity of the city government. The city government and its departments today offer fewer impediments to the flow of new ideas and provide a far greater ability to evaluate those ideas and, where appropriate, apply them. They are infinitely more alert to the problems of management and more open to subordinates and citizens.

There were no scorecards in Tacoma identifying dollar savings from innovations and improvements, but a few significant savings were realized. The reduction in crew size on refuse collection trucks saved approximately $99,000 in its first year and somewhat more thereafter. The shift, in the Fire Department, from a fifty-hour to a forty-eight-hour week without additional personnel required the department to manage with 4 percent fewer men on duty at any time. Further changes in company manning represented a saving of nine positions—the equivalent to $115,380 per year—all of which was applied to the creation of new rescue units.

The Unions

Tacoma has generally been a strong union city for many years. Labor is an important influence in local elections. About 60 percent of the city's own workers are unionized, represented by thirteen unions. No one union represents more than 11 percent of the total work force.

Unions have been prominently involved in the fate of productivity programs in three departments. The characteristics of these three union-management relationships are different, ranging from outstanding cooperation to strong traditionalism.

In the Fire Department, Chief Reiser already was considering ways to flexibly redeploy, reduce, and better utilize the work force when Donaldson and Totem One came along. Consequently, one of the early projects with Boeing involved use of the New York City Rand Institute fire station siting model to assess the change in response time likely from closing one station and converting another company from a conventional fixed district to "roving" duty over a broad sector of the city. The likely impact was found to be slight. At about the same time, the first 5-inch hoses were being introduced in selected companies to speed the line-laying preliminaries to fire attack.

These projects, and the department's productivity program generally, entered into the 1973 contract negotiations with Tacoma Fire Fighters, Local 31. Donaldson had announced his conviction that there was enough mileage to be gotten from innovations to keep everyone happy; he would support straight inflationary raises, and beyond that he would be glad to partition productivity gains—the fire fighters getting the equivalent of any dollar cost savings and the public getting more effective service. It is likely that a reduction in weekly hours from fifty to forty-eight would have been a major bargaining demand in any case, but, as it happened, the issue was raised in the context of productivity. In effect, the union traded cooperation with productivity measures for the two hours. What is most surprising is that union representatives themselves brought up the issue of reducing overall field-manning levels as part of the trade. Reiser considered manning such a volatile issue that he had not intended to broach it.

The bargaining position taken by its representatives caused a major crisis within the fire union. Some members felt, and still feel, that too large a concession was made; they believe that tying a reduction in the work week or an improvement in fringes to productivity savings was a poor precedent for the future when ways to cut costs would get harder and harder to find. But John Willis, the union's business representative for twenty years and chief engineer of the agreement, prevailed on the basis of the trust he commanded.

The 1973 contract was signed with a memorandum of understanding calling for continuing technical review of cost-saving projects, with savings to be reserved for hours reduction and fringes. (See Exhibit 9-6.) And in its wake came changes—reduction of eleven engine companies from four to three workers and the closing of one company and redeployment of another—which would be major in any fire department. What is more, the union has actively cooperated in a number of projects since that time, including equipment tests, recruitment and special training of minority fire fighters to meet Affirmative Action targets, the design and construction of rescue rigs, the displays for Fire Prevention Week, and the initiation of the hospital burn center.

The fire fighters union is widely regarded as cooperating actively in Tacoma's innovations. Changes of comparable impact have occurred in Public Works, however, without cooperation from Teamsters' Local 313, which represents refuse drivers and assistants. After conducting a thorough route analysis, the Department's Refuse Utility Division made plans to equalize route loads and at the same time reduce crew size from three to two. Negotiations with the Teamsters over incentives and pay to the crews or companies involved in the change began during the summer of 1974 but bogged down. So the Department decided to make the move first and then to negotiate incentive payments.

In preparation for this, the Division filled positions temporarily wherever possible for several months. Then, in March 1975, the change was made experimentally in five crews, using volunteers. The union was notified but had no strong reactions. Based on a smooth experience in this pilot, the change was made citywide on April 21st. The union was told that any wage settlement agreed to through continued bargaining would be retroactive to then. After going to mediation, the contract has now been approved by the City Council.

The department where union and worker resistance to change has been strongest is Police. In December of 1974 Tacoma Police Union Local 224 passed a vote of no-confidence in Chief Lyle Smith. Many issues were mentioned in the list of grievances, but there were two major ones. The first was a stand Chief Smith took on holidays. In an effort to create enough slack so that his resched-

Exhibit 9-6
Productivity Language from Labor Contracts in Tacoma

1. From 1975 Addendum to Master Agreement with Automotive and Special Services Union Local #461 (new language)

ARTICLE XIII–PRODUCTIVITY

During the life of this Agreement, the Union may call to the attention of the Labor Relations Director a significant increase in productivity by an employee or employees under this Agreement. Meetings by a committee appointed by the Labor Relations Director shall be held for the purpose of analyzing and determining the effect of such increased productivity and to report their findings. The committee's report, together with the recommendations of the Labor Relations Director, shall then be forwarded to the City Manager and the Director of Utilities, with a copy to the Union, for their consideration.

2. From 1975 Addendum to Master Agreement with Tacoma Firefighters Union Local #31 (language unchanged since 1973)

MEMORANDUM OF INTENT AND UNDERSTANDING
W I T N E S S E T H:

WHEREAS, it appears that the costs of providing adequate fire protection in the City of Tacoma increases substantially each year, and

WHEREAS, substantially all employees of the Fire Fighting Department of the City of Tacoma had a duty week which is ten hours in excess of the work week of all other employees, and

WHEREAS, both parties hereto agree it would be mutually advantageous to decrease, if economically feasible, the hours of duty of members of the fire service if such hours can be reduced without prejudicing or impairing existing fire protection in the City of Tacoma, and

WHEREAS, it appears that the most practical way to accomplish said end is to conduct one or more surveys or reviews of existing procedures and methods in order to ascertain the most efficient mode of operating the Fire Department consistent with its existent standards of protection;

NOW, THEREFORE, the parties hereto do hereby jointly declare their intent to accomplish said result, and do agree generally as follows:

That both parties recognize and agree that this memorandum of intent and understanding outlines in very general and basic terms the desired results and hoped for accomplishments of a review study and survey program, and that the implementing of any such program will of necessity be subject to further study, review and where appropriate, additional agreement. That both parties agree to cooperate to the fullest extent, one with the other, to establish and maintain a technical survey or review procedure of existing fire fighting methods and modes of operation of the Tacoma Fire Department expressly for the purpose of determining whether or not modifications and changes thereof will result in increased efficiencies and economies in the operation of the Fire Department.

That such technical survey and review shall be more or less continuous in nature and be conducted jointly by the City and Fire Fighters Local #31;

It is understood and agreed that the aim or purpose of any such technical survey or surveys is to maintain or increase the efficiency of the fire fighting department in performing fire protection services which will result in the diminution of the costs of the operation of the Fire Department to the City of Tacoma without a resulting loss in fire fighting coverage and efficiency.

It is further understood and agreed that, in the event any changes are recommended as a result of such study and survey which may be adopted or implemented by the Fire Chief and other administrative officials of the City of Tacoma and there exists a savings as a result of the adoption of said change, then such savings shall be used for the purpose of shortening the duty week or other fringe benefits. "Savings", as used in this

Exhibit 9–6 Continued

paragraph, shall mean that the costs of reducing said duty week together with the costs of administering the changes made, shall not exceed existing budgetary appropriations for the operation and maintenance of the fire service.

It is understood and agreed that the parties hereto shall hereafter adopt detailed rules and regulations for the implementing of any such changes and a procedure for the evaluation of recommendations made as a result of said survey; PROVIDED: That nothing herein contained or hereafter adopted shall in any manner diminish or impinge upon the lawful right of the administrative officials of the City of Tacoma to administer, operate, and maintain the fire service, it being understood and agreed that the duty of such supervisory officials is constant and continuing and entails, among other things, a duty and obligation to improve fire service operations within the City of Tacoma.

It is understood and agreed that both parties hereto will in a reasonable manner, attempt to implement any changes arising out of the recommendations of said technical surveys.

It is further agreed by both parties hereto that the execution of this memorandum of intent and understanding shall not constitute a waiver of either party, or any person or employee represented thereby, of any right or privilege existing under and by virtue of the ordinances of the City of Tacoma, and particularly those ordinances relating to personnel policies and pay and compensation, and any changes made or implemented as a result of said survey shall be binding and effective only after adoption in accordance with the laws of the State of Washington and the ordinances and regulations of the City of Tacoma.

It is agreed that this memorandum of intent and understanding may be cancelled at any time by either party hereto upon the giving of written notification of its intent to terminate said agreement at least fifteen (15) days prior to the date of the proposed termination.

It is further agreed that no right, privilege, obligation, or duty of a specific or precise nature shall arise or exist because of the execution of this Agreement, but that the same shall arise and exist only after subsequent and additional agreements and understandings have been executed by and between the parties hereto.

---

uling efforts could provide training days together for patrol teams and also cover high-crime evening hours densely, Smith ordered an end to the traditional compensatory days off for holidays worked. By paying time-and-a-half instead, the department would have fewer erratic leave days to interfere with the tight schedule. But this also would reduce the actual number of days off for members of the force, who often had used the accumulated days to extend vacations.

The other large issue in the no-confidence vote was based on reorganization in 1972 of the Department's detectives, who previously had kept regular daytime hours, into a more flexible squad of investigators who could be assigned rotating shifts to allow immediate work on more crimes. Disputes about rank and pay fueled a protest that also included the status of the previously more elite unit. The immediate furor blew over, but it showed a strong resistance to change in the department. It also prompted the Chief to initiate the organization development effort discussed earlier.

Despite its considerable use of teams, the flavor of Tacoma's Police force, like others, is set by the individual responsibility and prerogatives of officers.

From this independence has flowed resistance to new reporting procedures to make investigators accountable by case for their time, objections to the phase-out of Traffic Division motorcycles (which are unusable most of the time in Tacoma's wet climate), and even complaints that the new personal radios that replaced car radios in 1975 are an infringement on privacy.

More generally, Tacoma's labor policy is leaning toward productivity bargaining. In addition to the TFU contract already mentioned, the 1975 contract with Automotive and Special Services Union Local 461—a Teamsters affiliate representing a wide range of crafts, technical, and clerical workers—contains a general productivity clause. Within its provisions the union can call attention to significant increases in productivity, which are then analyzed by a fact-finding committee as a basis for optional further discussions. (See Exhibit 9-6.) Labor Relations Director Hugh Judd prefers the explicit form of the TFU clause. He does not share the concern of some labor negotiators that a general management prerogative approach to productivity changes is best. And considering the quality of cooperation from the Tacoma Fire Fighters, he has some basis for his judgment.

An Overview

Among the many efforts to improve performance and productivity in American cities during the last decade, the experience of Tacoma is unique. Programs in other cities have developed, often with imaginative local applications, from a general concept of good management practice based on a critical, cost-conscious, and analytic perspective of city operations. This concept plays a limited and secondary role in Tacoma.

Instead, Tacoma followed the very different ideas of Bill Donaldson. There was no effort to introduce comprehensive work measurement or citywide program or management analysis. Indeed, there was no build-up of a strong central analytic staff, a characteristic of nearly every other city program. The reason was that Donaldson wasn't much interested in doing any of those things. He was aided by the fact that Tacoma was already reasonably well managed and without major budget-financing problems.

Donaldson's Tacoma had none of the strong sense of purpose, common in other improving cities. There was no great push to effect productivity savings. The technology projects sometimes had a potential for budgetary savings—and sometimes they did not. Where there was a potential for reducing work force, it was rarely emphasized. In fact, the productivity gains—whether realized in budget savings or better performance—over four years were rather modest and confined largely to the Fire Department and refuse collection.

All the things that Donaldson didn't do would have impeded his basic objective. He wanted to induce, not force, the departments to take a more open view, to think out their problems rather than follow some traditional standard operating procedure. Tighter, more critical, more demanding central management might have produced some earlier gains but intensifying the usual adversary relationship between the manager's office and the departments would have killed the effort to change departmental thinking. The Donaldson strategy worked remarkably well with, of course, marked variations among departments.

The effort to induce new thinking in the city departments goes to the heart of the problem of management in American cities. Municipal departmental administration is typically oriented toward established professional standards of operation rather than managerial standards of performance. Departments are often ingrown and insular, distrustful of change and especially of outsiders. They resist, usually successfully, the intermittent efforts by mayors and managers to force basic changes on them. Periods of innovation tend to come in brief and infrequent flurries when happenstance brings an innovative administrator to the head of the department. Tacoma's rare effort based on the power of education and example may well be the only way in which a sustained change in departmental management can be introduced.

Tacoma has successfully entered a new style of city management, based on technical innovation and much improved communication among top administrators. Bill Donaldson, who supplied the central stimulus for that new style, has left to become manager of Cincinnati. Now, under Erling Mork, the city has a new and different style of leadership.

Donaldson was a charismatic and strongly innovative outsider. Mork is a popular and seasoned Tacoma native, less flamboyant but also less likely to move on elsewhere in a few years. Even in the middle of the uproar of 1969, he was able to maintain respect and working ties with all factions.

The change in managers seems to involve no slackening of interest in organization improvement; indeed, Mork was heavily involved in the Job Talk project and has taken initiative in starting training sessions with his own staff. With technical projects, he may be somewhat more critical of the terms of outside funding. Donaldson tended to accept any available money and match it with city staff time on the assumption that something interesting could be done with it, while his successor is perhaps slower to commit city time. Mork does not expect Tacoma to be the perpetual demonstration city that Donaldson envisioned.

Another crucial individual has been Harvey Singleton, whose style of technology transfer and taste for organization development set the tone for much of Tacoma's productivity program. His personal, unrushed style is giving way, on the level of central coordination, to the brisker style of Technology Center Director Regina Glenn, whose skills are more administrative and contacts more political than Singleton's. But beyond the shift of personalities, the form of transfer is changing to a city-funded institution, the Center, which seeks to establish formalized linkages to support the research and development contracts of the future. There is a key difference in purpose and organization. Totem One was designed for the funding and management of the *initiation* of a technology applications program; the Center is intended to be a means of a *continuing* effort built into the structure of the city government.

The city's portfolio of technical projects includes some that will involve moderate to substantial local investment for implementation. A key example is the multiuse harbor service vessel now entering its hull design phase. Capital cost for a fully designed craft would be an excellent deal for Tacoma, compared to cost of a standard fireboat to replace the city's old one. But development costs narrow the margin of benefit from innovation, and federal funding sources seem firm on demands for substantial hard local match. Ultimately, this pressure to assimilate much research and development expense into a capital investment framework will be of major impact to the future of hardware projects. Any reduction in special subsidies for development of prototypes increases the risk of local involvement.

The experience of department staffs in sizing up development opportunities may be growing enough to absorb such setbacks. Research and development activities are already well-integrated with long range purchase plans in the Fire and Public Works Departments, and both exert pressure through professional associations and directly on manufacturers to improve the state of the art expressed in production models of garbage trucks, street sweepers, hydrants, fire-fighting nozzles, and the like.

The survival of newly acquired sophistication in research and development clearly will depend on future leadership in departments as well as the city manager's office. The directors of a number of departments including Fire, Transit, and Police are all one-to-five years from retirement.

The city's organization improvement program seems well implanted. In addition to Mork's support, it profits from a new Training and Development director, Dwight Faust, who is beginning to share workshop leadership with the outside consultants and can be expected to take on more of the work as Drs. Bell and Rosenzweig taper off their relationship, which they never intended to be permanent. It remains to be seen if an outsider's impartiality is critical to the workshops continuing as well as to date. But internalizing this function is clearly a sign of acceptance of the tools and opens more opportunities for extension of training downward to line supervisors and work crews.

Whatever the impact of training on them, it seems likely that city employees will be affected increasingly by a productivity perspective in collective bargaining. This trend is too new for union responses to be clear, but a promising beginning has been made.

Notes

1. Muldoon, J.T., *Totem One Program—A Perspective from the Boeing Technical Team*, City of Tacoma, undated.

2. Fath, A. Frederick and Fawver, Courtland D., "Scheduling Techniques for Municipal Court," American Institute of Aeronautics and Astronautics, 3rd Urban Technology Conference and Technical Display, Boston, Mass., September 25–28, 1973, AIAA Paper No. 73–980.

3. Donaldson, William V. and Esquivel, Severo, "Participatory Management–Employees Are Creative," Labor-Management Relations Service, U.S. Conference of Mayors/National League of Cities, June 1973, p. 8.

10 The Unions

The extent and the power of employee unions vary widely among the eight local governments surveyed in the foregoing chapters. The union problems of, say, Dallas are of a different order of magnitude than those faced by New York. Yet, the threat—actual or potential—to productivity improvement programs posed by union power is a concern common to all eight jurisdictions.

One does not need to search far for the reasons. The more dramatic union problems in our largest cities are the stuff of national news, and city officials all over the country are, as a result, at least generally aware of the experience with unions in New York and San Francisco. At the same time, it is almost universally assumed that the advance of unionization in local government is inevitable and irreversible and that eventually even Dallas and Phoenix will have to contend with strong and aggressive employee unions. Yet, this forecast of the future begins with an overstatement of the status of unionization today. The highly publicized union-government conflicts have, in fact, occurred in a handful of cities, and, overall, local government unionization is still barely beyond its infancy.

The police, fire fighters, and school teachers have long been organized in most of the larger metropolitan areas. However, the right to bargain collectively has only gradually been extended to public employees, and not until the 1960s did the unions become a major power in the determination of public employee salaries, benefits and working conditions.

Even now, public employees in smaller cities are often unorganized or still in ineffective unions. Even in many of the larger cities, the role of the unions is still limited. Frequently, negotiations do not cover questions of fringe benefits or workload or productivity. New York and Detroit may be indicators of organized labor's future in American local government, but they are far from representative of the situation as it prevails today in most American cities.

The situation is changing rapidly. State laws, in the local decade, have authorized collective bargaining for hundreds of additional government units. Federal collective bargaining legislation for state and local government has been proposed. In the meantime, union gains in wages and salaries and fringe benefits have made an impressive case for unionization for public employees everywhere.

215

Unionization is spreading and, what may be more important, serious unionization is spreading.

Even in those governmental units still without unions or without collective bargaining, the union issue may have a powerful impact on unilateral government determinations. The government management that sees unionization near its door step is likely to make concessions that it believes will reduce the incentive for unionization. Moreover, the salary gains achieved in some jurisdictions have provided a standard that tends to have its impact on many other jurisdictions.

While spreading unionization appears to have had significant effects on municipal salaries, workload and productivity issues have been relatively uncommon in collective bargaining in local government. Even in the leading case of New York City, workload and manning provisions in collective bargaining contracts do not, except for the contract with the United Federation of Teachers, appear until 1965. Even where the unions have had workload concerns, the impact on productivity seems, in most cases, to have been slight. In Milwaukee, for example, there is only one case of a productivity improvement actually stopped by union action, and that was done by judicial determination. Nassau County's effort received the unwavering support of the major employee union right up to the demise of the program in the Board of Supervisors. Only in New York and Detroit, among the eight jurisdictions studied, have productivity improvements been successfully opposed by employee unions.

It is important to distinguish among productivity improvements in terms of their impact on employees. Productivity improvements require, without exception, some change in working conditions, work organization and method, or average employee workload. The change need not have adverse effects on the quality of the employee's work life; indeed, often work is less burdensome as a result of productivity changes. Increased productivity reduces the number of employees required for any given workload. This may not require a reduction in the existing work force if workload is rising, if improvements in work quality are needed, or if the existing work force had been unable to perform all assigned work. If a reduction in the work force is indicated, it may sometimes be achievable by attrition without firings.

Despite the variety of impacts, there is a presumptive union interest in any productivity change. A change that requires employees to work harder or under clearly less desirable or more hazardous conditions is the most obvious and the most legitimate source of union interest. A change that involves the termination of some employees is also clearly a matter of strong and justified union interest.

Unions have, in addition, sometimes opposed other change that have no direct adverse immediate effect on their members. Most common is the change that will permit a gradual or future reduction in staffing through attrition. This will, of course, tend to reduce future union membership and dues income—a seemingly minor matter. But it also may reduce employer dependence on that employee group and thereby reduce the power of the union. The union may see the change as an opening wedge that makes it possible for management to undertake drastic reductions in the future.

Union obstacles to other changes without significant adverse effects may be simply a matter of bargaining strategy. If the union is powerful enough to block such changes, it may be questionable practice, but it is not irrational to demand a price for the union *nihil obstat,* not because the change imposes a burden on union members but because it is worth something to the employer.

Changes that involve the addition of secondary duties that either fall within the purview of some other union or involve working "out of title" or "out of job classification" are special problems. Cases of this kind are relatively uncommon in government compared to industry, but they do exist.

There are some areas of genuine union concern that are usually ignored. In New York, the more professional employee groups, especially the teachers, have their own ideas on how the job should be done and have opposed productivity improvements that conflicted with those ideas. Actions reducing employee autonomy and increasing supervision have similarly been opposed. These relatively few cases suggest the possibility that employee resistance to management dictation of work organization and method may be an important underlying factor in a broader range of cases of union opposition to productivity improvements.

We tend to think of unions as monolithic entities although every union embraces a wide diversity in opinion among its individual members. What a union leader is able or willing to do in collective bargaining will depend on the divisions within the union, the current temper of the union members, the challenges to leadership, and, ultimately, on who the leader is and how much weight he carries among his peers. A union leader with a tenuous majority, threatened by a more militant faction within the union, may well have serious difficulties in making any concessions on workload and productivity. Indeed, even a small minority critical of productivity concessions could easily force insecure leaders away from such a position—because the concessions would make them vulnerable to criticisms from every perspective. Some members will believe *any* workload concession to management shows the lack of adequately tough negotiation. Others will prefer the lower workload to higher pay. Lastly, there are always some who will argue that a high enough price for the productivity agreement was not exacted.

On the other hand, more usual settlements involving fairly straightforward increases in pay and benefits are easier to defend, chiefly because they do not seriously disrupt the status quo, but also because they will be regarded as within expectations if they can be seen as at least as generous as a recent settlement accorded a competitive labor group.

It seems clear that in some situations in recent years the temper of union membership was such that there was no agreement, within reason or probability, that a beleaguered union leader could sign. One of the effects of the increasing use of independent fact finding, mediation, or arbitration panels is to help take the union leader off the hook.

The behavior patterns and attitudes of unionists, their leaders, the city's representatives, and its citizens will all tend to reflect the political nature of the environment. Unions are powerful allies in politics, and any politician would prefer not to alienate friends. Nor is it surprising if unions seem tougher in negotiations with administrations to which they are politically opposed. What the citizen thinks and says of teachers or police officers or sanitation workers in the community may, in many different ways, affect the course of negotiations. Strikes in critical municipal services like the fire, police, or sanitation forces, or in school teaching can have devastating effects on citizen attitudes toward both the negotiating politicians and the workers involved.

The institutional arrangements for approval of contracts or the budgeting of funds to pay them are also important. Many school districts require school budgets and tax rates to be approved by referendum. The defeat of school budgets has become increasingly common, and the underlying issue is not infrequently the size of the salary increases provided the teachers. Required approval by a city or county council or school board may raise similar uncertainties. Clearly, these arrangements have an effect on the bargaining by both parties. Any external approval process probably tends to moderate the level of union demands and the militancy with which they are pursued. On the other hand, the requirement for membership or union delegate approval of contracts will, in any case where this is more than a formality, tend to moderate management resistance.

The size and complexity of the government and the density of the community probably also have impacts in several respects. In the rural, suburban, or small-city school district, the head of a school board can translate a union demand into tax rate effects—and all parties will understand what it means in terms of probable citizen resistance. In the large complex, multifunction city with multiple revenue sources, the effect of a union contract on city finance or what the city can afford may be obscure not only to the union representatives but also even to the city's own negotiators. A city claim that it cannot afford a proposed settlement is unlikely to cut much ice.

The climate toward unions in metropolitan communities is more likely to be favorable or, at least, tolerant; employee identification with the employing government tends to be weaker, the sense of anonymity higher, personal relationships with the management group rarer, and grievances against the employing government greater than in smaller places. All these factors contribute to a climate more conducive to strong union action. The big city, moreover, is infinitely more vulnerable to strikes, work stoppages, and job actions. For these reasons, unions tend to be more powerful and more demanding in larger metropolitan areas than in other areas. This is unlikely to change.

In larger governments, labor relations also tend to be more professionalized on both sides. Unions are more likely to have professional permanent leadership, the cities more likely to have full-time labor relations directors. The professionals on both sides tend to be united by a shared realism; their major problems increasingly tend to be in educating their principals to what they regard as the realities of the situation.

Union negotiations in the private sector are all, to varying degrees, subject to the discipline of the economy. In competitive industries, the firm must have a combination of wages, rates, and productivity that permits it to compete. Even in less competitive industries, unit production costs will affect demand and the volume of production. Union leaders and negotiators are not unaware of the situation and, for example, commonly accept as norms the wages being set in competitive firms. The public sector has no comparable discipline save the ultimate resistance of citizens to increased taxes.

There is another important difference in collective bargaining in the public sector. In private industry, job rights are determined by the collective bargaining contract. In the public sector, the employee is independently protected by a civil service system. In the usual case, he or she can be removed only on charges (aside from a general reduction-in-force). Pension rights are guaranteed. Promotion opportunities are frequently protected against outsiders by promotion exams limited to peers within the agency. The public employee has retained in the new age of collective bargaining the generous vacations that were once an attractive offset for low public sector salaries. Moreover, the civil service reformers and the employees themselves have created enough pressure on legislatures to restrict non–civil service appointments to a mere handful and to limit the use of outside contracts and other alternatives to civil service.

The tenure of management in public collective bargaining is typically brief and subject to the vagaries and uncertainties of politics. Management is consequently susceptible to agreements involving costs that may not come due until after they have left office. (Some pension benefits are of this character). The top management of a city may have less than the bare minimum of education in either city affairs or collective bargaining before they must engage seriously in deals involving millions of dollars in public money.

The mayor's game, the politician's game—is, in fact, an odd one to place atop the complexities of collective bargaining. The negotiations must be conducted with an awareness that both the union members involved and the taxpayers who will eventually pay the bill are constituents. The substance is important, but to the politician the image before the citizens is his or her only stock in trade. Depending on the circumstances and the nature of constituencies, any settlement may have to be regarded as superior to the damage a serious strike might inflict on the politician's career. Under other circumstances, a tough stance with a union may be regarded as politically advantageous, even at the risk of a strike.

The political calculus is probably biased toward conservative management strategies. To persist in a productivity-increasing demand in the face of strike threats is a risky business for a politician. Even raising the issue may mean trouble from the adverse response it may produce in the union or from the ignominy of an eventual defeat on the issue. Department heads, whether political or career, are likely to reach similar conclusions. Numerous perceived improvements may simply never be proposed "because the union would never buy it."

There are solution-oriented aspects of the process. With both sides having an external constituency to be convinced, cooperative and mutual posturing and dramatization are encouraged. Yet, the process is tough enough on the dollars and cents, the meat and potatoes of collective bargaining; the real question is the extent to which the added weight of a productivity consideration can be borne.

Yet, while the complications may make it difficult to bargain on productivity, an increase in productivity has the inherent capacity to benefit both sides. It is not a zero-sum game where one party can gain only at the expense of the other. There is, by virtue of the productivity gain, a saving to the government which can be divided between the government and labor. There are, on the other hand, serious obstacles to deal making. Either side, of course, may decide that the game is not worth the candle. There may be real uncertainties that the productivity gain can actually be realized. Perhaps, most important, established parity relationships among the salaries of different employee groups may make it very difficult to reward productivity increases in one group.

Where productivity increasing changes are negotiated, the arrangement may be of several different kinds. One is the productivity incentive contract, which provides for incremental salary or wage payments if specified productivity standards are met. A second arrangement sets workload standards on the contract as a *quid pro* quo for general increases in salary. A third arrangement leaves productivity standards and changes to management either by explicit provision or by deleting prior work standards. A fourth may establish agreement to make changes in equipment, staff location, and other elements affecting productivity.

The formal agreement (or disagreement) between a public employee union and a local government agency is only one form of relationship on productivity programs. The extent to which questions of workload or work performance are subject to collective bargaining varies among jurisdictions. Some public jurisdictions will not bargain on a matter they regard as within managerial prerogatives. Such a jurisdiction may unilaterally make changes affecting workload and productivity. Once that is done, the union, presumably, makes its own decision whether or not to challenge the action and, if so, how. It represents, if unchallenged, something of an agreement that, for the time being, the government has the authority to act unilaterally. If challenged, it may establish more explicitly the range of government action and authority.

The failure to negotiate formally may, actually, disguise informal agreement, either explicit or tacit, designed to obtain the benefits of productivity increases to both sides without the great difficulties of negotiating formal agreements.

Both formal productivity agreements and tacit or unopposed productivity changes of this kind have antecedents in workload limitations imposed either under formal contracts or longstanding employee practice. Contractual workload standards have come with collective bargaining and are, by and large, a relatively recent development. Far more important have been the work standards or conditions accepted as a matter of course over long periods of time. They have persisted at least in part because no management challenged them. They vary in significance, but some are, obviously, extremely sensitive and likely to be strongly defended by employees.

All this suggests that the impact of unionism on municipal productivity will tend to vary from one city to another, from one service or function to another, and from one situation to another. Kuhn, Horton and Lewin,[1] in fact, argue for a theory of diversity of municipal union behavior. They point out that the union situations in New York, Chicago, and Los Angeles vary now, because unionism is at different stages of development in the three cities. But they add that there is no reason to believe that the diversity will disappear when union-government relations have matured in all three cities. The argument rests fundamentally on the continuing cultural and political differences among the three cities.

Indeed, even aside from the differences among communities, there would be a diversity of results reflecting simply the differences in actors and in specific situations. Collective bargaining is, moreover, basically a two-party game for which there is no equilibrium solution. Differences in results are inevitable.

Yet, with all the observed diversity and the theoretical justifications for its existence, a review of some of the cases of bargaining or disputes between local governments and unions on productivity issues does suggest, at least tentatively, some generalizations. The cases discussed below are necessarily drawn from those situations that have drawn the attention of students of labor relations in the public sector; they are, hence, presented as illustrative rather than representative. It should be remembered, however, that our concern is only with those situations in which productivity considerations were dominant, a very small proportionof all cases of local government-union bargaining.

The Productivity Incentive Contract

The incentive or bonus contract is one of several forms of productivity bargaining. Such contracts provide for incentive or bonus or productivity payments to employees if they meet certain work performance levels. This suggests, of course, that the potential savings from a seemingly achievable increase in productivity are large enough to yield advantages sufficient to pay off the worker and still leave some real gain to local government.

The incentive contract means that there must be enshrined in a collective bargaining contract some base production level above which incentives are payable. This base will obviously become a standard for output. Incentives and premiums for productivity are likely to be measured for the indefinite future from the level set in the first contract. At its worst, it might suggest over the years the development of a pattern like that in the railroads, where a day's work was set for years at the distance in miles that represented a full-day trip in the pretwentieth century heyday of the railroads. At its best, it would eliminate hassles and save time in initiating an incentive program.

The best known contract of this character was that between the City of Detroit and Local 27 of the American Federation of State, County and Municipal Employees, Detroit's sanitation workers.[2] The move toward the incentive contract began when Detroit decided to replace its existing refuse collection trucks with new 24 cubic yard compactor trucks in the hope of reducing maintenance costs and down-time, cutting overtime (because of the reduced number of trips to the dump), and increasing loader productivity (since the larger truck would be available a higher proportion of the day for collections).

The drivers of sanitation trucks argued with the Civil Service Commission that the slightly larger truck justified a new job classification. It was an argument with limited merit but the Commission agreed. This 15-cent per hour increase for the drivers made it virtually impossible to deal with the packers on a basis solely determined by actual productivity. It took nearly half a year, two slowdowns, and the threat of a strike before the city agreed to pay a bonus of 15 cents an hour, in effect, in return for union agreement to a productivity incentive program that would encourage full utilization of the new trucks.

The city estimated the first year's savings from the new trucks at a maximum of $2.3 million. Under the agreed upon productivity plan half of the actual savings would go into the productivity pool for distribution to the workers. The amount paid to the workers would be determined by formula.

A 50 percent weight was given to a reduction in paid man-hours per ton of refuse collected. The proportion of that amount payable was the ratio to the estimated maximum reduction, the top 0.1 percent of the 1972 collections. That took a hefty cut from 3.14 man-hours to 2.48 man-hours, but it was actually exceeded in the first quarter of the new plan.

Route completion was weighted at 20 percent. None of that amount was payable unless more than 90 percent of the collections were made on time. The full amount required that all collections be made on time. Routes completed on overtime were not counted. In the first quarter only 69 percent of the routes were completed on time and, hence, no part of the bonus attributable to was payable. The 69 percent was apparently an improvement over the experience in many past quarters.

Overtime reduction was the third factor and related to 20 percent of the bonus. It was payable in the proportion by which overtime hours were reduced from the prior year. The first quarter reduction in overtime was 14.59 percent, which, when multiplied by the weight of 20 percent, allowed only 0.0291 of the total bonus amount. The last factor was quality of pickup, which covered 10 percent of the bonus but for which measures not had been developed by the department.

The total amount actually paid to the workers in the first quarter of the plan was 0.3291 of the maximum bonus. This represented about $100 per worker for the quarter or about $7.74 per week. It would have been more if the plan had been limited to packers, but it covered nearly everyone in the department.

The average incentive payment ($7.74) may be compared to the $6 a week received from the unconditional increase of 15 cents per hour necessary to secure union acceptance of the plan. The total payment of $112,873 may be also compared to overtime payments in the same quarter, which, despite the lower use, amounted to over three-fourths of a million dollars.

After a year of operation, total savings in operating costs had been $1,960,000 of which $307,440 had been paid out in worker bonuses leaving a net saving to the city of $1,654,403. If the plan had been in operation from the first of the year, savings to the city would have been about $2.2 million before allowance for the costs of the new trucks or the administrative costs of the productivity bonus. The city benefited not only from significant dollar savings but also from a marked decline in public complaints about sanitation service.

City officials were, however, disappointed at the failure of the plan to achieve the standards set for it. Overtime hours dropped by the last quarter of 1973 to about half the historic rate, and paid man-hours per ton collected were significantly less than in the prior year. Route completions, however, failed to reach the 90 percent standard, and the quality index was never applied.

The average worker collected $265 in bonuses from the first three quarters the plan was in operation, about $350 on an annual basis but lost about twice that amount in overtime. In addition both AFSCME and the Teamsters began to raise many questions and doubts about the appropriateness of the formula, the employees eligible for distribution, and the city's responsibility for providing an adequate number of trucks and efficient facilities.

Donald Wasserman, of AFSCME's National staff, commented in November 1974 that

... the Detroit Sanitation Agreement ... no one can understand except the consultant who devised the program. The union does not understand it, and management does not understand it ... both parties must live with the damned thing and they really do not understand its implications. Originally, the Detroit sanitationmen thought they would get more money.... And they did get more money. On the other hand, ... there are a couple hundred fewer sanitationmen, and those still on the job feel they are working too hard. Additionally, they lost much of the overtime they previously earned. As a result, some workers are taking home less money.

... our guys do not know how much trash they pick up and have to take the city's figures on faith. You can say that is sloppy bargaining because of the lack of monitoring.[3]

The productivity incentive provisions were dropped in 1975, failing to survive a full two years of experience.

Flint, Michigan introduced a similar incentive payment scheme for its much smaller waste collection operation under similar circumstances during the same year.[4] Flint's waste collectors began a slowdown in the summer of 1973 after the Civil Service Commission rejected a reclassification proposal worth $250 per man per year, and the City turned down a request for an increase of 10 cents an hour. The city reopened negotiations and introduced the productivity issue. The Flint scheme was aimed primarily at the reduction in overtime. The formula provided for the payment to the workers of half the funds saved through higher productivity. The maximum payment was made only if (1) overtime had been reduced by at least one-fourth, (2) valid complaints were no more than 5 percent of the number of stops, and (3) seventeen of the twenty daily routes were completed without overtime. The amount was reduced if complaints were greater and/or if average routes completed were fewer. The union accepted the plan and dropped its demand for 10 cents an hour.

The program was successful with a net saving in personnel costs of almost $17,000. Overtime was down 44 percent, and a bonus was paid for the year of $261 per employee, more than the increase initially sought by the employees but less than overtime lost. Any crew also had the advantage under the scheme of being able to go home after six hours if its route was complete and, if assigned then to another route, receiving overtime after six hours rather than after eight. Workers were not eligible for overtime to complete their *own* routes until after eight hours.

Flint also reported that nonlabor costs increased more than enough to offset the savings in direct labor and that its waste collection division consequently showed a net drop in productivity overall during the plan's first year. This reflected the higher costs of the new trucks.

A vote taken in mid-July 1974, by the shop steward was 25 to 15 in favor of continuing the incentive plan, with about twenty employees not voting. Those dissatisfied were apparently concerned with the loss of overtime. The six-hour day seems to have been the clincher. The average employee gained $261 in incentive pay, lost nearly $500 in overtime, and gained two hours a day plus about sixty hours from reduced overtime. The union and the city negotiated for an extension of the plan for 1975.

The Flint program has been twice extended and modified—in mid-1974 and mid-1975—since the initial agreement. Changes were made to permit employees completing their routes to leave after five hours instead of six. In addition, the bonus was reduced pro rata for each employee to reflect time missed due to unexcused absence or lateness. The bonus pool was increased by $200 for each job reduction in waste collection.

The union's involvement in determining work rules and work organization has gradually increased. A management decision to unilaterally reduce the number of waste collection routes in 1975 resulted in a one-day walkout and an arbitrator's decision to require the City to negotiate over the number of routes and procedures for counting collection stops. Work rules are now incorporated into the labor contract, and a union-management committee has set out a precise procedure for counting collection stops. The union is increasingly interested in measuring total savings—direct and indirect—and in claiming its share of them.

The city achieved further important gains after the first year. Controllable overtime was virtually eliminated. Division staffing dropped from 64.5 in fiscal 1973 to 60 in fiscal 1974. As a result, both savings to the City and bonuses paid increased. In 1975, the bonus was $458 per worker before reductions for unexcused absences.

The evaluation team from the Urban Institute and the Labor Management Relations Service found employee satisfaction mixed. One point, however, is crystal clear. The task system permitting the workers to reduce the working day by as much as three hours is at least as important as the cash bonuses, particularly since the latter are well below the prior level of overtime payments.

The basic elements of performance in refuse collection are, in the main, subject to worker control. If sanitationmen work harder and faster, they will collect the garbage more rapidly or with smaller crews. Not so for police where the impact of standard police patrol or investigation on levels of crime or law enforcement is uncertain.

Despite the difficulties, the City of Orange, California introduced an incentive payment plan for its police force in 1973.[5] This came in response to a pay increase request from the Orange Police Association justified as a reward for the low crime rate in Orange compared to nearby communities.

Incentive payments were made if reported crimes of a repressible nature (rape, robbery, burglary, and auto theft) were reduced. A 3 percent reduction in crime over the first seven months of the program would have produced a 1 percent salary increase and a cumulative reduction of 8 percent by nineteen months was worth another 1 percent pay increase. The maximum increase of 2 percent at seven months and 3 percent more a year later needed a 6 percent crime cut in seven months and a cumulative 12 percent reduction by the nineteenth month.

Over the program's twenty months, the monthly rate for the four crimes covered by the program dropped 5.6 percent. Crimes where the suspect was apprehended at or near the scene of the crime were, however, not included in the totals subject to incentive payments. With such crimes deleted, the decline in the specified crime rate was 12.5 percent. The police earned the full bonus of 5 percent over the contract period.

The crime reduction achieved came largely from fewer burglaries, although auto theft was cut in the first phase and rape in the second phase of the contract period. Part I crimes in total actually increased but by smaller proportions than in nearby communities. Some new personnel were added to the force over the period, providing greater staff time to work on crime rate reduction.

The Urban Institute and the Labor Management Relations Service agree that the incentive system did contribute to a reduction in covered crime. Widely expressed doubts about the likelihood of accurate police reporting were largely dissipated by an audit of crime reports by the California Bureau of Criminal Statistics. The program did not and was not designed to reduce city expenditures, but it did produce citizen benefits in the reduced number of burglaries; the 243 burglaries "prevented" in the first phase of the program represent $73,000 in citizen savings at an average of $303 per burglary.

The incentive program applied to all personnel, sworn and unsworn, in the Orange Police Department excluding only the Chief and the two captains. The department appointed a crime prevention officer (trained at the National Crime Prevention Institute) and a new five-member Special Enforcement Team at the beginning of the incentive program. A third effort was a Crime Prevention Advisory Committee, a group of eleven officers from various units in the department, who met monthly with the chief to discuss ways to reduce the crime rate. All three seem to have given the department a set of specific, focused crime prevention programs and activities.

The crime reduction effort was a departmental program involving new units and new departmental programs. John Greiner's early report and the later Urban Institute-Labor Management Relations Service evaluation team indicate that police officers believe it increased cooperation with the department and made all officers more conscious of crime prevention.

The incentive program was suggested by management. Some police officers believed that the city was trying to put something over on them to avoid giving them a raise, but were reported as "well satisfied" with the program after the initial payment. As in Detroit, the incentive program was *not* a substitute for a conventional salary increase. The agreement with the Police Association included a 7.5 percent salary increase effective at the beginning of the contract and an additional 6 percent a year later.

The program was not renewed after twenty months for several reasons. Further significant crime rate reductions did not appear feasible, and the limitations on new hires seemed to be putting too much strain on the force. There was, in addition, an adverse reaction to the outside criticism of the project and doubts as to the integrity of the reporting system.

The replicability of the program seems limited. The opportunity for self-serving misclassification of and failure to report crimes is so great that the approach would scarcely be feasible for larger urban police forces. The small size of the Orange police force and the high average level of education of police officers, both apparently important to the project, also limit the places where the effort might be replicated.

Better strategy, better tactics and more aggressive police action can reduce the incidence of some crimes by some minor fraction below the levels they would otherwise have reached. Given the propensity to criminal behavior in the population and the level of law enforcement effort, there is probably a practical maximum to the crime reduction potential. Over time unusually effective police work will, in other words, reduce the opportunities for cutting crime below the trend. Moreover, if the propensity to criminality is increasing very rapidly in the population, the incentive police effort is unlikely to produce absolute reductions in crime or crime rates but, rather, to merely hold down the rate of increase. On the other hand, the imminent decline in our juvenile population, which, *ceteris paribus,* should result in a decline in crime rates, might reward police for results with which they had little association.

In Detroit, Flint, and Orange City, conditional productivity incentives were applied to a single city service. The experience in those cities provides convincing evidence of the difficulties of setting standards for productivity and effectiveness and of providing genuine incentives for employees while saving money for the city. A governmentwide productivity incentive program would, in this light, be a formidable undertaking, requiring the development of standards for a large number of separate services.

Nassau County's effort to introduce a governmentwide productivity incentive program stands as a case apart, with hard bargaining on the terms of the productivity incentive almost totally absent. I have suggested in Chapter 5 that Nassau's general productivity formula, had the Board of Supervisors accepted the notion, would have merely deferred until later the business of resolving the tough concrete issues of productivity incentive payments.

Most important, however, is the vast difference in situation between Nassau County, on the one hand, and the three cities on the other. Detroit and Flint turned to the productivity incentive contract as a means of solving a problem that seemed otherwise intractable. For Orange County, the productivity incentive was an experimental approach to the specific objective of reducing the crime rate. In Nassau County, on the other hand, the productivity incentive contract arose from a general theory that employee incentives and union cooperation would be necessary to increase government productivity. Hopefully, by enlisting union cooperation and sharing benefits from the outset, possible future employee and union resistance to increased productivity would be eliminated. The theory may well be correct, but in the absence of concrete union-government productivity issues, there was an unreal quality to the negotiations. Unlike the unions in Flint and Detroit, Nassau County's CSEA was not asked to sacrifice anything or risk anything. Rather, the program merely established a "price" for productivity improvements; if the union behaved like the rational economic person, it would accept those improvements for which the productivity reward was greater than the value placed by employees on the concessions required to achieve it. This assured, at a minimum, compensation for productivity improvements imposing little or no burden on employees without requiring acceptance of more disturbing changes.

The Non-Negotiated, Unwritten Understanding[a]

There is no generally accepted workload standard for the collection of refuse despite the existence of a significant private refuse collection industry. Obviously no single dimensional measure would make sense. Even within one city, collection productivity will vary from one area to another depending on density, traffic, parked cars, and distance to the dump or transfer station. Crews on the most productive routes may collect twice as much refuse as those on the least productive routes. The credibility in one city of work standards developed in another is, consequently, likely to be low.

At the beginning of 1970, the New York City Sanitation problem had become a public problem. The streets were dirty. Too much of the garbage was not being collected on time. Moreover, the public regarded sanitation as a soluble problem. The big problems of crime, ghetto education, and jobs might be insoluble but a mayor ought to be able to get the garbage picked up. Mayor Lindsay recognized the situation, and sanitation became the first priority for additional manpower in his 1970–1971 budget.

The issue was not productivity. Productivity in sanitation was regarded within the administration as virtually a lost issue. It emerged again with the public release by the Office of the City Administrator of a study indicating that the city might save one-fourth to nearly one-half of its refuse collection costs by using private cartmen in lieu of city employees. The city's Environmental Protection Administration (of which the Department of Sanitation was a component) issued a rebuttal analysis arguing that the City Administrator overstated the cost differences. The Citizens' Budget Commission reviewed both studies and issued a third analysis of comparative costs supporting the notion that private costs were substantially lower than the city's. None of the analyses had any apparent impact on public policy.

A new EPA Administrator and Sanitation Commissioner, Jerome Kretch-

---

[a]The accounts of the improvement productivity in refuse collection and in vehicle maintenance in New York City's Department of Sanitation are summarized from an unpublished study of change and innovations in four New York City agencies that I conducted as an Adjunct Professor at the State University of New York at StonyBrook with financing from a National Science Foundation grant to StonyBrook's Urban and Policy Analysis Program.

mer, engaged the management consulting firm, McKinsey and Company, to review the problem in early 1970. The McKinsey analysis led to the creation of an Office of Productivity, manned by sanitation officers. Using manuals prepared by McKinsey and supported by McKinsey analysts in the initial months, teams from that office analyzed collection productivity and set targets in each of the fifty-eight sanitation districts. Two districts were completed each month, and the entire department took over two years to complete. Over a period of three years, the department increased refuse collection productivity by about 25 percent. There was no specific financial incentive.

The Uniformed Sanitationmen's Association was one of the city's most powerful and important unions. Its president, John deLury, had led the union for many years and had obtained for its members a level of pay and benefits unique in the United States both in dollar value and in proportion to police and fire pay and benefits. Kretchmer and Herbert Elish (Kretchmer's deputy and successor) met with deLury on a regular weekly basis. Despite this, Elish initiated the productivity effort without prior discussion with deLury. DeLury learned immediately of the dispatch to the field of the first productivity team and demanded a meeting that day with Kretchmer and Elish. The city officials held firm to the need to proceed with the program. DeLury was ambiguous and undecided. Elish remembers, as he left, deLury's principal aide saying: "You do what you *want* to do and we'll do what we *have* to do." Elish wondered whether it was a threat.

But deLury did not block the program nor did he publicly support it, although he now regards himself as a cosponsor. DeLury says that his members understood that an increase in productivity would have favorable effects at the bargaining table and that it did have such an effect. There were never any negotiations or written agreements on the productivity program and no bonus or incentive pay identified as such in the later collective bargaining contract.

One can only guess at the relative causal importance of the various factors in this complex situation. DeLury, himself, was old fashioned enough to believe in a day's work for a day's pay and smart enough to understand the importance of pride in work and to know that the criticism of the department was undermining that pride in his members. He let Elish go ahead but without commitment, leaving himself and the union free to "wait and see."

Elish internalized the determination of productivity targets using the best career officers, custom-tailoring the targets to the specifics in each district, and requiring agreement between the productivity teams and the district chief. There was, hence, no problem of outsiders (e.g., the McKinsey analysts) "coming in and telling us what to do." Nor even of "headquarters not understanding that Morrisania is different." As a result, Elish created few new problems that would impair DeLury's ability to support him.

Trust played a big role. DeLury's membership trusted him and respected him; no other city union leader could have secured member acceptance of a 25 percent increase in work performed by just passing the word that it was ok, and the union would be taken care of. DeLury's willingness to stick his neck out related in turn to his growing trust in Elish and confidence in his managerial ability. To deLury, it was a rarity to have a commissioner who was fair, honest, nonpolitical, and a competent manager as well; he had not seen the likes of Herbert Elish since John P. Morton was deputy commissioner in LaGuardia's first term. DeLury speaks, too, of the importance of the best access to city hall and to the mayor that the union had ever enjoyed.

Contrast this cozy situation with the historic sanitation strike of 1968 only a few years earlier. The union delegates rejected the contract DeLury had negotiated with the city. When the city refused to sweeten their offer, the union went out on a strike, and John DeLury was sent to jail for fifteen days—all for a $25 per worker per year. The garbage piled up on the streets, and a desparate mayor finally asked the governor to call out the National Guard to collect it. That led to the bitter public confrontation between Lindsay and Rockefeller that supposedly killed the latter's presidential hopes. All this for $25! How could a union so militant and so volatile accept a substantial productivity program so easily? Certainly, the situation changed in the subsequent four years. Union-city relationships had become very good. The department had an able administrator for the first time. But the major factor may be that deLury lost control of the money issue to his own members in 1968 while he proved able to manage and control the handling of the productivity question four years later.

An Authoritative Standard

Among the few external standards that have any inherent credibility among workers are the time estimates for various motor vehicle repairs taken from the flat rate books issued by the manufacturers. The flat rate books are used throughout the country by private garages as a basis for work scheduling and billing. The flat rates are relatively undemanding since they should be achievable by nearly all garages and regular shops. In fact, it is common for the garage owner to split savings with mechanics who work faster than the flat rates. A well-managed repair operation should be able to beat the rate book on most repair jobs.

The flat rate books played a major role in the effort to improve vehicle maintenance and repair in New York City's Department of Sanitation in the 1970–1973 period. The department's failure to keep the city clean was one of the frustrations of John Lindsay's first term as mayor and one he intended to relieve in his second term. One major aspect of the problem was that an average of 30–40 percent of the department's collection trucks were out of service for repairs. A team from the Mayor's Project Management Staff had started work on the analysis of the problem at the end of the summer of 1969. Over the course of the next year or so the Project Management Staff recommended a series of corrective actions, including new repair facilities to reduce the congestion in the central garage, scheduling systems to control truck movement through the repair process, and a new parts inventory control system. These measures had some significant successes.

The early PMS reports had suggested a major productivity problem on the basis of comparisons with private repair operations and general observations of employee work attitudes at the sanitation repair facility. A PMS analysis in depth, completed in 1971, put the issue beyond doubt. A sample of hundreds of repair jobs showed that the Department's mechanics were performing on the average at less than half the productivity of the flat rate book standards.

Sanitation Commissioner Herbert Elish met with the head of the mechanics union to show him the results of the analysis and to advise him of the department's intention to impose the flat rates on the mechanics in the repair shop. The imposition of the new standards was delayed while the data were reviewed by the union leadership. The union objected to the standards, questioned the accuracy of the study and left Elish wondering whether he dared impose the standards without union agreement. On the other hand, the mechanics unit was not militant and by repute was neither aggressively nor competently led. A threatened strike could have devastating effects, however, especially if it occurred while there were still real prospects for further snow.

Meanwhile the Bureau of the Budget acceded to a Sanitation Department request for sixty additional mechanics. The new mechanics, when hired, were organized as a separate repair unit and did not work with mechanics already on board. The new mechanics could be dropped by the city without an explanation at any time during the six-month probationary appointment period. The mechanics were advised that the department would regard performance at the flat rate standards as evidence that probationary standards had been met. At the end of the six months, nearly all the probationary mechanics had met nearly all the workload standards.

Elish finally decided to put the new standards in force with minor modifications that came out of the discussions with the union representatives. The union then suggested that the standards be specified in a union-city agreement. This would put the standards beyond effective challenge but, at the same time, would protect the union against further unilateral productivity increases. Elish agreed to the written agreement. Some mechanics refused to meet the standards, but the union agreement left them without resource against departmental disciplinary action. The standards were applied with the result that productivity nearly doubled over the next year, and trucks out of service declined to 10 percent and less of the inventory.

In effect, Elish had left the union and its leadership intellectually defenseless. How could the union publicly reject standards being met in shops all over the United States? How could they argue that they could not meet the standards when the Department was able to show that the standards had been met for six months by a group of sixty mechanics newly recruited to the department? The national application and uncomplaining acceptance of the flat rates gave them authority and credibility that the city could not conceivably secure, say, for standards custom designed by its own industrial engineers and tailored to the special situation in the city's own shops and garages. The only defense—that New York was different—was strained, and the ingenious sixty-worker pilot project made it totally untenable.

The mechanics were not given any financial reward for the higher productivity. They were already better paid than their private counterparts, especially when pension benefits were taken into account. Elish had taken the position from the beginning that comparable pay (or better) entitled the city to comparable work.

The union was, in effect, strong-armed. One must wonder, despite the authority of the city's position, whether a stronger union would have tolerated the treatment. One minor mystery is the fact that flat rates seemed not to have entered the many prior discussions of the problems of the vehicle maintenance operation. Elish's impression was that the head of the mechanics union was distinctly surprised to find performance so far below flat rates. All this says something of the insular tendency not to look outside for standards, to regard civil servants and city problems as 'different.'

The Wilmington Fire Force[6]

A new mayor, Thomas Maloney, took office in Wilmington, Delaware on January 1, 1973. One of his major objectives was to stop or slow the continuing rise in expenditures, which had averaged about 15 percent annually over the prior four years.

An early target had been solid waste collection. Wilmington's collection trucks operated with five-person crews on a task basis permitting them to quit work on the completion of routes. An analysis showed that the average actual work week was twenty-three hours. After detailed analysis, the city unilaterally reduced crews to three workers each, without, however, any layoffs. This precipitated a strike which was eventually settled by an agreement to submit the matter to impartial arbitration. The arbitrator ruled in the city's favor, and the three-worker crews were retained. The city gave the collectors an unsolicited pay raise.

The structure of the fire force in Wilmington had remained essentially as it was in 1921. Studies prior to the Maloney administration had indicated that fire-fighting costs in Wilmington were comparatively high and suggested the possibility of work force reductions. However, a fire underwriters survey and a study by a former fire official of another city had both supported the current manning level.

The city government began a new review of the situation. It was decided that any change in manning must be negotiated with the union in view of a "maintenance of standards" clause in the existing contract with the Association of Fire Fighters, AFL-CIO. In preparation for bargaining, a six-month research and analysis effort was undertaken. Wilmington's Department of Planning and Development did a survey of fire departments in thirteen comparable cities and found that all spent less per capita than Wilmington despite Wilmington's longer work week and lower pay schedule. Other cities were operating fewer companies, each with fewer men.

The principal analytic effort was carried out with the assistance of the New York City Rand Institute. Rand's contribution was the application of a sophisticated mathematical model for simulating responses and response times to alarms for alternative fire company deployments. The Rand analysis indicated that the city could eliminate two of its nine engine companies without appreciable effect on response times. Moreover, the changes of a major conflagration requiring all nine engine companies was remote. All nine companies had been deployed that year for a major paint factory fire, but a review of the prior year found no occasions during which more than six companies had been out of the fire houses at the same time.

The city elected to retain the four-person engine company but to bargain for the elimination of two engine companies, eventually proposing a reduction of one immediately and one fifteen months later when the impact of the first cut could be evaluated. With seventeen vacancies in the force, no layoffs would be required.

The possibility of an incremental productivity payment to the fire fighters as compensation for the additional workload on the remaining companies was explored informally with the union. This possibility was rejected by the union because it would break established parity with the police, probably to the longer term detriment of the fire fighters.

The union rejected the proposed reductions, and bargaining continued past the expiration of the existing contract. This restored the city's authority to act unilaterally on matters covered by the expiring contract. A final city offer provided for: the elimination of a single engine company; a revised work schedule to eliminate city liability for the massive amounts of overtime that might be necessary as a result of new amendments to the Fair Labor Standards Act; and increases of 7.5 percent in the first year and 7 percent in the second year of a proposed two-year contract. The union committee agreed to put the proposal before its membership—where it was overwhelmingly defeated. A parallel proposal to the police union was also defeated.

Nearly a month passed before another meeting with the union. It proved unproductive. Shortly thereafter, however, with the aid of a federal mediator the city reached agreement with the police union on a somewhat higher settlement in exchange for a three-year contract. The settlement was unexpected, and it threw the fire fighters into disarray.

The fire fighters launched a major public relations campaign. A picketing line was set up before city hall and maintained almost every day until the contract was settled. On the day picketing was started, some 300 delegates from the union's international convention in Baltimore descended on the city to support the pickets. A public relations consultant to the union was engaged. Petitions were circulated. Press releases were issued. Calls made to local radio stations. All argued that the cut would make the city unsafe. The fire fighters pleaded their case before the City Council and won the support of the City Council president. The Council was sympathetic but elected not to become involved. The city countered with its own lower key public relations effort and won editorial support from the local newspaper.

Both sides agreed to request the intervention of a federal mediator. With the help of the mediator, a contract was agreed on after a twenty-one-hour session. It maintained parity with the police, eliminated one engine company, retained the work schedule changes but added $100 to the $50 uniform allowance as a kind of productivity increase. The contract was put to the membership and narrowly rejected. The city responded by unilateral action eliminating one engine company at 8:00 a.m. the next morning.

The unilateral action apparently speeded a settlement by removing the issue from the bargaining table. A last minute problem arose when the fire fighters demanded a reduction in the work week from forty-eight to forty-two hours. The city began examining prototype programs in other cites for the assignment of firefighters to police patrol-type duties during the low-alarm periods. The union dropped the demand when it learned the conditions under which the city would consider it. The contract ultimately reached and approved by the membership maintained parity with police but included no other significant changes from the contract last rejected with one exception. It made no provision for the elimination of the engine company—or for its retention. The city's action to eliminate the company remained in effect.

There are several significant aspects of the Wilmington experience. First was the extensive work in building the case that Wilmington's fire force was above the standards prevailing in comparable cities and that the repercussions on fire safety would be negligible. Second was the high vulnerability of the union to such an argument, because staffing was, in fact, the highest among the cities compared as it had been in the city's garbage collection operations. Third was the fire fighters' posture in three respects: the unwillingness to break parity with police; the greater capacity to *accept* the engine company cut than to *agree to it;* and, the apparent disinterest in strikes or job actions. The latter accords with traditional attitudes of firefighters—but more militant attitudes are beginning to emerge in many fire forces.

The fire fighters' position is curious in another respect. They adamantly resisted the engine company reduction for months although the reduction would have minimum effects on the force except for the members in the affected company. On the other hand, the reduction in the work week—the major nonsalary focus for negotiation in American fire departments for the past three decades— was brought in only as an afterthought in the last of three sets of negotiations.

The possibility of accepting engine company reductions and applying a part of the savings to lowering the work week seems never to have entered the bargaining.

The changes in both fire fighting and garbage collection produced significant savings for the Wilmington City budget, but they scarcely made Wilmington a leader in productivity achievements. Rather they raised the workload-staffing relationships in these two services to or near the levels long routinely accepted in many other cities.

Buy Outs and Big Deals

The simplest form of productivity contract provides for a supplemental increase in salary or wage rates in return for union agreement to increased productivity or to the elimination of some obstacle to increasing productivity. There is a fundamental economic attraction to the buy-out contract because typically the value of the work restriction to the employees is less than its cost to the government.

One instance of a buy-out was the case already discussed of the elimination of the contract limit on the number of cases to be handled by social case workers in New York City's Department of Social Services.

In a second case, the workers in the municipal hospitals were, in the early 1970s, processing an average of only 2.5 claims for Medicaid and Medicare reimbursement per person-day, an informal standard supposedly enforced by the union representing them. The City's Office of Labor Relations negotiated a doubling of the daily work standard to five cases per employee at a reported cost of $500 per worker in additional salary.

Both cases represent "good deals" for the city, returning benefits vastly in excess of costs. They also reflect the unusual limitations on management in New York's 'mature' labor relations environment. In the social worker case, the contract can be seen as the recovery of managerial prerogatives lost in a prior contract. The Medicaid processors' case is more questionable. The workload limit previously in effect had no legal status, had never been agreed to by the city and seems, simply because output was so readily doubled, to have involved deliberate substandard performance. The case, as reported, carries the sweet smell of extortion—and, yet, almost certainly remains the easiest, fastest, and the cheapest method of increasing productivity.

Other New York City cases involve productivity-related work rule changes in a regular collective bargaining contract without any identifiable separate price. One was the chart day provision in Sanitation, which permitted the city to shift work schedules to place more workers on duty on Monday and Tuesday— the heavy collection days. A somewhat different case was the inclusion in the fire fighters' contract of explicit authority for "adaptive response"—curiously a program that *reduced* workload by cutting back on the number of pieces of apparatus responding to a routine fire box alarm.

New York City has also made three attempts at overall productivity bargains. The general productivity clause introduced during the second Lindsay term had negligible impact with respect to police and fire. There are some who believe that it provided the basis for union acceptance of productivity improvements in other areas of city government. This is, however, subject to question. The union-government Productivity Council introduced into labor contracts during the Beame administration's first two years yielded no productivity savings. A successor arrangement coming into operation in mid-1976 had, at this writing, yet to be tested.

Some Concluding Observations

One can scarcely make generalizations about municipal unionism without first disposing of New York, the most widely known and most extreme case. Nowhere else do employee unions play so powerful a role with respect to proposed productivity improvements. This is partially because the city's basic collective bargaining ground rules give the unions a legitimate basis for challenging any changes affecting the work life of the employee. But it also reflects New York's relatively long experience with unions and, especially, the frustration of the city's civil servants with the rising problems of the city in the 1960s.

Despite the problems posed by unions, many determined and soundly conceived efforts to increase productivity in New York were successful. Only in fire, police, and the public schools did union positions and worker attitudes block significant productivity improvement, and, even here, opposition has softened under the pressure of the fiscal crisis. No one can doubt that the unions have made productivity improvement substantially more difficult. Yet, Victor Gotbaum, the head of the AFSCME local, seems clearly correct in saying that the major problem is deficient management rather than union behavior.

Four of the seven other local governments reviewed in this book have well-developed city productivity improvements programs. These include Dallas, Milwaukee, Phoenix, and Tacoma. Among them, there is only a single case where a proposed productivity improvement was blocked by a union. That case involved a successful union recourse to the courts in Milwaukee, invoking an anticontracting provision in the collective bargaining contract to stop a city effort to contract for custodial services for a municipal building.

The absence of effective union vetoes of productivity improvements is certainly in part due to the inclusion in the four of only one city from the midwest and northeast where unions are strongest and most oriented toward workload issues. Indeed, one could support the argument that productivity improvement programs have tended to concentrate in areas where unions are least powerful. It also seems apparent that these four cities have probably done a superior job in the management of employee and union relations. Finally, all four cities have dealt cautiously with productivity in the police and fire services, the sectors where successful union opposition was most likely.

Union problems in productivity programs have been concentrated in refuse collection and disposal and, to a much lesser degree, in fire protection. This is partially because productivity programs have placed heavy emphasis on these areas, especially refuse collection. But it also reflects a tendency for unionization to develop more rapidly and to be more militant in these areas than in other municipal functions.

The experience to date in dealing explicitly with productivity in collective bargaining is ambiguous. Ray Horton has suggested that productivity bargaining tends to arise when the government seeks to recover through productivity increases the large salary gains it has yielded to strong unions. The productivity bargain tends to be as one-sided as the prior salary bargains, because it cannot change the basic power inbalance between a strong union and a weak government.

The productivity incentive contract has proved no panacea in its limited application to date. Of the three widely publicized cases, only Flint's refuse collection contract has survived. It has proved no small matter to detail managerial responsibilities, work conditions, quality standards, and productivity base lines. The continuing development of the Flint program is illustrative. The definition of the eligible work group has proved a problem, and there are some underlying issues in relating individual motivation to benefits payable on the basis of group performance.

Moreover, the incentive payments have not been large enough to clearly outweigh the burden of additional work and the loss of overtime. Flint's success seems to arise from the combination of an incentive payment with a shorter work day.

The problems and eventual termination of the Detroit and Orange County plans should not obscure the fact that all three programs resulted in substantial increases in productivity, improvements in performance, and (in Flint and Detroit) large savings to the city. The potential for productivity improvement was, thus, clearly established. The issue is the incentive structure needed to achieve it and sustain it.

In neither Detroit nor Flint was there an effort to develop any standard of performance from either industrial engineering studies or the experience of other cities. Rather, the productivity baseline was set on the basis of existing performance. Despite the qualifications that must accompany efforts at intercity comparisons, it is useful to calibrate the Detroit and Flint results against refuse collection productivity elsewhere. Detroit achieved first-year gains varying among quarters from 18 percent to 29 percent but still fell marginally short of New York's 1973–1974 productivity of roughly 10 tons per truck shift. Both cities use three-man crews including the driver, and Detroit has the advantage of 24 cubic yard trucks compared to the 20 cubic yard trucks used in New York. Flint, with two-man crews, averaged 0.537 tons per manhour based on an eight-hour day, nearly 30 percent higher than the comparable figure for New York City. If it is assumed that the average crew in Flint completed its route in six hours, the actual productivity would be 0.716 tons per person-hour; with an average five-hour day now permitted, the figure would rise further to 0.849 tons per person-hour. Phoenix's one man manually loaded 29 and 33 cubic yard trucks run far above all the others with productivity per manhour ranging from 0.875 tons to 1.25 tons. With due allowance for differences in the many other factors affecting productivity, the dominant factors in these comparisons are almost certainly the different notions of how much refuse a worker should be expected to lift in a working day.

These intercity differences underline the general absence of accepted performance standards even for the most measurable urban services. Moreover, data on the performance of other cities—which might serve as a surrogate for more scientific standards—are rarely readily available. Industrial engineering standards, such as those used in Phoenix, can be developed, but they will tend to have little credibility with strong and aggressive unions. More often than not, productivity discussions proceed without any clear notion on either side as to how much work ought to be reasonably expected.

There is at least one case that suggests the potential high value of authoritative standards. This was the use of the manufacturer's flat rate books to set standards in New York for the repair of sanitation vehicles. The flat rates gave management a virtually irrefutable basis for establishing time standards for various repair jobs. Without them, the city would have never dared demand a near doubling of productivity, nor would the union have accepted such a standard.

The flat rates are, however, a rare case. In most cases, the cities must at best depend on other less definitive sources of standards, most usually practices and performance in other local governments. One example is Wilmington's use of intercity comparisons of fire service staffing. These comparisons showing Wilmington to be the most heavily staffed of the departments covered had a significant impact in convincing the mayor that a reduction in staffing made sense and probably in persuading the union of the vulnerability of its argument for maintenance of the status quo.

A totally different approach was that used to set performance targets for refuse collection in New York City. The targets were developed locally, but they acquired unusual credibility because (1) they were developed by a team of sanitation officers rather than by outsiders and (2) they were custom-tailored to the differing conditions in each of fifty-eight sanitation districts.

Logically, performance standards or incentives should apply to individuals or working teams such as truck crews, rather than to the entire unit as a group. In refuse collection and many other municipal operations, this would require the modification of the group standard to reflect the special opportunities and problems of each individual job or assignment. To do this, a significant investment in work measurement would be needed.

The application of standards also assumes good managerial performance; a refuse collection crew, for example, can scarcely be penalized if trucks are frequently not available or break down in service. Overall, productivity incentives or work performance standards will demand more data, more analysis, better understanding of operations, and better management than most cities are readily able to provide. It would represent in many of them a sharp shift from long traditions of intuitive and sloppy management styles to an analytical and statistical mode of operation more associated with the Harvard Business School than with municipal government.

In addition to the technical and workload problems of developing standards, there are special problems in detailing all of them in a collective bargaining contract. Whether aimed at the determination of incentive payments or the establishment of minimum performance standards, there is a need to set out factors determining the variation in standards among different jobs, to spell out the responsibilities of management, and to set up rules governing the handling of certain situations should they arise. In many cases, to do all this goes beyond the knowledge and understanding of operations available in most cities. Furthermore, the detailing of all the factors brings a new and undesirable rigidity to management. At the same time, the failure to cover such matters can lead to dissatisfactions of the kind articulated by Wasserman with respect to the Detroit contract. These problems are probably unavoidable in the productivity incentive contract, but they are not an essential aspect to productivity bargaining generally.

There are indications that productivity contracts pose special problems for public employee union leaders. The Wilmington fire fighters' ability to *tolerate* but not approve the elimination of a fire company is instructive. Patrick Murphy has noted that, as Police Commissioner of New York, he found the militant and aggressive Patrolmen's Benevolent Association unwilling to formally agree to certain proposed changes but quite willing to accept them if they were first tried in a few precincts without producing serious protests from police officers. The refuse collection case in New York is a more fully developed example.

These cases suggest risk avoidance on the part of the union leaders. One can at least glean the suspicion from these cases that productivity bargaining is a tough and sometimes impossible problem for union leaders. Some leaders seemingly would prefer less formal arrangements where all the "p's and q's" are not incorporated in a contract that must be approved by the membership. Others would prefer to leave productivity issues to management. Neither position is feasible, however, unless management is adept enough to handle the matter without raising problems with the rank and file of the unions.

The argument comes around full circle with the recognition that the conditional productivity incentive contract is a means of handling productivity considerations without a union commitment to some specific workload level—but reintroduces some of the same problems in the specification of the conditions and terms under which the incentive is payable.

In the strong union cities, many productivity issues will tend to be difficult to negotiate and even more difficult to handle without negotiation. In such situations, the incentive benefits to workers probably must typically be more generous, less complicated, and less ambiguous than they were in Detroit. The technical difficulties of setting performance standards are, however, much less serious in many other areas of city operation than they have been in sanitation. In some activities, for example fire fighting and the public schools, productivity is largely a matter of manning ratios rather than work performance. In others, such as vehicle repair, there appear to be fewer problems in the application of common standards to all employees. Throughout, the experience suggests that productivity bargaining demands a higher standard of management performance than has been common in our larger cities. Indeed, the successful handling of productivity issues with unions has been characterized by the extraordinary care and effort with which the cities have developed their cases.

Productivity-based compensation schemes of any kind face some obvious but barely encountered problems with salary relationships among different employee groups. This is evident in the refusal by the Wilmington fire fighters to consider a productivity bonus that would increase salaries above those of police officers. Another aspect of the problem arose in Detroit with the extension of the incentive scheme to employees not engaged in the collection of refuse. The point need not be belabored, but it is clear that productivity increases may raise serious questions of both equity with employee groups without comparable opportunities for increasing or, sometimes, even measuring productivity and parity with those employee groups for which there are long established intergroup salary relationships.

With the single exception of the unusual police contract in Orange, California, the reported cases of productivity bargaining have come in the older more strongly unionized cities of the northeast and midwest. They represent, in every case, an effort by city management to buy out of low-productivity situations that have been fixed by practice or occasionally by earlier contracts. The unions have resisted changes in a situation that has typically resulted from long managerial inattention to productivity considerations predating effective unionization.

In cities such as Dallas, Phoenix, and Palo Alto, growing unionization is encountering a far different situation. With city management highly oriented toward productivity and work performance standards, employee productivity tends to be relatively high and performance standards well understood. This is especially true in Phoenix. Productivity bargaining seems less likely in these cities, and, if it does come, it will probably be directed—not toward the recovery of lost ground—but rather toward the application of new and emerging technologies.

There are few reported situations where the unions constitute the critical factor in productivity improvement. The exceptions nearly all involve police officers, fire fighters, sanitation workers, and, occasionally, teachers. It is noteworthy that the union-oriented productivity strategies in Nassau County and, except for the sanitation workers, in Detroit, found the unions virtually indifferent to proposed productivity improvements. This is consistent with the fact that, except for refuse collection, most productivity improvements have not significantly increased the burden on workers. Most improvements have depended not on simply demanding more work from employees but rather on changes in work organization or new equipment.

In the most difficult union situations, it may well be that the real issues are sociological and psychological rather than economic. To the rank and file in a large organization, aggressive union behavior has been an antidote to the feeling of powerlessness, to grievances against an insensitive management, to public criticism and complaints, and to just being pushed around. Such a situation probably symptomizes the need for new styles of management rather than new approaches to union-management relations.

Notes

1. Raymond Horton, David Lewin and James W. Kuhn, *The Impact of Collective Bargaining in the Management of Government: A Diversity Thesis,* prepared for delivery at the 1975 National Conference on Public Administration, Chicago, Ill., April 1-4, 1975.

2. The discussion of the Detroit productivity incentive contract is based almost entirely on information drawn from the following two publications: *Detroit Sanitation Productivity—Eveyone Wins,* Labor Management Relations Service Report, no. 18, Labor Management Relations Service, Washington, D.C., and *Improving Municipal Productivity: The Detroit Refuse Collection Plan,* National Commission on Productivity, Washington, D.C., 1974.

3. *Motivating State Government Productivity Improvement Programs.* A collection of working papers and proceedings on the social and political environment and its impact on state government agencies. Presented at a workshop held at the Gideon Putnam Hotel, Saratoga Springs, N.Y., Nov. 18-30, 1974. Editors: Walter L. Balk, Edgar Crane, Bernard Lentz, State University of New York at Albany.

4. Information on the productivity incentive contracts in Flint and Orange has been drawn entirely from: John M. Greiner, *Tying City Pay to Performance: Early Reports on the Experience of Orange, California and Flint, Michigan,* The Urban Institute, Labor Management Relations Service, Washington, D.C.,

1974. John M. Greiner, Roger E. Dahl, Harry P. Hatry and Annie Millar, *An Assessment of the Impacts of Five Local Government Productivity Programs*, The Urban Institute and The Labor-Management Relations Service, Washington, D.C., December 31, 1975. (To be published.)

5. See note 4.

6. My knowledge of the Wilmington Fire Force case comes largely from a talk delivered by Mayor Maloney at a meeting in St. Louis in May, 1975 sponsored by the U.S. Conference of Mayors and from a written account distributed by Mayor Maloney at that meeting.

11

What Makes Productivity Programs
Work and What Have They
Accomplished?

The Initiators

Productivity programs are a product of choice, rather than of necessity. There
is no evidence of any underlying logic in the development of local government
that would lead to their creation. There is no instance of which I am aware—
either in the eight governments surveyed or elsewhere—of any significant pressure from citizens, citizen associations, or any other private organization to set
up productivity programs. Indeed, there are few indications of any citizen
interest in productivity. Not even the increasingly numerous and vociferous
opponents of higher taxes and spending have picked up the cudgels to fight
for productivity improvement.

　　This is important. To mayors or city managers, it means that if they do
not want a productivity program, they do not have to have one. In fact, they
will probably never have to explain why they do not have one. The only exception among our cases is Phoenix, where the City Council pressed the productivity
program upon the city manager. Even in Phoenix, the Council acted on its own
views rather than in response to any segment of external opinion.

　　There are some very good reasons for a mayor or a manager or a city
council to not want a productivity program. Productivity programs are potential
sources of trouble, because they can be implemented only by disturbing the
status quo. Trouble may arise from the impact of productivity changes on
municipal employees and relationships with the unions that represent them.
Changes in the character and magnitude of services provided to citizens constitute another form of disturbance that may create problems. Another effect
of productivity programs is the friction that results from increasing the exercise
of authority by the office of the mayor or manager or the bureau of the budget
over the department heads. Last, of course, is that failure in the effort is a real
possibility and one likely to have adverse effects upon the careers of the program
sponsors.

　　These factors underline the inherently political nature of productivity
improvement programs and the importance of political leadership to both their
initiation and success. Not even the strong budget agencies in some of the cities

surveyed could force productivity improvements on the operating agencies if those changes were likely to result in threats of resignations by department heads, serious employee morale problems, union action, or significant citizen protest and complaint.

In all eight of the local government productivity programs we have reviewed, political leadership was, in fact, crucial to the initiation of the program. In Phoenix, the City Council took the lead. In the others, with the possible exception of Milwaukee, the chief executive was responsible. In Nassau County, New York City, and Detroit programs were begun under the aegis of an elected executive. In the others, city managers, with the support of their city councils, started the programs.

Although most productivity programs have been initiated by chief executives, acceptance by the city council is usually critical. The solidly established programs in Phoenix and Milwaukee have achieved that status in large part as a result of the sustained legislative involvement in and backing for the programs. The Multi-Municipal Productivity Project in Nassau County died quickly when it failed to obtain the approval of the Board of Supervisors for its employee incentive scheme. The Palo Alto program faced a tenuous future until the council became convinced of its value.

Because productivity does raise real political issues, the top-level support may waver over time with circumstances and may not extend to programs, departments, or people in what is seen as more protected positions. Program efforts seem, for example, to rarely place much pressure on police departments, and the fire department will typically be handled with rather more circumspection than, say, the water department. A city manager may find, as did George Sipel in Palo Alto, that relationships with some department heads require protecting those departments from the direct scrutiny of the productivity staff. Some obvious productivity issues will seemingly be ignored until the leadership finds the time propitious to take them on. In the very complex case of refuse collection in Milwaukee, that propitious time did not occur for fifteen to twenty years after the problem had been clearly identified. In Dallas, some actions waited the retirement of a long-established department head.

Productivity improvement efforts initiated by department heads without pressure or encouragement from above seem rare. Some department heads seem to welcome the pressure for productivity improvement, but—even when they have definite productivity improving ideas—they appear infrequently to have either initiated or advanced them for top-level approval. Most department heads have to be persuaded and some coerced to undertake productivity improvements. Indeed, in every city, there appear to be reluctant dragons among the department heads, who are at best minimal participants in the program and, often, seemingly resist any involvement.

One of the explanatory factors must be the unwillingness to take the risks involved without top-level support or orders. Another factor is the absence in most municipal departments, even in larger cities and counties, of analytical staff to develop and manage innovations. At the same time, resistance to ideas pressed or imposed from outside is understandable. Some department managers may be unwilling to jeopardize internal relations by undertaking efforts that would cut back the department's budget or work force. Perhaps the largest single factor is the rarity in all pursuits—including municipal government—of the innovative manager.

The initiation of a productivity program would appear from this discussion to be an irrational act contrary to the realities of politics and government. Yet, productivity programs are initiated. The obvious question is why. The most general answer applicable to all the cases studied is that the programs were undertaken because their sponsors believed that they served the public interest. One suspects that, like most other innovators, they were inclined to view possible problems from an optimistic perspective and with more than ordinary confidence in their ability to handle them. Going further, there seem to be two quite different situations under which productivity programs are initiated.

In the first of the two situations, productivity improvement tends to be undertaken as a low-profile effort in communities where the potential opposition to such a program is minimal. The sponsors of the program in such situations view the effort as simply a further step toward more prudent management. Political factors tend to be unimportant. Dallas, Phoenix, and Palo Alto are all cases of this kind.

In a second situation, the productivity program emerges as a more flamboyant act of political entrepreneurship. The environment is more political, and opposition is far more likely or even certain. The protagonist is likely to be a political maverick or a reformer—although not necessarily so. Lindsay probably best exemplifies the type. A political outsider, totally convinced of the need to restructure city government and dependent on a record of signal achievement for his political future, the productivity program fitted both his convictions and his needs. Donaldson, even though a nonpolitical city manager, has some of the same characteristics. A strong personality with a unique view of city government and a commitment to innovation, he was virtually certain to effect important changes in the Tacoma city government. Like Lindsay, his future opportunities would be advanced by a national reputation. In Coleman Young, newly elected as Detroit's first black mayor, there is evidence of a similar commitment to change and a desire to establish a reputation for effective management.

In at least three of the local governments, there were fiscal problems that created a powerful rationale for improvements in productivity that would help cut expenditures. New York and Detroit were in the midst of major budgetary difficulties at the time productivity programs were inaugurated. Caso was concerned with the need to tailor county expenditures to a future where economic growth was certain to be slower. Even in rich Palo Alto, a deterioration in the city's fiscal situation contributed to an increased city council interest in productivity improvement.

For the elected politician willing to take the risk and confident that it can be done, the productivity program is an opportunity for "show and tell," a chance to build a reputation with the electorate. But, to date, productivity programs have made heroes out of few, if any, politicians. For most mayors and, probably, most city managers, initiating a productivity program is something of an act of faith. Few mayors have a clear notion as to how well or how badly services are performed in their cities or the magnitude of improvement that might result from a productivity program. Where risks are clearly apparent, most officials can have little advance indication that the game is likely to be worth the candle.

There are some signs of a rise in innovative leadership in local government. Part of it is due to the financial squeeze on the cities. Part is a new climate. Local political leaders became notably more cautious and circumspect as the turmoil of the 1960s increased the risks of change. This seems to be changing, and more mayors are taking strong public stands on public expenditure issues. For example, Mayors Maloney in Wilmington and Uhlman in Seattle have taken on major battles with employee unions and won. In like vein, New York's feisty unions have pulled back in the face of the city's fiscal crisis.

The Political Environment

The politics are tougher and the risks greater in some cities and communities than in others. The problems posed by productivity programs may be easier to handle in some government structures than in others. The limited evidence suggests that productivity programs are more likely to flourish in cities in the south and west with city manager forms of government. There may be good reasons for this.

The city manager system, by making the executive an employee hired and fired by the legislature, eliminates many of the frictions and competition common between an elected mayor and Council. The manager, unlike the elected executive mayor, will rarely march off in a direction opposed by the Council. Moreover, as a professional, he is likely to propose actions that satisfy his professional standards and that may enhance his professional reputation, leaving the political judgments to the Council. The Council, on the other hand, benefits by its ability to defend its actions as based on the recommendations of a professional manager.

In most of the west and southwest, local politics seem far less intense and shrill than in the cities of the northeast and midwest. Municipal government tends, in the west and southwest, to provide fewer services, to be less important as a source of employment, to be less subject to traditions of patronage, to have fewer cases of corruption, and, perhaps, to be regarded overall as less important than in the east. All these factors probably make it easier to undertake productivity programs.

Whether or not they operate under city manager charters, the dominant tradition of municipal government in the west is professional and managerial, while in the east, the tradition is, in the main, political. There are, of course, local governments that deviate from the dominant model in their respective regions. Milwaukee is far more political than most western city governments, but it is clearly tilted toward the managerial model despite its midwestern location. On the other hand, Tacoma in its pre-Donaldson turmoil seemed to be moving away from the managerial orientation.

James Q. Wilson has suggested a similar dichotomy of police departments in his *Varieties of Police Behavior*. Not surprisingly, the political departments tend to be in the east and the professional-managerial departments in the west.

The differences seem pervasive in both the government and the community. It is a difference in perspective on the management of government, a difference in the way in which citizens view government, and a difference in the attitudes of civil servants toward their jobs.

The eastern and midwestern cities are older and more densely developed. They retain many of the ethnic divisions left from the immigration from Europe before World War I. Local economies in most of the east and midwest have lagged behind the high growth rates characteristic of much of the west. More municipal employees are organized, and more of the society is organized both politically and socially. The eastern city is a "tighter" community than its western counterpart with less freedom for maneuver. Density, snow, and Irishmen create an environment in Boston almost wholly alien to the traditions of local government in Phoenix.

Whatever the cause, the odds for productivity improvement programs seem decidedly better in the west. Programs there can be initiated with less difficulty and will encounter less resistance than in the east. In the east and midwest, successful productivity programs will depend to some large degree on political entrepreneurship of an uncommon kind.

Talent

The productivity improvement effort in local government can, as I have noted in the first chapter, be regarded as only the most recent of a long series of efforts to raise the quality of management in local government. Productivity improvement shares with the Planning-Programming-Budgeting System, which came into vogue in local government circles in the late 1960s, a common perspective of the problem. The early productivity programs followed PPB in placing the major emphasis on the development within local government of an analytical staff capacity. The proponents of these programs saw the principal—or at least the primary—problem of local government as the lack of a capacity to either see the deficiencies in its performance or devise means of doing the job better.

The argument for analysis and program development can be divided into two strands. The first is the case for establishing staffs with that responsibility. The second was an argument for new kinds of expertise, especially systems analysis, following McNamara's example in the Department of Defense.

Neither aspect sat well with those who saw local government as a simpler managerial problem with improvement well within the capacity of its operating officials. To this group, the principal problems were politics and labor relations, and improvement would come from attention to these areas rather than analysis. To many, the analyst seemed a useless addition, too detached and alien from the work situation to understand what was feasible. The systems analyst and the operations researcher were likely to be even worse, neither understanding nor capable of being understood.

The history to date is an almost total vindication of those arguing the necessity of an analytical staff. The best performers in the productivity game are those that have taken the straightforward position that productivity improvement requires work. The successful cities and counties have all made an investment in the additional staff needed to develop and administer the program. There is simply no evidence of cheap or effortless governmentwide productivity programs.

Among the productivity staffs, there is only a scattering of individuals trained in systems analysis, operations research, advanced statistical techniques, or even industrial engineering; New York City is a limited exception to this general rule. Most cities have followed the practice of the better state and local budget offices in recruiting from recent public administration graduates. Advanced and esoteric analytic techniques are rarely used, and there is little indication that they have been needed.

Several qualifications must be added. The first is that the more advanced skills lacking in government staffs are sometimes provided when needed by the engagement of consultants. Second, the skills are most relevant when the scale of operations is very large. The scale factor is apparently important only in New York City, but there it is evident that some problems could not have been solved without the use of rather high-powered analysis. Lastly, I would agree with a comment made by John Stewart, former Director of the National Productivity Commission, that the introduction of specialists in work processes—industrial engineers and the like—will nearly always identify additional opportunities for improvement in any sizable or complex operation.

The productivity program has been conceived in most local governments as an expansion of the concept of central oversight. Typically, productivity staff are centralized as a unit in the budget agency and work as an adjunct to budget. The staff tends to benefit from budget support and to suffer, in some cases, from budget's adversary relations with the agencies.

Consultants have also been important, especially in program initiation. Milwaukee's management analysis unit was established on the basis of a Griffenhagen recommendation while Phoenix's analytic approach was launched by a Booz, Allen and Hamilton study. Consultant Richard Hughes aided the first steps in the development of the Palo Alto Service Management System. McKinsey and Company and the Rand Corporation were important in the early days of New York's program analysis effort while Meridian Engineering designed and virtually administered the city's capital project management system. Boeing played a crucial role in Tacoma's technology transfer program from the beginning. In all these cases, the consultants served as effective transfer agents of techniques and methodologies of which the cities had limited knowledge.

Nearly all the local governments involved have continued to use consultants and outside researchers for some projects. Most prefer to use their own staffs, but internal staffs are rarely able to handle all the needed work. Moreover, the outside consultant will often provide added credibility with the operating agency involved or skills not available on the city payroll.

The establishment and staffing of analytical and productivity units in most of the governments can be regarded as an important step toward the institutionalization within local government of a capacity for self-criticism and innovation. Much less progress has been made, usually by design, in building the same capacity into the operating departments.

The linkage between analytic capacity and leadership should not be ignored. Analysis and innovation survive when they are supported and used by leadership. In Milwaukee, the analytic approach has survived a quarter of a century in a situation of high leadership continuity and joint executive-legislative involvement. In New York City's more divisive political climate, the painfully developed new capacities were in shambles barely a year after a change in mayoral administration.

The Think Tanks

Of the eight local governments studied, only New York City extended its effort to build a supporting analytical capacity to the establishment of a separate research institution or "think tank." The New York City Rand Institute was not, however, a unique endeavor. The think tank for state and local governments was a concept that attracted wider interest, and a number of such institutions were established in the later 1960s:

1. The New York City Rand Institute was the largest of these with an annual budget at one time of about $2.5 million.

2. The Los Angeles Technical Services Corporation was also a nonprofit

corporation with a much smaller budget and a less direct connection to the city government.

3. The Office of Newark Studies was a branch of Rutgers University functioning for all practical purposes as an in-house analysis shop for the mayor.

4. The Illinois Institute for Social Policy was set up as an independent entity with the state's Department of Public Aid.

5. Far earlier than any of these was the Institute of Community Studies set up in 1949 by Homer Wadsworth of the Kansas City Association of Trusts and Foundations.

All these organizations received Ford Foundation support, and some had grants from other foundations. They were primarily dependent, however, on governmental funds to perform specific study or research projects.

I wrote in June 1972 of these organizations:

> The way of the pilgrim is hard. The newer of the pioneer reserach institutions discussed in this volume have those who love them, but they have not yet gained the support and acceptance necessary for long-term survival. Troubled by financing, they face the legislative budget process or contract renewal with uncertain support and unknown prospects. Their requests are vulnerable to both fiscal and political pressure. They seek money from Washington, from foundations, and from local philanthropy. They solicit work and contracts. Most have yet to build a secure long-term financial base.
>
> The newer institutions are not universally admired, and they are fair game for politics and for criticism. They have found only a limited number of government clients that want them and can use them effectively. A few have experienced the vulnerability associated with involvement in highly controversial public issues. Only a few can feel confident that they would survive the election of a new governor or mayor. They are only beginning to produce a record of accomplishment that may demonstrate their value to the unconvinced. And they are finding that even good performance is not always translatable into a persuasive case for their survival.[1]

Since that time, the New York City Rand Corporation, the Los Angeles Technical Services Corporation, and the Illinois Institute for Social Policy have all been dissolved. The Office of Newark Studies continues serving the same mayor and maintaining, compared to the others, a low profile and modest pretensions.

The New York City Rand Institute pioneered in the application of systems analysis techniques to the problems of a city government producing a vast volume of work—much of it superb in quality. The Institute developed a strong relationship with the Fire Department but, in other agencies, failed to achieve the same degree of continuing support. The Institute was not adroit in its relationships with the agencies and totally unprepared for New York's fierce political climate. It was associated with John Lindsay and fair game for any of his critics. The Institute saw its funding cut back after the inauguration of Mayor Beame; later it became one of the first casualties of the city's fiscal crisis.

The Illinois Institute for Social Policy was a target for legislative criticism from its inception. Even during Governor Ogilvie's term, it came within a few votes of having its funding eliminated from the appropriation bill in the state legislature. With Ogilvie's defeat for reelection, the demise of the Institute was expected and occurred.

The Los Angeles Technical Services Corporation could survive so long as it could persuade the agencies of the city and county governments that it could perform research and analysis for them more effectively than could others. With a peak level of only about $500,000 annually, LATSC never achieved more than a tenuous hold. Ultimately, it became clear that adequate support was not forthcoming.

During this same period, the Department of Housing and Urban Development created ten so-called "Urban Observatories," an arrangement under which HUD and the Office of Education financed research to be provided by a university or a group of universities for the government of the city in which they were located. The research agenda was to be determined jointly by the city and the university except for some nationally designed projects. HUD has maintained interest in this effort and has recently funded an additional ten observatories. The effort has yet to realize the hopes expected of it. There have been a handful of modest successes and some failures. It is fair to say that the observatories have not became a major source of problem solving for any of the cities in which they have been created.

All these unsuccessful experiences underline some of the problems in establishing links between local governments, on the one hand, and universities or reserach institutions on the other. An effective relationship in a purely technical sense demands a mutual accommodation with the academics and systems analysts learning about city government and the bureaucrats learning about the capacities and limitations of researchers and academics. Under the most favorable circumstances, this takes time. At worst, it simply doesn't work. At the same time, the political climate may range from indifference to hostility. There are few places in the United States where the idea of academics or high-powered researchers working on local or state government problems has much intrinsic appeal or credibility with the public, politicians, or bureaucrats. It is a Washington idea developed by those with federal government experience. In state and local governments, the seed is likely to fall, as it has, on stony ground. Any such arrangement is likely, hence, to be highly vulnerable and a potential casualty of budget cutting or politics. The application of intellect to local government problems is a suspect activity in America. The more academic, the more intellectual, the more pretentious the effort, the greater its vulnerability.

Obstacles to Productivity Improvement

Employee unions are widely regarded as the principal obstacle to productivity improvement in local government. As the discussion in the last chapter shows, the honor is unearned. Only in a handful of local governments and in a small number of municipal services have the unions been a serious impediment to increases in productivity. Only a few productivity improvement proposals have been blocked by the unions. Even in New York City, it proved possible to launch a large, broad-scale, and effective productivity program.

In the relatively few places with strong, aggressive unions, there is little doubt that the process of introducing productivity improving changes tends to be slowed and that some possible improvements are simply never advanced. In a far larger number of cases, productivity improvements have proceeded without either union resistance or employee objections. Indeed, the efforts in Nassau County and in the Detroit Productivity Center to involve the unions from the beginning both failed to generate much union or employee interest in specific productivity projects. It seems, in fact, highly probable that most productivity improvements in most local governments are viewed with equanimity, if not indifference, by most municipal employees.

The attitudes of department heads and civil service employees in managerial and supervisory positions probably pose a more widespread problem for productivity improvement than do employee unions. We see evidence of the problem in Lindsay's search in New York for department heads who could and would undertake innovation, in the opposition to productivity improvements by some of Palo Alto's department heads, and in the opposition or lack of cooperation of many of the middle managers involved in Nassau County's productivity improvement projects. Clearly, many factors are involved including resentment of external interference, reluctance to take risks, low credibility in the possibility of constructive change, the desire to protect subordinates, and more generally, the absence of any tradition of innovative management.

Except for Nassau County and, to a limited extent, Palo Alto, local legislative bodies do not figure in our narratives as a source of opposition to productivity programs. In all but a few cities—such as Detroit and New York, with very strong mayor charters—executive authority to reallocate funds or establish new positions is tightly constrained; expenditures for a productivity improvement program would ordinarily require explicit Council approval. The anecdotal evidence suggests that most mayors, city managers, and county executives would face difficulties in attempting to sell their councils on expenditures for productivity analysts or consultants to undertake a productivity improvement program. A determined executive may sometimes be able to undertake the job without additional resources or, perhaps more often, to obtain federal financing for the project.

Opposition by citizen groups does not appear to be a major problem in productivity improvement. Local government officials tend to be somewhat more cautious in modifying services that impact directly on the public but, only New York of the eight governments surveyed, has had changes blocked by citizen action. It is also true, however, that to some unknown extent, governments avoid productivity initiatives of a kind that is likely to generate adverse citizen reaction. The circumspection with which police departments are treated in most productivity programs probably reflects the ability of the police to engender citizen support for their objections to outside interference.

Transfer of Ideas

There is evidence, in the communities with productivity programs, of an appreciable but yet limited drawing on lessons learned and ideas developed elsewhere. There is little indication, however, that any major effort was motivated or induced by the example of another community. There are several patterns of technology transfer.

The first comes from the movement of people from jobs with one local government to jobs in another. Bill Donaldson's work on technology in Tacoma obviously reflected the continuing development of his initiatives as city manager of Scottsdale. George Barbour applied in Palo Alto ideas he had acquired or developed while heading the productivity projects of the International City Management Association. Harry Kelman brought his knowledge of the productivity improvement program in New York's Sanitation Department to his job heading the Work Planning and Control system in Phoenix. Ron Contino came from the same experience to head the San Diego County productivity program. There are former Phoenix hands in both Palo Alto and Dallas. The "movers" bring not only experiences from other situations but also a more cosmopolitan perspective of outside developments.

The second group of transfer agents are the consultants, who have, as I have already noted, played an especially important role in the initiation of programs. Consultants also figure in nearly all the system building: Work Planning and Control and Program Analysis and Review in Phoenix; the Service Management System in Palo Alto; Project Management and Planning-Programming-Budgeting in New York. There are many examples of comparable consultant work in other cities. Management consultants are probably especially well equipped to undertake assignments of this kind.

A third form of transfer comes from knowledge of the experience of other cities. There are several examples in the subject cities. In refuse disposal, Dallas reviewed the Phoenix system, and, earlier, Phoenix had surveyed Scottsdale and Inglewood, California before local decisions were made. Both Dallas, in analyzing its water department, and Wilmington, in analyzing its fire department, made cost and staffing comparisons with other cities.

A fourth source of ideas comes from the professional communication channels, including recent efforts explicitly designed to encourage transfer. Most of the eight local governments had some experience with Public Technology, Incorporated, most commonly with the fire station locator model. New

York City's Rand Institute's fire response model was used in both Wilmington and Tacoma, and "taken into account" in the Dallas analysis.

A fifth source of ideas was industry. The transfer method was apparently ordinary product marketing. Its importance is difficult to judge and probably tends to be understated. The Shu-Pak refuse collection trucks, Roto-Broom, Rapid Rail, the Addressograph Total Copy System, the Honeywell 2000 building monitor are only some of the hardware items that figure in the productivity narratives of the individual communities. The availability of the hardware made the productivity improvements possible, and it is likely that the first knowledge of the hardware often came from company sales representatives.

With all the evidence of transfer, it seems a small part of the overall effort. This is partly due to the fact that every new idea, whether it is developed indigenously or imported from outside, must be modified, adapted, and detailed to fit the needs of particular local situations. Technology transfer is seldom a ready-to-wear suit. More commonly, it provides superior inputs to a process that still depends on a substantial amount of custom tailoring. Even hardware that needs no modification must be fitted into a service system of which it is only one ingredient. In addition, however, present transfer processes are clumsy, imperfect, and often almost accidental. A far superior effort is clearly possible.

Implementation

In New York City, the implementation of productivity and performance improvements was a major problem. Mayoral decisions would often literally be lost in a maze of complications within the huge bureaucracy. The problem was solved only with the creation of a Project Management Staff, initially in the Mayor's Office and later in the Bureau of the Budget, to schedule and monitor the implementation of improvement efforts. The inauguration of the formal productivity program in 1972 was, in fact, an extension and formalization of the same approach establishing a schedule of performance targets for which the operating agencies were responsible and against which they were required to make regular progress reports to the mayor.

None of the other local governments with productivity improvement programs seems to have faced similar problems in the management of implementation. Usually, budget office staff in these cities have stayed close to implementation, often assisting the operating agencies. But formal project management systems are virtually nonexistent. Implementation has usually proceeded on a timely basis without any special tracking system.

The differences between New York and the smaller cities are chiefly a reflection of the enormous difference in scale and, to a lesser extent, variations in the quality of management. Most of the other governments have been among the best managed in their size categories. In New York, the frequently high technical and professional capabilities in the city's staff have not been matched by a parallel tradition of managerial excellence. The quality of management has long been generally low.

In nearly all the governments, reporting and data collection on city agency performance is extensive. Phoenix's work measurement program probably demands the most detailed reporting, but all the others gather output and performance information on a regular and systematic basis. None, except in New York's productivity programs, include performance targets or objectives. Except in New York, arrangements for review and follow-up seem to have been spotty, rarely involving a staff effort of appreciable magnitude.

Targets and Achievements

If we were to eliminate refuse collection from the list of productivity improvements, the accomplishment of the typical productivity program would shrink to half its size. It is one of the curiosities of local government that in the first half of the 1970s so many cities elected to take on the garbage collectors. There were major improvements in refuse collection productivity in Dallas, Detroit, Flint, Milwaukee, New York, Phoenix, Scottsdale, Tacoma, Wilmington, and probably many other cities. In most, it was, usually by a wide margin, the largest single productivity saving.

There are good technical reasons for the choice. Refuse collection is a service that lends itself to measurement and comparison to a much greater degree than most municipal services. It is also a materials-handling problem for which basic technology is strong and to which industrial engineering techniques are especially appropriate. Moreover, performance had apparently typically or at least frequently fallen well below achievable standards. On the other hand, sanitation unions in most localities are relatively strong and likely to resist workload changes. The success in handling the unions may be a matter of timing in that most of the improvements come after the period of peak union militancy in the 1960s.

One insight on refuse collection escaped me until I visited Milwaukee. This is the fact that refuse collection practices in northern cities were, until perhaps 1950, dictated by the problems of collecting coal ash. The replacement of coal by oil, gas, and electric heating after the war must have reduced aggregate refuse weight to a fraction of its previous weight—but manning and work standards geared to the heavier job of ash removal apparently tended to persist to some substantial degree. In many cities, this left large potential productivity gains to be harvested at some future date.

After sanitation, fire departments were the object of the most attention, but here the gains were smaller and sometimes questionable. New York, Tacoma, and Wilmington actually cut back the number of fire companies. Dallas and

Milwaukee merely slowed or stayed the expansion. The fire fighters' unions were more effective than the sanitation unions in resisting change. Often, they had the support of the fire chief and top officers.

The other target areas tended, like sanitation, to involve output that is easily measurable. Building inspectors, meter readers, pavement repair crews, building maintenance and cleaning staff, and mechanics all have this characteristic. Blue-collar labor areas seem to have predominated.

The limited attention given the police may be due not merely to political sensitivities and the strength of the police unions but also to the ambiguity of police output and the consequent difficulties in its measurement and analysis.

Health and social service programs also seemed to have received little attention partially because they are typically minor elements in municipal budgets and, now, more commonly handled by the state or the county. Some of these programs also have some of the same ambiguity of output as characterizes police.

Some seemingly obvious targets are not as common in productivity programs as one would expect. Paper work management, especially in finance, vital statistics, police, and register of deeds and licenses and permits, has tended to offer major opportunities for savings. The management of cash balances is another area of similar opportunity. Neither appear with much frequency in the programs reviewed.

On balance, the productivity programs seem to have been properly opportunistic, concentrating with few exceptions on functions that offered a rather high promise of savings and on agencies where cooperation was high or potential resistance low. One result is that some of the tougher productivity improvement prospects still lie ahead.

Those prospects are substantial. The future model of refuse collection will be the one-person mechanized truck. This innovation is already functioning in Phoenix and Scottsdale, and the technology permits the development of the variants needed for the denser cities of the east and midwest. We are on the threshhold of totally new concepts for the organization of fire forces with smaller but more self-contained attack units and speedier second-alarm mobilization capacity. The breakthroughs in police work are not yet as evident, but the increasing study of police performance and the growing recognition of the many low-value uses of police manpower both promise to bring that issue to a head.

Cities have gone through only a first phase in computer usage with at least as much to do as has been done so far. Not the least of the impacts will come from minicomputers, microcomputers, and the miniaturized "chip." The computerized algorithms, already available, for optimum scheduling, routing, and allocation will see wider usage, as will new programs developed for virtually every routine paper handling and analysis done in the typical city government.

To realize the potential will require more analytic work and more complex work by the cities and vastly more help from outside in the development of standard models of application.

The experience to date would indicate that any city able to generate annual productivity savings equal to 1 percent of the city budget is doing very well. This understates the effect of the improvement since most savings continue annually for the life of the operation. Hence, newly implemented savings annually at an annual rate of 1 percent would lead aggregate savings in ten years running at a continuing rate of 10 percent assuming other functions had not increased in real terms.

This is not negligible, but it is dwarfed by other factors affecting municipal budgets. Under the conditions in recent years, inflationary increases of 10-15 percent have been quite common, and, even in more normal times, 2-3 percent per annum is virtually a minimum. Moreover, the national economic significance of municipal productivity programs will be miniscule so long as so few cities undertake such programs.

From the broader perspective of overall state and local government, city government is dwarfed by the expenditures of state and county government and the school districts. Education, welfare, medicaid, and health constitute about three-fourths of all nonfederal government expenditures, but they are included in comparatively few municipal budgets. Washington, D.C. and New York City are among a handful of exceptions. The attention paid to these social, education, and health service areas from a productivity perspective seems to have been minor compared to the scrutiny now being given to municipal programs.

Note

1. Frederick O'R. Hayes and John E. Rasmussen, eds., *Centers for Innovation in the Cities and States* (San Francisco Press, 1972), p. 429. All of the institutions mentioned in the section on Think Tanks are described in detail in this volume.

12

Research and Technical Assistance for Productivity

For decades, the key word of choice for those concerned with the quality of government management of its responsibilities has been "efficiency." "Productivity," in this context, carries, perhaps, a somewhat broader meaning, but the current use of that word in lieu of efficiency is more a symptom of a change in semantic style rather than one of meaning.

Yet, there is a difference. Efficiency is curiously situation-bound in most of its uses and most properly applied to an individual firm or government, a program or operation. Productivity, on the other hand, is a meaningful concept with respect to the national economy and its growth.

The new interest in the old issue of government performance has produced a broader response partially because of the new name. "Thinking about productivity in government" is not quite the same as "thinking about government efficiency." The term "productivity" reminded the economists, as "efficiency" never would have done, of the fact that no one had ever developed any means of valuing government output, except by its costs, in our national income accounts; as a result, our estimates of gross national product and national income have simply assumed a zero growth rate in government productivity.

A subject given scant attention during a decade of off-and-on debate on national growth and productivity rates suddenly acquired the needed cachet. The Congress, the General Accounting Office, and the Executive Branch became interested not simply in increasing government efficiency but in knowing the trends in productivity in the federal government. In a rather short time, some estimates based on empirical examination were developed and published. The same interest extends to the equally important but more difficult area of state and local government.

Evidencing this new interest, Jerome A. Mark published, in the *Monthly Labor Review* of December 1972, estimates of the effect of different assumed productivity growth rates in government on the rate of increase in national productivity. If, for example, productivity in the private sector is increasing by 3 percent per year, and the government sector has not increased in productivity.

259

the national rate would be 2.5 percent. If the federal government is, as some recent studies indicate, increasing its productivity by an average of 1.9 percent a year but state and local governments remain unchanged, the national rate would be 2.7 percent.

What Mark and others are telling us is that productivity in state and local government (and in government, generally) has national economic significance, indeed, greater significance than ever before because of the record state and local government share in gross national product. One result is the emergence of a new and legitimate area of research interest rather unrelated to programs and efforts to increase state and local productivity. This is the concern for adequate measurement of productivity changes in the state and local government components of national product accounts and, more broadly, the role of expenditures by these governments in the national economy.

Quite separate from this arena of research is that research specifically aimed at understanding or aiding the process by which state and local governments might increase the productivity of their operations. This in itself is a research area of very broad scope.

The genesis and implementation of productivity and performance improvements in local governments involve a wide range of different actors and processes. In the fully developed case or model we can identify the following distinct processes as relevant to productivity increasing action and potential subjects of research:

Policy decision processes involving the city or county council, the chief executive, department and program heads, the electorate, and the general public.

Program analysis and design, the means by which problems and opportunities are identified, and improvements planned and designed.

Negotiation and bargaining with interested parties.

Work process and organization, the work force required to do it, work methods and technology, hardware and equipment used and the nature of output.

Adjustment procedures to accommodate productivity changes potentially affecting both workers and program clients.

Evaluation to determine costs, effectiveness, and results from any change.

This schema bears some resemblance to that used in Chapter 1 but differs from it to reflect the emphasis here on process. Considered as an outline research agenda, this listing would embrace a number of different disciplines as well as several different research areas within those disciplines. Political science, sociology, psychology, economics, engineering, and systems analysis are only the more obvious of these.

This structure without addendum would assume implicitly that the individual local government and its community existed quite independently and self-contained with perfect knowledge of its options and their probable results. We know, to the contrary, that the individual local government is dependent to varying degrees on knowledge, techniques, and tools from sources external to the government. The stimulus to initiate a productivity improvement may come from knowledge of an experiment conducted in some other city or, for example, from a convincing presentation by an IBM salesman. These are, of course, only random examples from a very large number of different kinds of impact from the outside world. We might shorthand this as the process of *external communication.* Research and technical assistance are, of course, concerned primarily with the development of material useful for introduction through this communication process and with the communication process itself.

We can categorize very simply the kinds of information that might be usefully developed to better stimulate and support local productivity improvement programs. In terms of sheer volume, the largest component would be drawn from the relevant experience of other local governments. This experience has the special value of a presumptive credibility, because it reflects *de minimis* the political-bureaucratic environment common to all local governments rather than the quite different economic environment of private enterprise.

Note that information of this character may be equally useful if its deals with failures rather than successes and that it may be concerned with any of or all the local processes discussed above. It may be *descriptive,* simply a case study of a local program or some aspect of such a program. It may be *comparative,* attempting to assess different programs or efforts, one against the other. It may be *analytical* and *evaluative,* focused on the identification of the extent of success and the factors most important to its achievement. Or the research may go one further step to develop and support a *prescriptive* approach setting out the best approaches seemingly indicated by a review of experience.

There is little material of this character available today and what there is, with some few recent exceptions, tends to focus heavily on work process, the problems of technique, technology, and work organization. To many a mayors or city managers, this may seem the least of their problems; they may be far more concerned with the problem of union negotiations or city council involvement. Quite aside from the narrow focus of much of the existing material, the small volume is a genuine handicap given the extraordinary diversity in local government and the environment in which it functions. The value to a local official of any productivity program experience in any other local government will vary directly with the extent the local official can see in that experience elements common to his or her own situation. The important elements may be community size, climate, geographic location, physical characteristics, political environment, labor relations, governmental structure, or any of a host of others. The diversity of American local government in such respects virtually dictates the usefulness of a broad approach to the researching of relevant experience.

There are, of course, lessons to be learned from experience in situations external to local government. Many perhaps need to be developed to more clearly apply to local government situations. The Mayo-Roethlischberger experiments at Hawthorne say something seemingly useful for the conduct of work in any organized setting, but it may be lost without the effort to translate its significance to the particular setting of local government. Technology applications tend to appear first in businesses but transfer to governmental problems and processes may demand further development. Despite the often serious problems of adaptation to a governmental environment, there are parallels in the private economy to nearly all the processes of innovation and productivity improvement in government.

In all the above, the objective of reserach would, in effect, be to develop the lessons from relevant experience within and without local government and by articulation, comparison, analysis, and adaptation make it both communicable and useful to local governments or to those who serve local governments. This strong experiential focus of research seems inevitable given the fact that this is the dominant learning mode in the disciplines concerned with the social and political processes that are central to governmental innovation. Research on work process and technology has some similar characteristics, certainly in the effort to identify best existing practice. Efforts to develop new techniques and technology are more akin to invention, but, even here, the typical research aims at utilizing already known and applied techniques and technology in new combinations to fit special problems.

The last of the component processes in local government productivity improvement programs mentioned above was the evaluative aspect, determining the effectiveness and results of the supposed improvement. This deserves some special attention if only because it has been a matter of high interest to researchers drawn from the economic profession.

The central concern is with the measurement of the product or output of the process. One problem is the difficulty in developing any measure aside from the volume of inputs for the measurement of the output of certain services, for example, police. There is the further problem that even if output were measurable at least comparatively through some index formulation, the value of that output would depend on its impact on, say, the crime rate—a value that cannot readily or definitively be determined given the many causal external factors. Closely related is the problem of quality of the product. An increase in quantity of output achieved with a constant resource input is not regarded as a gain in productivity if it results from a reduction in the scope or quality of the service provided. A conceptually adequate measurement system must consequently measure the quality of output as well as its quantity.

Much of the research concern is not directed at the needs of local government for better evaluation but rather toward the problem of valuing governmental output. To the local government official, some of this is useful, but much of it is esoteric. In most local governments, a reduction in the sanitation force made possible by less frequent collections would be regarded as a gain in productivity (despite citizen complaints) and there would be little sympathy for the economist's concern with the value of the reduction in quality attributable to less frequent service. On the other hand, if higher productivity has resulted in more garbage spills and dirtier streets and alleys, local government is likely to be interested in better methods for quality control and evaluation.

Research is, of course, only one aspect of the problem; a second aspect concerns the means by which research results can be brought to local governments and used in the development and administration of programs to increase productivity. This is a far more complex issue than has usually been recognized. The problem exists despite a highly developed communications network embracing the professional and even the political officials of local government. There is little doubt that most of these officials are exposed through professional meetings and through publications that they receive regularly and routinely to the existence of more effective or more efficient program configurations in other local governments. The availability of that knowledge seems to have produced comparatively little interest in emulation.

A single paragraph in a public administration periodical is, however, only a teaser, rarely detailed or evaluative enough to provide meaningful guidance for its replication in another city. It suggests the need to develop "how to do it" material. The opportunities for an enriched "how to do it" approach have become very extensive, now including computer programs on magnetic tape with sample taped data files, film strips, video tape, slides, movies, programmed instruction, and others.

The best of the "how to do it" material may still leave substantial problems in adaptation of an innovation to a particular local situation. This suggests that the packaged material will often be useful only if it can be supported by the assignment of technical experts to assist and aid the process of adaptation. There have been efforts to provide this help.

There remain a large number of American governments, probably a majority even of the larger ones, on which the many performance and productivity improvement efforts have had little impact. This is a motivation question on which there is little systematic and objective data. We know, at least in an anecdotal sense, that the absence of public pressure for improvement, the risks of failure or confrontation incident to any change, skepticism about the innova-

tion or its adaptability to that particular situation, and the lack of staff qualified to analyse the issue or administer the program are all factors in executive
reluctance to undertake innovations. The pragmatic question is the character
of the inducements and the protections against risk that might produce a
different pattern of behavior.

The National Science Foundation

Out concern here is primarily with those who carry out research and provide
technical assistance, rather than the organizations that fund it. However, the
role in urban research and technology transfer assumed by the National Science
Foundation in recent years is too significant to be ignored.

The NSF Intergovernmental Science and Research Utilization and the
Experimental R & D incentive Programs (now the NSF/RANN Intergovernmental Programs) have financed a variety of experimental efforts to provide
technological and scientific inputs for local and state government decision
making. These include the Urban Technology System and the Urban Consortium, both managed by Public Technology, Incorporated and discussed elsewhere
in this chapter. Tacoma's "Totem One" Technology Transfer Project, the Four
Cities program in California, the Mayor's Science and Technology Advisory
Council in Philadelphia and the engineering extension agent program in Geneva
and Anniston, Alabama have all been supported by NSF grants. The common
element in all these programs is to provide to the local governments the services
of an individual trained in technology application.

Science and technology development in the states has involved support
for a Governor's R & D Priorities Conference, which led to the creation by the
State of Oklahoma of a Foundation for Research and Development Utilization,
for a Center for Public Technology at Oklahoma State University and for
another Governors' R and D Priorities Conference that led to state establishment
of the Ohio Development Center. The Technology Information Exchange project
has prepared "technology packages" for state and local governments on energy
conservation, land-use planning, and manpower productivity.

In the Foundation's Research Applied to National Needs (RANN) program,
public sector productivity research has accounted for roughly $15 million in
annual expenditures. RANN has financed evaluations of policy-related research
in nineteen areas of municipal operations and twenty areas of human resources.
A series of investigations have been commissioned in a systematic effort to explore productivity measurement problems in municipal services. Another group
of projects aims at identifying the effect of organizational structure on municipal service delivery. The impact of alternative types of federal grants is covered
by a related set of projects. The relationship between government regulation and
economic productivity is another major research area.

The Foundation's Intergovernmental Programs have been the most visible

part of NSF activities to the local official. The Foundations's major efforts
in technology transfer seem to have all had some measure of success. The RANN
effort is becoming more visible with the publication of the thirty-nine state-of-
the-art reviews and with the proliferation of projects in which one or more
local governments have been involved. No other urban government research
effort has been so systematic in its coverage. RANN projects have progressed
through the obvious cases of fire protection and refuse collection to such areas
as purchasing, auditing, real property assessment, and pension fund management. Research specifications almost always call for user manuals or other
output designed to bring the results to users.

Twenty million dollars a year has made the Foundation the single most
important entity in urban governmental research. The proof of the value of the
Foundation's work would, of course, be evidence of its widespread use and
application. Much of the research output is getting used but primarily by the
researchers and academics concerned with these problems; the state-of-the-art
evaluations, despite a wide variation in quality, constitute the best example of
such use. The Foundation's only entry into nationwide research and technology application in local government has been through its grants to PTI—but
PTI has not been a vehicle for the application of the Foundation's own research
results. One may suspect that a truly effective nationwide dissemination and
application will require more substantial funding than the research itself.
Whether NSF will be willing to make such a commitment or able to obtain it
from the Congressional financiers is subject to some doubt.

The Urban Institute

The Urban Institute, a nonprofit research corporation, established at the instance of the Department of Housing and Urban Development in 1969, has
been the largest single source of user-oriented research on productivity in local
government. A large proportion of the Institute's recent work in the area has
been sponsored and financed by the National Center on Productivity and
Quality of Working Life, while some of the earlier work was financed by HUD
and the District of Columbia government.

The Institute's work has had several different aspects. One has been a
concern with program evaluation and effectiveness. *Practical Program Evaluation
for State and Local Government Officials* was prepared by Harry P. Hatry,
Richard E. Winnie, and Donald M. Fisk with HUD financing in 1973. *How Clean
is Our City? A Guide for Measuring the Effectiveness of Solid Waste Collection
Activities* by Louis H. Blair and Alfred I. Schwartz was published in 1972, the
results of a joint project with the District of Columbia Government, partially
aided by HUD funds. This was followed by a parallel effort in transportation,
Measuring the Effectiveness of Local Government Services: Transportation,
another HUD-financed study by Winnie and Hatry.

The Institute collaborated with the International City Management Association in preparing for the National Commission on Productivity, *The Challenge of Productivity Diversity,* a four-volume mimeo report dealing with the measurement of productivity in solid waste collection and police-crime control and including, in addition, six case studies in innovation. In 1974, *Measuring Fire Protection Productivity in Local Government* was prepared by Philip S. Schaenman of the Institute staff and Joe Swartz of the National Fire Protection Association and published by the NFPA.

The Institute also prepared for the National Commission on Productivity the report, *Managing Human Resources in Local Government; A Survey of Employee Incentive Plans* and a far more comprehensive successor volume, *Employee Incentives to Improve State and Local Government Productivity.* A report was prepared on the productivity incentive collective bargaining contracts for sanitation workers in Flint, Michigan and for police officers in Orange, California. All these were published by the Commission rather than the Urban Institute. A more recent study, *An Assessment of the Impacts of Five Local Government Productivity Programs,* includes a later assessment of the Flint and Orange cases. The study was prepared in collaboration with the Labor-Management Relations Service and financed by the Department of Labor.

The Status of Productivity Measurement in State Government: An Initial Examination was prepared for and published by the National Commission on Productivity in 1975. More recent reports include: *Program Analysis for State and Local Governments* and *Measuring the Effectiveness of Basic Municipal Services—An Initial Report;* the latter was done collaboratively with the International City Management Association.

The Institute's research team on state and local government under Harry Hatry has become an important resource, particuarly with its increasing knowledge of important developments in state and local efforts to increase productivity. No other organization save the National Center for Productivity and Quality of Working Life itself has made a significant effort to prepare "how to do it" guides and manuals for state and local government officials. Few others have surveyed and analyzed local government experience for the cases useful to other local governments. Even in its more limited preparation of case histories, the Institute is one of the few organizations with an interest in the preparation of such material. The Institute staff is beginning to provide the continuity of perspective—despite its relatively short existence—that we might expect from a federal department for local government, had we such an organization. Its work has been solid and well-developed throughout.

The National Center for Productivity and Quality of Working Life

The National Center for Productivity and Quality of Working Life, (formerly the National Commission on Productivity and Work Quality) in existence for only five years, has no independent research capacity and a very limited budget, and must necessarily devote primary attention to productivity in the private economy rather than in government. Yet, it has provided significant assistance to the effort to improve productivity in state and local government.

The Center has functioned through three different approaches. First has been its publication program. In addition to the reports prepared for the center by the Urban Institute, the Center has published the following:

1. *So, Mr. Mayor, You Want to Improve Productivity; Jurisdictional Guide to Productivity Improvement Projects, A Handbook for Public Officials,* a catalogue of local productivity improvement efforts;
2. *Opportunities for Improving Productivity in Police Services,* a guide prepared with the aid of an expert advisory committee;
3. *Improving Police Productivity: A Brief for Elected Officials;*
4. *Opportunities for Improving Productivity in Solid Waste Collection* and the companion *Brief for Elected Officials,* prepared, like the police hand-books, with advisory committee aid;
5. *Improving Municipal Productivity: The Detroit Refuse Collection Incentive Plan,* a case study and analysis of the experiment with a productivity incentive bonus for workers;
6. *Productivity in State and Local Governments, Report on the Wingspread Conference;*
7. *Improving Productivity and Productivity Measurement in Local Govern-ments;*
8. *Governmental Productivity: Organizational Activities.*

Other Center publications in process include pieces on work measurement systems, on the use of private sector for the performance of public services, on the productivity potential from the use of university extension services, and a productivity guide for City Council members.

The widely distributed Center publications represent an effort to bring to state and local government officials generally usable knowledge of the many productivity improvement efforts undertaken in state and local governments, ideas about the significant opportunities for productivity increases in selected areas, and expert guides on how a productivity program might be launched.

A second thrust of the Center's effort has been a series of conferences with local government officials held during 1974–1975 in collaboration with the International City Management Association in the various regions of the country. More recently, the Center has created a special advisory council of state and local government officials to help pursue its objectives in this area.

Lastly, the Center staff has worked with staffs of other federal agencies, notably the Department of Housing and Urban Development and the National Science Foundation in the development of efforts related to state and local government productivity. This is probably especially significant with respect to the NSF, which has undertaken a program of research grants to explore various aspects of state and local government productivity.

One could scarcely hazard a guess as to the impact of the Center's work program on state and local productivity. There is, however, no doubt that the Center's program has made a large proportion of our top state and local officials conscious of the existence of a potential for productivity improvements and of the programs in other jurisdictions that might serve as models. Nancy Hayward who heads up the Center's public sector work has done an extraordinary job of evangelism in bringing the productivity message to local government officials.

Public Technology, Incorporated

Public Technology, Incorporated (PTI) was set up in the early 1970s by the International City Management Association with the aid of a Ford Foundation grant. The purpose was to bring technology to local governments. PTI functions under a board dominated by representatives of the various nonprofit organizations for state and local government: The ICMA, the National Association of County Officials, the Conference of Mayors and the National League of Cities, the National Governor's Conference, and the Conference of State Governments. The President of PTI is Porter Homer, former manager of Dade County, Miami, and several other former local government officials are members of the top staff of the organization. PTI is, in few words, user-dominated.

PTI's basic modus operandi starts with the users of technology, the officials of local government. In each major area, such as, for example, fire fighting, PTI creates a user committee of local officials, typically the heads of principal using departments in various local governments. The user group develops a statement of its principal technology needs. PTI brings in appropriate technologists to help develop an approach meeting user specifications. The technologists may be drawn from PTI's own staff, from university or other research groups and, for hardware, from the manufacturers of equipment. An approach, once developed, is tested in a sample of localities and eventually made available for wider distribution.

Thus far, this process has produced a new longer-lasting, but more expensive road patching material, new breathing apparatus for firemen, the Hughes Probe-Eye infra-red heat detector, and the Grumman automatic nozzle for fire engines. There has been, also, an increasing development of software: a fire station locator model, a sanitation truck routing model, a packaged motor vehicle maintenance system.

These innovations are provided to cities with paid subscriptions to PTI and ordinarily PTI staffs have been made available on a limited basis to help with the problems of putting the new device or method to work. Subscribers now include over 100 counties and cities.

PTI has also received funding from several federal agencies including NASA. It has explored possible application in the cities of technology and techniques developed for the space program. A project on shorter distance radio communication for the fire service is an example of this program.

PTI is widely known among city officials especially in cities functioning under the city manager plan. Most city managers and many other top local officials have become familiar with its objectives and with the specific programs it is offering to improve local government productivity. The development and testing period has precluded any widespread application of new hardware, but a large number of cities have used PTI's analytic models, especially the fire station locator model.

There are some who are critical of the PTI effort. It is argued that the modus operandi, especially on hardware, results in an unnecessarily slow process of problem identification and solution development and that, moreover, the user domination means an emphasis on marginal and peripheral changes that avoid any serious threat to traditional methods of operation. The PTI fire station locator model has been criticized as technically limited and not applicable in many situation where a more sophisticated model could be useful. The new pavement repair material now appears likely to be so expensive that it will offer only a modest advantage over conventional paving material. The Grumman nozzle will carry a price tag of $12,000 or more, enough to discourage its purchase in many fire departments. Finally, some critics are perturbed by the partnership between PTI and profit-making manufacturing firms, such as Hughes and Grumman.

There is almost certailny some merit to the criticisms. It may also be true that most of the problems were unavoidable if local officials were to be persuaded of the advantages of technological change and if manufacturers were to be convinced that development costs for technology for cities could be recovered. The argument should not, however, obscure the fact that PTI has had some genuine success in educating local government to the potential of new technology and new techniques. This is particularly striking in the many small cities involved.

The fire station locator model is a good example. Fire station location has historically been handled by what might be called informed intuitive judgment in a municipal service that has usually been very resistant to interference from the powers above. The PTI, in effect, made available a "black box" (albeit a simple black box) method of solving the problem. It is one of a large family of computerized algorithms developed during the last decade that have relevance to municipal problem solving. Despite some resistance to "black boxes" among local government operating officials, the fire station model has become in a few short years probably the most widely known and widely used example of the technique in American local government. This reflects the power of PTI's user dominance and user orientation.

I have encountered various criticisms of the fire locator model in almost
every city in which I examined productivity improvement efforts. This seems
to have had little adverse effect on the willingness of the cities to work with
PTI. PTI is, to local officials, a member of the club; this has spared PTI the
destructive effects of public criticism in these early years of program development and even deterred withdrawal by managers skeptical of the alleged benefits
of membership.

Whatever the merits of the model, it has been, in every case I examined, an
effective means of opening up the issue of fire station location and fire force
deployment. Knowing the PTI model existed, city managers had an alternative
to the professional judgment of the fire chiefs. That was enough to launch
a process in which the solution that emerged, whether or not with the aid of the
PTI model, was significantly different from the approach initially recommended
by the fire department.

In July 1973, the National Science Foundation awarded to PTI a fifty-
three-month contract for the development and management of an experimental
Urban Technology System (UTS). Under this program, technological support
is provided to twenty-seven small- and medium-sized general local governments.
For each participating government, a resident technology agent has been employed by PTI; the agent was selected by the local government from a list of
candidates designated by PTI. Backup technical support is supplied for each city
by a university, nonprofit research organization, federal government laboratory,
or a profit-making research firm under PTI-financed contracts.

The primary objectives of the project are to test the effectiveness of the
UTS model in increasing technological innovation and the diffusion of innovation among local government. It will also be evaluated on its success in aggregat-
ing the local government market to stimulate private research and development
and in assisting the federal government in setting research and development
priorities.

By November 30, 1975, $2.5 million in National Science Foundation Funds
had been invested in the program; to this amount, the participating local governments had added over $4 million. At that time, the technology agents had been
resident in the host jurisdictions for seventeen months, the first twelve months
of the program having been devoted to program organization and development.
The seventeen-months work had, according to PTI, produced annual savings,
actual or anticipated, of nearly $6.3 million in the operations of the local
governments involved. That amount is described as including cost savings, cost
avoidance, and productivity gains. Hence, each federal dollar had generated a
local investment of 1.7 dollars, and each dollar of total investment had produced
potential annual savings of about the same amount. The ratio of savings to investment will, perforce, increase, since most of the savings will continue at the
same annual rate although the related investment expenditure has been completed; meanwhile, program resources will be invested in new projects that will
yield further savings.

The PTI accounting of savings includes sixty-four different projects in twenty-two of the twenty-seven participating local governments. Seven jurisdictions account for over 60 percent of the projects. These are: Lower Merion Township, Pa. (8); Pueblo, Colo. (7); Hampton, Va. (6); Sioux City, Iowa (5); Jersey City, N.J. (5); Little Rock, Ark. (4); and Pasadena, Cal. (4). A review of some of the projects with relatively large annual savings will cast some light on the varied nature of UTS projects.

Energy conservation projects account for $1.2 million in estimated savings, largely in three cities: Jersey City, Nashville, and West Hartford. Jersey City's projects include a new total energy system for the Medical Center and a boiler modification project both designed by Exxon Research and Engineering, the technical back-up organization. Other projects emphasize control of and economy in energy usage.

The largest savings—$1.1 million—are attributed to a multiproject Operations Improvement Program in Pasadena. The project under the direction of the technology agent is setting up new budgeting, evaluation, accounting, information, and performance auditing systems. Over $200,000 of the estimated savings had been achieved; the balance is a project goal.

Solid waste collection and disposal projects have total estimated savings of $1.2 million in Little Rock, Lower Merion Township, and Evanston. Evanston's technology agent restructured routes and proposed the use of larger trucks; the system is in operation. Work force was cut from fifty-seven to thirty-six for annual savings of $315,000.

Nine-hundred-thousand dollars in public safety improvements comes from projects in St. Petersburg, Pueblo, and Sioux City. The St. Petersburg project reassigned fire fighters to create three flying squads covering all structural fires, providing additional service that would have required forty-four more men and $500,000 under prior assignment practices. Sioux City was able to save $180,000 in airport crash rescue and fire protection services by relocating an existing fire company at the airport.

There are a handful of automation projects (e.g. building heat and lighting in Henrico County, Virginia and gasoline dispensing in Oklahoma City) and many applications of routing, scheduling, and allocation models.

Even with some attrition in claimed but yet-to-be-achieved savings, PTI's claim that the project pay-off will exceed costs is almost certainly valid. The project should, when completed, provide a convincing demonstration of the value of higher-than-usual levels of technical assistance. PTI concedes some failures in selection of back-up institutions and in choice of agents. It has also had problems with personality clashes between technology agents and city representatives and with cities that have proved very difficult to work with. Adaptation to meet these problems is one of the tests of UTS management.

More recently PTI has launched another program, the Urban Consortium in which the twenty-six cities and six urban counties over 500,000 are participants. The Consortium began with modest financing in 1974 and has now re-

ceived funding of roughly $1 million from the National Science Foundation and
the Department of Transportation. It will attempt both to bring new technology
to the participating cities and to provide a forum for interchange of experience
in relevant areas.

The Labor-Management Relations Service

The Labor-Management Relations Service (LMRS) was established by the
National League of Cities, the United States Conference of Mayors, and the
National Association of Counties to provide information and assistance to
local governments on relations with labor and with employee unions.

LMRS under the direction of Sam Zagoria has been much aware of the
productivity issue in labor relations and has given that aspect of labor relations
considerable attention. It has, as a result, become one of the major sources of
information and guidance on that subject to municipal and county governments. While not intended to be a research organization, it has been able
through federal and other grants to undertake analyses of some important labor
relations–productivity cases. LMRS prepared, for example, the first nationally
distributed analysis of the Detroit sanitation workers' incentive contract. It was
also responsible for evaluations of the Productivity Center program in Detroit
and the Multi-Municipality Productivity Program in Nassau County, New York.
The LMRS monthly newsletter is a model of the genre, perhaps the best of all
newsletters and bulletins of any kind directed toward local government officials.

LMRS illustrates the advantage of subject area focus in issues of emerging
significance. It has, undoubtedly been able to do more and achieve attention for
its results than could its sponsoring organizations within their own structures.

The Council on Municipal Performance

The Council on Municipal Performance (COMP) describes itself as "a non-profit,
educational corporation established to develop and disseminate objective and
detailed measures of comparative municipal performance." COMP was established in New York City in 1973 by economist John Tepper Marlin with the
aid of grants from the Robert Sterling Clark Foundation, POINT Foundation,
and the Rockefeller Family Fund. COMP is a fledgling, now in its fourth year.
Its capacity for survival depends on its continuing ability to attract the grants
necessary to supplement the necessarily limited income from subscription to its
reports.

COMP had issued by mid-1976 six Municipal Performance Reports (MPRs)
analyzing intercity differences in conditions and performance in various areas
of concern. Reports have been issued on City Crime, City Housing, the Wealth

of Cities, City Budgets, City Air Quality, and City Transportation. Depending on the availability of data, comparisons typically cover about thirty large cities and are made on the basis of a rather exhaustive analysis of readily available data and some not so readily available data.

The monograph, *The Wealth of Cities,* for example, includes comparative data for thirty-one cities on median per capita income; the proportion of the population below the poverty line; the aggregate poverty income gap and the average gap per poor person; comparable data on a group with somewhat higher incomes described as "deprived" rather than "poor," coefficients of income inequality; aggregate income above the poverty line for city populations; costs and beneficiaries of antipoverty programs; an analysis of employment by degree of diversification, self-sufficiency, and employment in durable manufactures; the ratio of nonworkers to workers in the population; current and ten-year average unemployment rates; instability in employment levels; proportions of unemployment and low income in poverty areas compared to that for the area as a whole; and, finally, a narrative review and comparison of city economic development programs.

The Wealth of Cities is a representative example of COMP's output. Like most of the reports, it provides a great deal of information on differences among cities in a particular area of interest but tells us very little about the differences in performance among the municipal governments in those cities. Rather, it concentrates on the differences in the particular condition or aspect of urban life. This is partially because COMP has selected for its research a number of areas where the dominant causal factors are largely or wholly external to municipal government. The quality of the local economy can, for example, rarely be attributed to the relative effectiveness of local economic development and antipoverty programs. Local housing programs represent only one input of rather limited importance in the quality of the housing stock. The government role is more important in public transportation, crime rates, and air quality, but—even in these sectors—external factors are usually more important.

COMP's analyses are, in the main, the products of desk research from published data sources, the literature, and, sometimes, reports from special inquiries to the cities involved. Productivity and performance comparisons of municipal government would, on the other hand, require either substantial field research or a heavy investment in the design of data instruments and the willingness of city governments to execute them. Without these extra and costly elements of the research, it is doubtful that effective productivity and performance comparisons could be made with respect to most municipal activities. COMP is interested in such comparisons but the costs have been beyond the capacity of its funding.

The reports are not, hence, Municipal Performance Reports but, rather, City Condition Reports. They are valuable in pointing up problems and in indicating the variations in the externally determined conditions with which different cities must contend. The reports show the range of difference even among seemingly like cities to be surprisingly wide.

COMP must struggle with the limitations in published data series. For example, the FBI's Uniform Crime Reports (UCR) are the only comprehensive sources of crime statistics by jurisdiction in the United States. The UCR depend on, however, data reported by local law enforcement agencies; the underreporting of crime is ubiquitous and the variation in the degree of underreporting varies enormously from one jurisdiction to another. The antidote is emerging, at least for large cities, in the new LEAA-Census crime victimization surveys—but, for most cities, crime rate comparisons must start with the unsatisfactory UCR data. COMP attempted to develop a new crime index using five-million home owner insurance policies and found that its new theft index—called "ingenious" by *Planning* Magazine—came up with virtually the same ranking as the LEAA survey.

The Census of Government's data are of higher and more uniform quality but are still dependent on the accuracy of the data submitted by the cities to Census. In its efforts to make data comparable, Census produces results that are unrecognizable to officials of the larger and more complex jurisdictions. These problems add to the need for a more direct approach on COMP's part to the cities and their operation.

With all the reservations that might be expressed with respect to the COMP research program to date, its reports have been both valuable and unique. It has carved out a mission for itself that badly needs doing and that no other organization has seen fit to undertake.

The Conservation of Human Resources

The Conservation of Human Resources research complex at Columbia University under Professor Eli Ginzberg cuts a far wider swath than the most liberal definition of productivity would allow. The project has been a prolific producer of research on a wide variety of loosely interrelated subjects—work force and labor markets, health care institutions and needs, collective bargaining in the public sector, and, more recently, local budgeting for human resource programs. It is the latter two topics that concern us here.

The project on human resource program budgeting has some special significance. The human resource programs are defined in the project to include all the income maintenance, social service, health care, and education (including higher education) functions in the New York City budget.

In 1973, these programs accounted for $7.2 billion of the then $10 billion New York City budget. The role of local governments in these areas varies from state to state across the nation, but overall these programs account for two-thirds to three-fourths of government expenditures; they are also the most neglected in terms of productivity and performance improvement efforts.

The lead piece in the research effort is Charles Brecher's *Where Have All the Dollars Gone? Public Expenditures for Human Resource Development in New York City, 1961 to 1971.* Brecher's purpose is modest, to distribute the ten-year increase in the costs of these programs by the cause of the increase. That modest objective, for these complex programs in a large and complex city, required a substantial research effort.

The relationship of the research to local government productivity may seem obscure but it is not. Brecher has, in effect, attempted to reach a more analytic statement of the problem of human resource expenditure by an *ex post* assessment of the ten-year increase in expenditure. He uses a simple and readily replicable analytic model. He, first, estimates the amount of the ten-year increase attributable solely to workload changes (number of public assistance recipients, children in the public schools, full-time equivalent university enrollment, and other similar measures) by multiplying the change in workload by 1961 average unit costs. The effect of inflation is, then, estimated by applying percentage increases in private sector wage indices to the personal services cost component and in the consumers' price index, or an appropriate component of that index, to other than personal services expenditure. The base costs to which the percentages are applied are essentially 1961 costs adjusted for subsequent changes in workload. These estimates of the amounts due to workload and inflationary increases are then subtracted from the total increases in expenditure, leaving a residual reflecting the composite effect of change in efficiency and program quality.[a] Where feasible, Brecher divides wage bill changes between the amount attributable to inflation and the "excess" wage increase that is, of course, part of the residual. In other cases, he is able to identify specific program change factors responsible for part of the efficiency-quality change.

The character of Brecher's results underlines the importance of the analysis. He found that he was able to explain, through workload changes and inflation, a widely varying and, often, surprisingly low proportion of the change in expenditures. In the welfare programs, these factors explained 73 percent of the increase in public assistance grants, 66 percent of the increase in home relief, and 97 percent of change in administrative expense. At the other extreme—the major health programs—only 8 percent of the increase in municipal hospital costs, 15 percent of the increase in medical assistance–Medicaid costs and 10 percent of the rise in mental health center costs were explained by workload changes and inflation. The education program fell in between with workload and inflation accounting for 32 percent of the change in public school costs and 35 percent of the increase in city university expenditures.

One case where Brecher was able to carry the analysis further was in the aggregate increase in instructional salaries (not total expenditures) in the public

[a]Brecher's technique justifies an academic footnote. He assigns entirely to inflation the effect of increased prices on increased workload. This is an old problem of the $\Delta p \, \Delta q$ term for which Ross and Burkhead lay out an elegant solution in a work discussed below. Brecher's simpler approach serves his purpose.

Exhibit 12-1

Analysis of Increased Costs of Human Resource Programs in New York City

	Increase: 1961–1971	
Explanation	Amount (millions)	Percentage
Workload	$ 47.5	7.7
Salary Increases	278.3	44.9
Inflation	(183.8)	(29.7)
Excess	(94.5)	(15.2)
New Programs:		
Smaller Classes	76.0	12.3
Paraprofessionals	22.1	3.6
Higher Teacher Ratio (to extent not reflected in class size)	117.3	18.9
Other	78.3	12.6
Total	$619.6	100.0%

Source: Charles Brecher, *Where Have All the Dollars Gone? Public Expenditures for Human Resource Development in New York City, 1961 to 1971* (Praeger, 1974).

schools. He breaks down those increases in Exhibit 12-1. Brecher's objective is, in effect, to narrow the question, to explain what he can of the increase in expenditures, and to identify factors contributing to the part of the increase not explained. The ultimate question is what we, the public, are receiving from the higher expenditure level and, in particular, what indications are there that increase in program "quality" have produced increases in program effectiveness. Brecher finds that the data and often the measurement concepts to do this are simply not extant.

Brecher's research is necessarily unfinished, almost a workingnote. It is an outsider's work that misses some of the technical factors in expenditure increases and some of the opportunities for further development of expenditure explanation. It discusses but fails to integrate the impact of important federal requirements and programs. The analysis is further subject to some technical argument, for example, on the choice of wage indices to measure inflationary impact on salaries. I fault the research on none of these grounds. The resources and time required for research that is exhaustive and definitive are not justified by the value of the product in the first cycle. Brecher has produced an excellent preliminary statement of the problem susceptible to significant further refinement over time. It is a good beginning for a continuing research program.

The next stage of the project is the development of better approaches to the budgeting of these human resource programs. An initial round of working papers has been prepared on budgeting in each of the major program areas. The papers concentrate heavily on the specification of the data required for better budgeting and the information system changes necessary to obtain them. The emphasis throughout is on measures of program impact or effectiveness and on the tracking of individuals through the system necessary to provide such measures.

A great deal of our frustration with social welfare programs is directly attributable to the limitations of traditional techniques of data aggregation. Standard reporting on public assistance programs, for example, tells us how much was spent on how many cases or people, how many new applications were received and approved, and how many cases were closed. But it gives us little sense of program dynamics—the characteristics of applicants, the reasons for applying, the characteristics of persons in cases closed, the recidivism rates, the effect of migration, and recipient work history. These insights come from tracking hundreds of randomly selected cases over time. Guy Orcutt's pioneer work in compiling individual economic histories and in microsimulation arises from the same need. Current computer and software capability has greatly expanded our ability to do this. The need is real and important, and the initial papers indicate that the Columbia group will provide a knowledgeable and valid commentary on its characteristics and how the need might be met.

Research on collective bargaining and labor relations in the cities is a separate research project of the Columbia group. The research conducted by James W. Kuhn, Raymond D. Horton, and David Lewin will examine the experience to date with collective bargaining in the cities, particularly as it relates to work force utilization. A general analysis of experience across the nation will be carried out from data collected by annual surveys of the International City Managers' Association and from a review of relevant literature. In addition, a more detailed analysis will be done of labor relations in America's three largest cities—New York, Chicago, and Los Angeles. Lewin has prepared an initial analysis of labor relations in Los Angeles, and Horton, earlier, published an analysis of labor relations in New York during the Wagner-Lindsay years. The project is still in first stages. The authors have, however, already suggested, from initial fact finding, the diversity thesis of public collective bargaining which I have discussed in Chapter 10.

Whether or not the research validates the hypothesis, the research design is a good one. Unionization and collective bargaining in the cities are matters of great concern, imperfectly understood because bargaining is a game-type problem without determinable or predictable results from managerial strategy. Understanding depends on the development of an analysis of the process and results of collective bargaining in perhaps hundreds of situations and scores of cities. The comparative analysis of three large American cities should be an important contribution. The broader but thinner nationwide analysis is not equally likely to produce a significant contribution, but it is needed to help provide a framing perspective for the three-city study. Perhaps, the most important is the need to establish continuing research efforts to accumulate, analyze and disseminate the results of our developing experience in local government collective bargaining.

State University of New York at Albany

The Productivity Research Project for State Government at SUNY's Albany campus is a Ford Foundation–financed project in the University's Graduate School of Public Affairs.

The Productivity Reserach Project has published two workshop reports: *Administering State Government Productivity Improvement Programs* and *Motivating State Government Productivity Improvement Programs.* These are collections of workshop papers, one from each of two research conferences or workshops held under the auspices of the project. Each of the conferences includes papers from both academics, chiefly productivity project faculty from SUNY, and practitioners.

Practitioner papers include descriptions of the productivity improvement programs in Florida, Nassau County, New York State, Washington State, and Wisconsin. In addition, other practioner papers approach productivity from special perpsectives—union leadership, Department of Personnel, Bureau of the Budget, legislature, and university-government relations. The papers vary in quality and in potential usefulness to administrators or planners attempting to develop governmental productivity programs. There are few cases where the papers provide very detailed descriptions of the particular productivity programs or the process by which they were developed or the problems encountered in doing so. Their main value is that they add to the scarce literature on state and local government productivity programs and provide some insights of value into those programs.

The academic workshop papers are of more consistently high quality and more systematic in their coverage. Professor Walter Balk and his colleagues in the project have a sophisticated understanding of productivity programs and of their functioning in a social and political context. They embrace perspectives from industrial engineering at one end of the spectrum to organization psychology and political science at the other. The coverage is genuinely comprehensive, and the handling of some technical issues, especially with regard to problems of measurement and managerial control, is masterfully done. Balk has incorporated much of this perspective in his book, *Managing Scarce Resources in Public Agencies: Some Policy Perspectives on Productivity Improvement Programs,* which was published in 1976 by Sage Publications.

The SUNY research group has completed a number of significant empirical research projects in state government productivity. One of the most important is an analysis by political scientist Edgar Crane and economist Bernard Lentz to identify the factors in the political environment associated with productivity programs at different levels of effort and comprehensiveness. State productivity improvement efforts are classed in four groups: (1) ad hoc departmental efforts; (2) centrally managed efforts; (3) comprehensive measurement and reporting systems; and (4) fully developed multiagency programs.

Research to date indicates that the level of the productivity improvement is associated positively with the following variables (among others):

1. Total population
2. Per capita income
3. Innovation index score
4. Partisanship (frequency of legislative turnovers)
5. A "moralist" political culture (less with "individualist" cultures, least with "traditional")
6. Location in the west or, to a lesser extent, in the midwest
7. Legislatures with higher legislative expenditures, more complex organization, program review capability, and high professionalism
8. Strong governor constitutions
9. Per capita state taxes, revenues, expenditures, and debt
10. Comprehensive and sophisticated budget and evaluation systems
11. Total number of employees and number per capita
12. Percentage of employees under civil service
13. Proportion of state employees unionized and their percentage of adults in state population

These associations, subject as they are to deviations, indicate that productivity programs are most likely in the larger, more advanced state governments despite the greater problems in those states of civil service and unionization.

The existence of a productivity program does not, of course, indicate that productivity itself is higher. Bernard Lentz's findings with respect to financial administration are that the adjusted revenue collected per employee tends to be higher in the less advanced states with lower degrees of both civil service coverage and unionization.

Another research group including sociologists Robert Quinn and Madeline Dillon has been examining the behavioral aspects of productivity improvement. One study on the process and outcomes of productivity improvement attempts to relate different classes of change (technological, structure, people, and task) of work and organization (formalization, size, task difficulty, task variability) and outcomes (twenty-three categories). Interviews with managerial personnel at all levels have been conducted in a number of states and a questionnaire sent to some 800 states managerial employees.

Quinn and Dillon are conducting a related study of the basis of recommendations by various managers in the New York State Department of Transportation with respect to 200 different proposed economies or productivity improvements. They have developed a judgment-mapping technique that locates proposals in terms of two characteristics, say, magnitude of savings and ease of implementation.

The researchers now see productivity improvement as a special case of innovation and to which most of the characteristics of innovatory process apply. Quinn believes that the strongest source of productivity improvement is "pain," for example the necessity to adjust to budget cuts. Manager's resistance is most likely to occur if change threatens the manager's job or organization. The strongest positive factor is a boss who insists on the change.

Quinn and Dillon conducted with systems analyst Edward LeBlanc a third project on the effect of management information systems on productivity improvement. System characteristics have been identified in the transportation and mental health agencies of a number of states and related to productivity improvement efforts and to different personality characteristics of managers. Productivity improvement efforts do tend to be stronger in agencies with well-developed, and productivity-relevant data systems. The style of management is a crucial factor with highly data-oriented managers most likely to use MIS output for productivity improvement and with subordinate managers tending to be responsive to a data-oriented superior even though their own styles are not data-oriented. Le Blanc is examining some of the broader issues of MIS in the articulation and coordination of units of large organizations.

A number of other studies were also done. Walter Balk studied employee suggestion systems, and Harold Adams examined effectiveness and evaluation in the unified services model for county-based mental health programs.

Syracuse University

The Maxwell School of Citizenship and Public Affairs has had for some time a Metropolitan Studies Program. The research conducted under that program has concentrated heavily on the fiscal aspects of urban and metropolitan government. The continuing research program was substantially expanded to encompass research performed under contract for the Temporary State Commission on Local Government and, later, for the so-called "Scott Commission," a special state commission on the management of New York City.

The Public Employment Project is an integral part of the overall metropolitan studies program. Its emphasis is on problems of public expenditure and employment rather than on productivity per se. The one significant exception is the monograph, *Productivity in the Local Government Sector* by Jesse Burkhead and John P. Ross published in 1974.

Productivity in the Local Government Sector is a state-of-the-art review of the problems of analyzing local government productivity written from an economist's perspective. It deals carefully and cogently with the concept of productivity and with the measurement of productivity and the allocation of productivity changes among input factors. Empirical studies of governmental productivity, federal and state as well as local, are reviewed and critiqued.

Two of the seven chapters deal with the ex post analysis of changes in government expenditures in New York State local governments. Increases attributable to changes in prices and in the quantity of output are estimated; this, in effect, parallels Brecher's work with similar conclusions. An effort is made to develop explanations for the residual increase incorporating all the changes in scope, quality, and productivity. The structure is simple but elegant, and a model approach to the problem. The empirical analysis encounters difficulties however, on the analysis of the residual; there are few program quality surrogates for which data are available and the choices made are not very satisfactory.

Only in the concluding chapter of the book do Ross and Burkhead address the problem of efforts to increase productivity in local governments. This is a summary of problems rather than an effort to provide answers. They call for increased research and development, better information systems, and the development and transfer of technological and managerial innovations to improve productivity.

As the above indicates, Ross and Burkhead have not addressed their work to the needs or interests of local government officials. It is, however, a useful and well-done introduction to the problems of measuring local government productivity and analyzing local government expenditure increases for researchers and analysts working on either problem.

The broader concern of the project has, however, been with the analysis of characteristics and trends of public expenditure and employment in state and local government and with forecasting probable future changes. The Ford Foundation–financed productivity aspects of the public employment project are concerned with interrelationships of public employment, productivity, and collective bargaining and public finance at the local level. This will include analyses of several cases: (1) CETA and Public Service Employment in Atlanta; (2) A study of comparative public employment experience in Buffalo, Rochester, and Syracuse and (3) the compensation impact on public sector collective bargaining in Detroit. The case material is supplemented by analyses of broader scope, often based on national data aggregates dealing with the determinants of future public expenditures.

Much of the empirical research performed under the Syracuse project is unrelated to local government productivity programs and, in fact, has only a limited relationship to local government productivity. It is, rather, serving another purpose. It is, first, providing analytically structured information on the character of local government expenditure experience over the last decade or two. The effects of inflation, of the emergence of municipal unions as a

powerful factor in those expenditures, and of the expansion of federal aid have
obscured any sense of normal standards in local budgeting and expenditures.
The Syracuse project is beginning to provide such a perspective by reviewing the
elements that have entered into these increases and by comparative analyses
among regions and among cities.

Other Research Programs

Some important research in problems of productivity and performance occurs
not in nationally focused efforts nor in broad academic research programs but,
rather, in local problem-solving efforts. Three important efforts of this kind
in New York City are worth comment.

The dissolution of the New York City Rand Institute in 1975 ended a
seven-and-a-half years relationship between the city and the Rand Corporation
during which about $12 million in research was performed for city agencies.
The magnitude of the program, Rand's high research capability, the sustained
continuity of the program and the complexity of the city government all contributed to an extraordinary research output.

The most widely acclaimed work of the Institute was that done for the
New York Fire Department. The development of "rapid water," which increased
water flow and reach through the addition of long chain polymers resulted from
the Rand program. Perhaps even more important was Rand's deployment and
response model permitting a comparison of the effect of alternative fire company locations and response patterns upon response time. The model has had
wide use in New York City. Its application led initially to the elimination of six
fire companies and the relocation of an additional seven; more recently, it
has been used to establish priorities for the reductions dictated since 1975
by New York's acute fiscal crisis.

During the same period, the Institute had also carried out analyses of police
patrol emergency response. The Institute solicited and obtained from the
Department of Housing and Urban Development a $200,000 grant to assist in
the application of Rand's emergency services response models to other cities.
Under this grant, the Institute worked with a number of other cities in the
application of the model. The fire response model was used in a number of
cities, including Wilmington, Delaware where it figures in the reduction of one
company from that city's fire force.

The Institute's work with fire and police constituted only a part of Rand's
extensive work program with the city. An elaborate analysis of resident income
distribution and housing costs established for the first time the shortfall in
tenant ability to provide rents sufficient to cover minimum opearting and
maintenance costs for rental housing. Similar insufficiencies have become the
most important causal factor in the rapid deterioration of the existing housing
stock in the poorer areas of many of our older cities. The Institute, as a result

of its analysis, recommended the Maximum Base Rent System designed to assure an adequate flow of funds to housing from tenants who could afford to pay the necessary rents.

One of the last major projects of the Institute was a collaborative study with the Human Resources Administration of the welfare system and the problem of poverty in New York. This was a massive statistical analysis providing the most detailed data on the poor available for any major city in the country.

These are barely a sampling from the Institute's work with the city. The areas covered and the number of reports prepared put it in a class where the Institute's output now constitutes by far the largest single research program on urban government problems. It has also been the largest source of published cases in urban public analyses. Much of Rand's methodology is replicable in other settings and applicable to other cities despite the unique characteristics of New York. A good deal of its value must be attributed to the fact that the Rand researchers were required to deal with urban problems in the concrete rather than in general and that that concrete context was the locus of the most difficult and complex problems of urban society in America.

More recently, the Fund for the City of New York has undertaken a significant program in government productivity. The Fund is a nonprofit organization set up by the Ford Foundation to make grants to projects of assistance to New York City. The productivity project was initiated with Project Scorecard, an effort to develop a systematic method of assessing street cleanliness in all parts of the city. Using a complex sampling and scheduling system, crews observe street cleanliness in samples of each of the city's sanitation sections every month. Observations are geared to a five-class schema of cleanliness. The quality classes are defined both descriptively and through prototype photographs. Regular public reports are issued as well as daily and monthly reports and special analyses produced for the Department of Sanitation.

A second Fund project aims at the monitoring of the adequacy of health care through comparisons of actual performance, as indicated in patient records, with standards of quality care specified by groups of expert physicians. This disease-specific, chart-review method has been tested at three hospitals in New York City for two prevalent chronic diseases, diabetes and hypertension. Additionally, the care provided to patients with a series of emergency department presenting complaints—acute asthma, urinary tract infection, and sore throat— has also been assessed. Finally, a pilot study extending the method to medical care in nursing homes has been completed.

This work is a path-breaking forward step in an area that has received little close and scientific scrutiny. Preliminary results indicate major deficiencies in care at all the project's sites and have provided information that can be used to improve the quality of care through increasing physician and staff compliance with the standards. The technique is wholly replicable and is currently being extended to other treatment areas.

An application of the monitoring-against-standard technique is now underway through a Fund grant to the New York State Board of Social Welfare, a regulating agency for the child welfare system. This project hopes to set standards for permanency for children in foster care and to assess comparatively the performance of the voluntary child-caring organizations with regard to their procurement of permanent homes for their caseloads. The Fund also expects to apply this monitoring technique to other social service areas over the next year.

The Vera Institute of Justice in New York is of longer tenure, established some fifteen years ago. The Institute has devoted its efforts during this period to innovation in the criminal justice system. It began with bail reform and has moved on to scores of other projects in the criminal justice system itself or with the handling and treatment of criminal delinquent populations. It has pioneered in the use of pilot project techniques for testing and evaluating the change and in the organization of private nonprofit corporations to carry out the new approaches for local government. Bail reform was succeeded by release on recognizance and work release programs. Therapeutic approaches have been substituted for arrests of intoxicated derelicts. Supported work programs have been developed for criminals and addicts. One of the first large-scale methadone treatment programs was undertaken by Vera. It introduced traffic and crime alert programs to prevent futile officer appearances in court. Vera's Director Herbert Sturz has long been interested in broader application of Vera's approaches; with support from the Ford Foundation, Vera has established new offices in London and in Cincinnati, Ohio. Its supported work program led to a proposal eventually supported by both the Ford Foundation and the U.S. Department of Labor for an eighteen-city supported work program administered through an independent nonprofit corporation established for that purpose.

An Overview of Productivity Research

The above discussion can make no claim to comprehensive coverage of research on productivity in State and local government. It does, however, cover virtually all the research and technical assistance programs that are having any impact of nationwide significance on state and local governments.

There is little in current research and technical assistance for local government productivity that could be called valueless, (although much of the academic research is not likely to have much direct value for local government). All the research and technical assistance taken together, however, could scarcely be called a program nor does its distribution approximate anyone's notion of relative priorities. It is, rather, a varied package reflecting the different interests of those able to secure financing in a very broad field in which little has been done in the past.

The case for a substantial expansion of resources for research and technical assistance seems so obvious as to be scarcely worth developing. We are suffering from a national inattention to local government and its performance that could arise only in our kind of federalism. Our level of understanding and performance in major sectors of our economy is, as a result, woefully short of our needs. The standard of productivity and effectiveness in local government seems clearly far below the demonstrated capacity of our society. Research, technical assistance, and experimentation are unusually important because of our current ignorance, a federal structure that dictates approaches to the problem that are largely indirect, and the great heterogeneity of local government. Any substantial increase in funding would produce benefits almost regardless of its particular focus simply because the marginal value of additions to our present investment levels is potentially very high.

The most perplexing issue is that of application of best practice. There are convincing demonstrations that the transfer of technology and technique works in communities interested enough to participate in a program to aid such transfer. The other side of the coin is the appalling fact that the majority of our local governments are not that interested. To some local politicians, the risks and disadvantages of innovation are seemingly determining. To others, the absence of any citizen pressure for innovation means "why bother?" I am reminded of the Jesuit development of the category of the "invincibly ignorant" to cover those of good faith who, even after exposure to the "true faith" could not believe. The barriers are sociological, and we still know too little about how they might be breached.

Expanded research and technical assistance programs should be a major and integral part of a national program to increase local government productivity. I have so treated them in the recommendations in Chapter 13.

13 For the Future

I am left with a frustrating sense of the minuteness of the current effort to improve productivity and performance in local government. Even with generous allowance for the unheralded and unpublicized improvements, only a small proportion of our larger local governments are engaged in serious continuing efforts to improve management and productivity. Within most of these more innovative governments, the effort is still far from comprehensive in its impact on the various local functions. We could do much better. In a technical sense, we could, in fact, easily do much better. The variation in the current quality of performance among local governments is enormous. If every function were carried out at the level of efficiency and effectiveness achieved by those governments at, say, the seventy-fifth percentile, i.e. those performing better than three out of four governments and worse than one out of four, the savings resulting would be enormous.

There are many reasons why the best practices do not spread more rapidly among state and local governments, but the most important reason is the peculiar isolation of these governments. They are isolated in the sense that program decisions are made in a local political market into which broader concepts of practice and performance have achieved only a limited penetration. Over the last thirty years, mayors, city managers, other local officials, and state officials as well have become vastly better educated on what is going on in other jurisdictions. But knowing, or more commonly, suspecting the truth creates no mandate to use it, gives it no protective political authority or credibility, and provides no help in implementing it through an administrative cadre that may be hostile or inept.

Most of the actors in local policy determination—employees, unions, senior bureaucrats, citizens, most elected officials, and the media—are conditioned almost entirely by local experience. A worker's sense of a fair day's work and a sensible work method reflects, primarily, actual work performance. Citizen notions of reasonable city service expectations are based almost entirely on the level and character of the services they are actually receiving. What is being done is legitimized by experience; what is proposed is speculative. It is scarcely surprising that so much of local government seems governed by a kind of law of the presumptive perpetuation of established practice.

The argument for change is supported almost entirely by experience outside the community, and information on that experience is rarely available in systematic and comparable form. One small hall would hold all the people in the United States with any understanding of how refuse collection in their own towns compared in efficiency with the same operation elsewhere.

The rate of change and improvement in local government will tend to be low and unsatisfactory until the environment of decision making is more effectively penetrated by relevant nonlocal information. This would encompass information on best practices in various functions, on comparative performance in terms of costs and effectiveness, and on performance standards where they exist. The problem is partially a matter of finding effective means of communication, but there is also a substantial need for the development of the information.

The most important use of information is in the education of the public. A mayor may be aware that the Fire Department is overstaffed or that refuse collection is inefficient and still decide that the remedy is too risky or too difficult to attempt. If, on the other hand, the same information is available to the local newspapers, the League of Women Voters and other civic groups, or to opposition members of the City Council, it will become a public issue with a high probability that corrective action will eventually be taken. Performance comparisons with other like communities are likely to be particularly effective where the local operation is among the least efficient. In other situations, a comparison with some achievable standard of performance may be appropriate. In either case, the data would provide yardsticks, now almost totally absent, for public assessment of local government performance.

It would be very much in the same vein to expose workers, supervisors, and department heads to practices in high-performance cities and counties. Here, the written word will rarely suffice. The worker and the supervisor typically need to see the operation in context to satisfy themselves as to its applicability to their situation.

Better information and wider understanding of performance in comparison with that in other communities or with standards is important in motivating change. It does not, however, provide the competence needed to implement productivity improvements. Complex changes may not be undertaken simply because no one is available to work on it, or because no one understands how to do it, or because some crucial detail needs more scrutiny. There is little doubt that the availability of technical assistance can relieve some of these problems and stimulate interest in change. The limited experience of Public Technology, Incorporated provides some evidence that this is so. A case of broader application is the role of the salespersons and engineers of the computer manufacturers in the widespread introduction of the computer.

A more fundamental elevation of the competence of local governments to improve productivity and performance requires the acceptance of new concepts of local government operations. The idea of a staff capacity for critical evaluation and for work process redesign and improvement is still alien to local government. Even the more general notion of staff support for program managers sees relatively limited application. Change and improvement come slowly because no investment has been made in the staff with that responsibility.

All the above is addressed to the failure of local government generally to do as well as the most efficient local governments are doing. In any area, there is a legitimate question as to whether and how the state of the art might be advanced or, in other words, how *best* practice can be improved. PTI, Tacoma's Technology Transfer, and some of the New York Rand Institute projects have attempted to do this in certain areas, but much more is needed. A particularly important need is for the development of model approaches for the use of new hardware and technology in complex operations. For example, a host of new developments in fire fighting needs to be integrated into an overall fire-fighting system.

The development of system and technique now embraces possibilities that even a decade ago might have seemed fantastic. It is currently possible for example to make available on time sharing computers all over the country (or to program on minicomputers) "add your own numbers and stir" programs under which *any* local government could, for example:

Evaluate its distribution of police patrol cars

Develop the most efficient routes for its refuse collection trucks

Find optimum locations for fire stations, ambulance stations or any other service provided by dispatch from fixed points

Determine the likelihood that an arrest for a given crime will result in conviction and the proportion of convictions resulting in prison sentences, the probable time imprisoned, and many other outcomes.

Estimate fire response times under different deployments.

There are only illustrative and, more important, the expansion potential is very substantial. Something of the same kind is becoming true of information and accounting systems that the computer has made astonishingly portable.

In virtually every aspect of aiding the process of innovation in local government, there are currently programs attempting to serve the need. One might cite deficiencies in the particular choices of priority, but the major problem is the lack of scale in the effort and the absence of any central program guidance.

A serious effort to improve the performance of state and local governments would require a relatively modest federal investment, but it would be many times the current level of expenditure on programs serving this objective. It would probably also require a new federal agency, either independent or perhaps within HUD, to carry out this mission.

It should embrace all the particular program thrusts discussed above including:

1. The development of valid comparative data on performance of various functions by states and major local governments
2. Programs for personnel education and exchange
3. A corps of qualified staff to provide technical assistance
4. The development of state of the art models for important programs and operations;
5. An advanced program of dissemination and communications.

One might add that the federal establishment could benefit from comparable substantive attention to its managerial problems, and it might well be done in the same context. Indeed, a National Administrative College or academy serving educational needs of all governments might be one aspect of such a program.

This should be a continuing program, because new opportunities and new problems are continually emerging. It should be possible to establish performance targets especially after initial experience provides some factual basis for so doing.

I have little doubt that an effectively designed and funded program could produce benefits equal to some multiple of its costs. It is even conceivable that it might pay for itself in direct federal savings in the expenditures for federally aided programs.

Index

About the Author

Frederick O'R. Hayes was director of the budget for the city of New York from 1966-1970. He came to New York from a career in federal service in Washington where he had most recently been deputy director of the Community Action Program in the Office of Economic Opportunity. Since leaving government, Mr. Hayes has taught as a visiting professor at Yale University, the State University of New York at Stoney Brook, and the New School for Social Research. He has carried out various studies and written numerous articles about urban government problems and was coeditor with John E. Rasmussen of *Centers for Innovation in the Cities* and States. Mr. Hayes received the M.P.A. and M.A. (political economy and government) degrees from Harvard University.